Praise for *Enough Blame to Go Around*

"New York City's labor unions have been luckier than they deserved to have had reporter and editor Richard Steier around to spotlight their occasional triumphs and their much more frequent failures. Like Murray Kempton, another great New York columnist who loved the men and women of labor but who never suffered the fools who sometimes ran their unions, Steier's columns are filled with news, insight, and always compassion for those who ride (and drive) the early trains and buses to work."

— Tom Robbins, CUNY Graduate School of Journalism

"Steier presents an impassioned case for public sector unions and the benefits they have won, along with fascinating tales of the machinations inside several of the largest unions in New York City— District Council 37, Transport Workers Union Local 100 and the 2005 strike that paralyzed the city, and the United Federation of Teachers."

— Alair Townsend, former New York City
Budget Director and Deputy Mayor

Enough Blame to Go Around

Enough Blame to Go Around

The Labor Pains of
New York City's Public Employee Unions

RICHARD STEIER

excelsior editions
State University of New York Press
Albany, New York

For information, contact State University of New York Press, Albany, NY
www.sunypress.edu

Production by Cathleen Collins
Marketing by Anne M. Valentine

Library of Congress Cataloging-in-Publication Data

Steier, Richard
    Enough blame to go around : the labor pains of New York City's public employee unions / Richard Steier
        pages cm. — (Excelsior editions)
    Includes index.
    ISBN 978-1-4384-4954-8 (pbk. : alk. paper)
    1. Labor unions—New York (State)—History.   2. Labor unions—Officials and employees.   3. Collective bargaining—Government employees—New York (State)
I. Title.

    HD6519.N5S74 2013
    331.88'113517471—dc23   2013005363

10 9 8 7 6 5 4 3 2 1

To my parents, who instilled in me an appreciation for the written word and offered a look at the fun side of the journalism business; and to Gilda, with love.

Contents

Acknowledgments

This book came about thanks to a suggestion by Rob Polner, who then provided a friend's guidance while helping me navigate my way to SUNY Press. My appreciation to Dan Janison, who when Rob floated the idea didn't dismiss it as silly.

My gratitude also to Jimmy Breslin, Robert Lipsyte, and Murray Kempton, whose work helped shape my sensibility; and to Tom Robbins, whose pieces for the *Daily News* and the *Village Voice* spurred more than one follow-up look at union funny business.

My informal education as a labor reporter was provided by officials from both sides of the bargaining table and a few neutral parties as well. They include Basil Paterson, Bruce McIver, Harry Karetzky, Bob Linn, Jim Hanley, Gary Dellaverson, Donna Lynne, Arvid Anderson, Marlene Gold, Steve DeCosta, George Nicolau, Jane Morgenstern, Estelle Karpf, Nat Leventhal, Stanley Brezenoff, Alair Townsend, Harvey Robins, Michael Jacobson, Bernie Rosen, Barry Feinstein, Bert Rose, Victor Gotbaum, Charles Ensley, Al Viani, Stu Leibowitz, Mark Rosenthal, Beverly Gross, Dennis Sullivan, Vinnie Montalbano, Norman Adler, John Toto, Jack Bigel, Jonathan Schwartz, Randi Weingarten, Jimmy Boyle, Nick Mancuso, Vinnie Bollon, Tom von Essen, Pete Gorman, Brenda Berkman, Sidney Schwartzbaum, Norman Seabrook, Arthur Cheliotes, Bill Henning, Larry Hanley, Eddie Kay, Jim Gebhardt, Tony Garvey, Bill Kelly, Floyd Holloway, Richard Wagner, Bob Croghan, Ray Diana, Phil Tacktill, and at least a dozen others who will be happy that I didn't mention them by name.

I owe thanks to my bosses at *The Chief*, Ed Prial and his brother Joe, who gave me the editorial independence needed to do the job right; and to other members of the Prial family—Frank II, Frank Jr., Jim, and Mike, who gave me the chance earlier to develop my skills and then write the column. Thanks also to Steve Jackel, a former colleague who is now the newspaper's lawyer, and to Harry Park, its head of production.

I am also grateful to those at SUNY Press—Michael Rinella, Cathleen Collins, and Anne Valentine—who believed in the book and helped shepherd it into print.

Introduction

Over the past 40 years, the wages of ordinary workers in the United States, adjusting for inflation, have risen by just 1 percent, even as compensation for top executives has grown exponentially. There are several significant factors that account for that widening income gap, including computerization, globalization, and the tilt away from a level playing field that began with the presidency of Richard Nixon and was solidified by Ronald Reagan's transformation of the political dialogue in America.

But there is also an inescapable correlation to the decline of organized labor as a force in American life over that period. Four decades ago, roughly 35 percent of the nation's workers belonged to unions; today just about 12 percent do. In the process, as private-sector unions have declined in size and influence, the one area where labor has gained strength has been in the public sector, where collective-bargaining rights were not even granted until the late 1950s. In what seems particularly ironic today, the first state to enact those rights was Wisconsin in 1959, a year after they were adopted for New York City.

New York was a ripe area for labor ferment during the 1960s, beginning with a strike by welfare workers in the middle of the decade that was as much about the treatment of their clients as it was their own salaries and working conditions. The march to the barricades continued with a 1966 strike by transit workers that paralyzed the city for 12 days and a couple of years later by a sanitation strike and a months-long teachers strike that was fought not over wages but rather a bid by black militants to exert "community control" over public schools by, among other things, firing white instructors they claimed were inadequately educating minority pupils.

Eventually the spotlight dimmed as labor unrest quieted; New York's unions were credited with helping to rescue the city from the brink of bankruptcy in 1975, although critics claimed that too-generous contracts awarded to them by previous mayoral administrations were a major factor in the financial crisis. The bullet was dodged, and the unions in New York (where I live) gradually consolidated their gains, even as public worker unions in other parts of the country also prospered.

For much of the three decades after New York's fiscal crisis, public employee unions operated largely below the radar of the national and New York City media, unless a major scandal bubbled to the surface or, as with the city transit workers union in late 2005, a potentially crippling strike briefly focused attention on labor/management conflict before evaporating once the crisis passed.

The *New York Times*, which used to have a reporter assigned solely to covering municipal labor, discontinued the practice in the early 1980s, relying on its City Hall reporters or its national labor correspondent to step in once an alarm had sounded. The *Post* hired a labor reporter (me) in 1989 and discontinued the beat after a strike at the paper ended with management busting out the Newspaper Guild four years later, entrusting most of its labor coverage since then to young reporters impressionable enough to slant their coverage to suit the prevailing editorial sentiments. The *Daily News* has a civil service column buried in the regional sections of the paper but usually reserves most of its news-section column inches for scandals involving greedy labor leaders caught with their hands in the till. And television, which generally finds its version of news in the morning papers, has responded accordingly to the drop-off in serious labor coverage.

But the crisis on Wall Street has brought a sudden surge of interest in public employee unions, although not for any reasons they would encourage. Some labor leaders contend that there has been a concerted effort, by the titans of the financial community, the media properties of Rupert Murdoch, and Mayor Michael Bloomberg to deflect attention from the cause of the city's financial problems by focusing it on the benefits that public employees receive and how good they seem in comparison to what's available these days in the private sector.

One of Murdoch's business publications, *Barron's*, early in 2010 had a cover story complete with a drawing of a cop and firefighter sunning themselves on a tropical island to dramatize its case that their pension benefits represented a greater threat to the long-term future of the national economy than the chicanery on Wall Street. The governor of Wisconsin, Scott Walker, elected in part through the financial largesse of two billionaire brothers with a distinctly anti-labor bent, has succeeded in largely disenfranchising the public employee unions in his state, although he exempted from his crackdown the police and fire unions that endorsed him (and which in many cities are the labor groups most likely to back Republicans for office).

Even New York's governor, Andrew Cuomo, whose father during 12 years of running New York State was a symbol (accurately or not) of old-fashioned pro-labor liberalism, has styled himself as a sort of kinder, gentler Chris Christie. Since taking office in 2011, he persuaded the two largest unions representing state workers to accept concession-laden contracts that included a three-year wage freeze and increases of up to 60 percent in employee payments toward their health care coverage. His tone was softer than Christie's, but his threat of up to 10,000 layoffs if the unions weren't willing to capitulate served as a potent bullhorn. In March 2012, Cuomo forced through the State Legislature a sharp reduction in pension provisions for future state and municipal employees.

Conservative critics have argued that public employee unions enjoy an unnatural advantage in their dealings with employers because their political support, or the withholding of it, can be the key to an officeholder's reelection, given their sway over their memberships and their ability to make large contributions of both money and campaign volunteers. Whatever advantage that offers has long been offset for the New York City unions in the media-framed battle for hearts and minds. The city tabloids, which because of their stridency often drive the public debate in a way that the more-reserved *Times* can't, tend to be particularly conservative when it comes to the rights and benefits of public workers. The unions have also slipped in the public relations arena because the strong personalities that once could be found running the bigger organizations have faded into retirement or died. Among the newer generation, perhaps the sharpest labor leader, Randi Weingarten, left the United Federation of Teachers in 2009 to head its national parent, and the most-militant one, Roger Toussaint of the Transport Workers Union (TWU), never overcame the losses, financial as well as political, that resulted from his ill-conceived city transit strike and eventually kicked himself upstairs to a secondary post in his international union.

While the municipal unions have a reputation for being able to influence city and state legislators to do their bidding, there has been relatively little significant legislation benefiting those unions or their members enacted into law in recent years. Their clout has surfaced not in what they are able to achieve but in their ability to block legislation that would harm them or their rank and files, such as Mayor Bloomberg's attempts to amend the law that requires that when teachers are laid off, it must be in reverse order of seniority, known as "last in, first out."

Municipal unions have had their image damaged by a few significant corruption scandals. Brian McLaughlin, who had headed the city's AFL-CIO Central Labor Council, the umbrella group for both public- and private-sector unions in New York, is now serving a 10-year Federal prison term for embezzling $2 million in members' dues money, campaign funds from his other role as a State Assemblyman, and from separate pots including that of a Little League founded by his original power base, Local 3 of the International Brotherhood of Electrical Workers. District Council 37, long the largest union representing New York City workers and once viewed as a beacon for progressive politics and minority advancement in the municipal workforce, in 1998 was found to have been systematically looted by a band of local-union presidents who took advantage of the gullibility and weakness of Stanley Hill, the 125,000-member union's first African American leader. And reforms have been slow to come to some troubled unions. DC 37's international union tightened controls over spending but left intact a voting system that gave local-union presidents rather than rank-and-file members the power to choose the union's leader.

An Amalgamated Transit Union local of school bus drivers was found to have been controlled by a Mafia family for more than three decades, but even after Federal prosecutors removed the union's two corrupt leaders, the international permitted another board member to take over the local's operation even though he refused to answer questions posed by an outside investigator whom the international itself had brought in, ostensibly to clean up the local.

The money stolen by these individuals, as well as by lawyers who used to represent the city's largest police union, paled in comparison to the hundreds of millions ripped off by the pirates of Wall Street, or even some corrupt consultants brought in to automate the city's time-keeping system because Mayor Bloomberg's budget director thought ordinary employees might be cheating the city out of a few thousand dollars by gaming the old punch-card process. But their wrongdoing has fueled the mentality that says "they're all greedy bums," even if most of those wearing labor hats are trying to achieve workplace safety while helping those they represent carve out a decent living and even ascend into the middle class.

The decline of organized labor in much of the nation and particularly in the private sector has made public employees the last bastion of robust unionism. Their unions have become a broader target in recent years, particularly for hard-right conservatives who view them as an arm of the Democratic Party.

I've had a unique vantage point to observe the gains, ruptures, and struggles of municipal labor in New York City. Since 1980, I've covered those unions and city government, part of the time as a reporter and labor columnist for the *Post* (during the 1993 strike at the paper, an op-ed piece I wrote for *Newsday* criticizing Murdoch ensured that I wouldn't be invited back once he quelled the brief uprising). Since 1998, I've been editor and featured columnist of the *Chief-Leader*, a 116-year-old independent newspaper that covers city and state government and their unions in greater detail than any other publication.

When I began writing the column "Razzle Dazzle," in 1998, municipal union corruption, which had been so limited in the past as to seem obscure in comparison to organized crime's grip on private-sector unions from the carpenters to the teamsters and longshoremen, was bubbling to the surface. Other issues, such as the growing cost of employee benefits, were not of prime concern, partly because the stock market was percolating so nicely that the pension funds were flush with money. In 2000, the Republicans occupying City Hall and the Governor's Mansion in Albany made a deal that improved employee pension rights in return for permission to take the excess profits out of the funds and plow them into their budgets. Having weathered a brief economic crisis in the mid-1990s that led to wage freezes for city and state workers until the lean times were banished by the boom on Wall Street, there was no talk of scaling back employee rights, never mind the threat of massive layoffs, unless the unions agreed to rollbacks of pension and health benefits.

This collection of columns written over the past 15 years reflects how New York's economic problems have altered the landscape, with declining government revenues as a result of the Bush tax cuts passed down to local governments, leaving public workers and their unions getting squeezed hard. They offer historical perspective on how much life has changed and why it has sometimes been difficult for the municipal unions to adapt as their viability is being challenged here and to an even more severe degree in other cities and states where public employee unions maintain tenuous footholds.

There is no question that the public employee unions have contributed to the problems that confront them today. Their leaders are not unlike the politicians who serve as presidents and governors and legislators, so intent upon preserving their own power that they often reflexively align with those who are best positioned to help them rather than living up to their mandate to act in the best interests of their members. Union democracy has sometimes suffered as a result, and when the political machinations lead to corruption and indictments, it damages labor's image and breeds cynicism and often apathy among the rank-and-file members as well as the public.

On the other hand, for all their flaws, the unions represent the best shot that ordinary people in this nation have for fair economic treatment; even those workers who do not belong to a union benefit when their employers improve wages and working conditions in order to stay competitive for top talent, or sometimes to diminish the desire to bring in a union. They deserve better than the gallery of cartoons served up by op-ed and editorial pages and in TV's limited, once-over-lightly coverage of labor issues.

The columns detail union corruption and the battles between labor and government, as well as examining the tensions that exist in honest unions over controversial matters. Contrary to public perceptions of police unions being the architects of the Blue Wall of Silence, some of the columns detail instances where union leaders have risked antagonizing even their own conservative rank and files to criticize oppressive mayoral policies that worsen relations in minority communities, and one focuses on a case where a police union aggressively but within bounds assisted members on trial in a racially charged case that because of its sensitivity left others hesitant to speak up on behalf of the accused. The columns also explore situations that can divide unions not only when reformers cross swords with regulars but when someone elected as a reformer begins acting in the same high-handed fashion that he or she had once rebelled against in challenging those they eventually displaced.

They also touch on internal communication problems the unions encounter, especially when trying to galvanize their members or work jointly with each other. Some unions, particularly those representing cops and firefighters, are strong because they have rank and files that ensure that union delegates are responsive to their needs and therefore demanding of those in charge. District Council 37 has grown weaker because its members are so spread out and in many cases so poorly paid that they can't find the time to be active in its operations. This problem has been exacerbated by shortsighted union leaders who figure that a disengaged membership is one that is less likely to disrupt the status quo. The largest of its locals, which was also the leader in the thievery of the late 1990s, in June of 2011 conducted an officers election in which just 4 percent of its 24,000 members took part, because rather than using a mail ballot it required them to come from all over the city to a single polling location at the union's lower Manhattan headquarters.

All this might seem almost tribal in a working universe that increasingly is nonunion. It is not. What some have characterized as "pension envy" reflects how the playing field has been tilted by media coverage: ordinary workers disparage public employees for having it so good rather than pressing for some of the benefits that were once taken for granted in private companies but have been stripped away or watered down in recent decades. There is a reason that ordinary workers find it harder to get as comfortable as their parents once did in an era when it was relatively rare to have married women providing a second household income.

During his first summer in office in 1981, President Ronald Reagan fired striking Air Traffic Controllers and ushered in an increasingly hostile climate for unions and workers as the balance of power began shifting in favor of management and the well-to-do in society, to the detriment of those whose futures lay in being able to find decent jobs that offered good benefits. What was also lost along the way was job security that stemmed as much from protection against arbitrary punishment as from the steadiness of the work or the industry in which it was performed.

To a large degree, New York's public employee unions still offer those protections, but they have begun to pay a steep price—as the wage freezes and benefit cuts forced by Governor Cuomo demonstrate—to do so while hoping to ride out a storm that is at least as much political as it is economic in nature. The unfortunate aspect of the battle is that, in more than a few instances, the leaders of some of those unions have undermined the interests of those they were elected to serve.

The columns are grouped in five sections; in some they appear chronologically, in others the story is best told by jumping back and forth in time to frame the issues. The dates listed reflect the issues of the *Chief* in which they appeared.

Acronyms and Abbreviations

AAA	American Arbitration Association
ACORN	Association of Community Organizations for Reform Now
AFSCME	American Federation of State, County and Municipal Employees
BCB	Board of Collective Bargaining
CLC	Central Labor Council
CSEA	Civil Service Employees Association
DOE	Department of Education
DOT	Department of Transportation
DROP	Deferred Retirement Option Plan
ESPA	Empire State Pride Agenda
HHC	Health and Hospitals Corporation
HRA	Human Resources Administration
MLC	Municipal Labor Committee
NYRA	New York Racing Association
OMB	Office of Management and Budget
OPT	Office of Pupil Transportation

PBA	Patrolmen's Benevolent Association
PEF	Public Employees Federation
PEP	*Public Employee Press*
TWU	Transport Workers Union
UFA	Uniformed Firefighters Association
UFT	United Federation of Teachers
VSF	Variable Supplements Fund
WEP	Work Experience Program

Unions on the Run

As president of the United Federation of Teachers, Randi Weingarten was often castigated by New York City tabloid editorial boards for her persistent advocacy on behalf of her members and resistance to mayoral attempts to reduce their rights. She also proved adept at reaching compromises with Mayor Michael Bloomberg on issues ranging from pensions to teacher discipline. Photo reprinted courtesy of the *Chief-Leader*.

In 1982, Mario Cuomo, the lieutenant governor of New York, was a decided underdog when he sought the Democratic nomination for governor. Most of the party establishment was aligned behind New York City Mayor Ed Koch, who had been essentially drafted into the race by the publisher of the New York Post, Rupert Murdoch, whose paper had helped propel Koch past Cuomo five years earlier when the two sought the mayoralty.

Koch had come to City Hall vowing to get tough on municipal unions and became the public face of management during the 11-day transit strike in 1980 by striding onto the Brooklyn Bridge and waving on commuters, who had been forced out of the subways and onto its footpaths to get into Manhattan, while harshly criticizing the union. Yet two years later, much of the city's labor movement was backing him. One prominent labor leader cited pragmatic motives: even if Koch were defeated, he would still have another three years in his second term as mayor.

Cuomo had the support of the largest of those unions, District Council 37, as well as its state counterpart, the Civil Service Employees Association (CSEA), to make up for some of the disadvantages he faced. The unions offered both money and a significant stream of volunteers to work phone banks and ensure that their rank and files came out and voted. Their assistance played a key role in his surprisingly comfortable upset win over Koch in the primary and his eventual election against a Republican opponent in November.

When his son Andrew ran for governor 28 years later, the landscape was different. He had compiled a strong record as state attorney general, and the embattled governor, David Paterson—who had gotten that job only after the incumbent, Eliot Spitzer, resigned from office after it was revealed that he had a taste for high-priced hookers—found himself overwhelmed by negative publicity and chose not to seek a full term. The younger Cuomo styled himself as a reformer who understood the need to cultivate business interests in New York, pledging to straighten out the state's finances by reining in its employee costs. This approach didn't endear him to labor, but he didn't seem to mind: unlike his father, he didn't need union support to give him a base, and he didn't solicit it. He gained election with 70 percent of the vote in November 2010 and was already being talked up as a possible contender for president in 2016. When he took office the following January, he quickly established that he had meant what he said about being less accommodating to the unions than the typical New York Democrat, and as he showed a deftness for navigating the treacherous political currents in Albany and bulldozed the state legislature into a budget that *erased a $10-billion deficit without raising taxes, his stature grew and his popularity soared.*

The way in which the budget was crafted, however, meant that no money was available for pay raises for the state's workers, whose contracts expired on the same day that the new budget took effect. Not only that, but Cuomo told labor leaders that unless they agreed to major concessions in other areas, he would lay off up to 10,000 workers to keep the budget in balance.

Eliot Spitzer during his brief, unhappy tenure in office had declared to one legislator that he was "a (bleepin') steamroller" who would flatten those who took him on. The unions soon discovered that Andrew Cuomo, who before his stumbling bid for governor in 2002 had a reputation for similar boasting, now lacked Spitzer's bluster but was more than capable of rolling over them.

A New Sheriff's in Town; The Town Is Nottingham

(August 26, 2011)

"Stop Coddling the Super-Rich" was the headline for the op-ed article by Warren Buffett in the August 15 *New York Times*, which the investment guru began, "Our leaders have asked for 'shared sacrifice.' But when they did the asking, they spared me . . . While the poor and middle class fight for us in Afghanistan, and while most Americans struggle to make ends meet, we mega-rich continue to get our extraordinary tax breaks."

At the same time many were reading his piece noting that he and fellow billionaires are paying taxes on a far-smaller percentage of their incomes than ordinary employees because their capital gains on investments are taxed at a much-lower rate than earnings from actual work, the Civil Service Employees Association was counting the ballots on a wage contract—a term that's used loosely here—that would freeze pay for three years, require employees to take nine days of unpaid furloughs, and increase their health-benefit contributions by as much as 60 percent.

Members were asked to hold their nose with one hand while digging so deep into their pockets with the other because Governor Cuomo made a political decision that he, too, should spare the wealthiest of his constituents from the sacrifice being asked of their fiscal inferiors. He took a campaign pledge not to increase taxes to an extreme level by steadfastly opposing a push to extend the income-tax surcharge on high earners that is due to expire at the end of this year.

Why Afflict the Comfortable?

Even when a compromise was offered by Assembly Speaker Sheldon Silver under which the surcharge would be eliminated for all those making less than $1 million in taxable income, the new governor said no. He was determined to get the state's budget in balance by sticking it to his workforce without afflicting the most-comfortable residents of the state. In the Orwellian world of tabloid-driven politics, this is known as exercising leadership. Public workers are like peasants being leaned upon by the Sheriff of Nottingham, with no Robin Hood in sight to balance the scales.

Even after a slightly-more-onerous deal was voted down by the law-enforcement wing of Council 82, Mr. Cuomo barely sweetened the pot on wages to offer two 2-percent raises in the final two years of the five-year deal. He knew he didn't have to rely too heavily on the carrot because the CSEA's leadership was focused on the big stick he held: the threat of up to 9,800 layoffs unless the unions met his demands.

"People are terrified of the [upstate] economy," said one veteran union negotiator who nonetheless had been skeptical that the deal would be ratified. A three-year wage freeze is unprecedented in state and city collective bargaining over the past 45 years, and even the two-year freezes of the mid-1990s did not come with additional givebacks as part of the package.

Of particular concern, said this negotiator, who spoke conditioned on anonymity, is that Mr. Cuomo is holding two more hammers over the state's largest union: his vow that next year his top priority will be gaining legislative approval of a Tier 6 pension plan for future workers, and the fact that the no-layoff clause that was a key element of the CSEA accepting the givebacks only applies to the first two years of the contract and would not prevent people from losing their jobs if agencies eliminate their units.

"If I'm CSEA and I made this deal and I didn't have an understanding on pensions, that's a major faux pas," this negotiator said. "If things go belly-up, that [no-layoff] language is something you can drive a truck through."

More Fearful of Boss than of Members

Deals like this get done when labor leaders are more afraid of the government official on the other side of the table than they are of the wrath of their own members. Yet it's not as if Mr. Cuomo's take-it-or-else stance didn't carry risks for him as well. As much as he may have spoken during the campaign about the waste in state agencies, knocking 4,800 people—never mind 9,800—off the payroll would have adversely affected the services his administration is expected to deliver. He spent part of last year encouraging union leaders to read a biography of Hugh Carey that pivoted on how that governor saved the city—and by extension, the state—from the 1975 fiscal crisis. When Mayor Beame laid off tens of thousands of workers, it had a devastating impact on city services; one of Mr. Carey's key accomplishments was using a Federal jobs program as a device to bring back a sizable contingent of those employees.

But Mr. Cuomo went all-in playing the layoff card, and CSEA President Danny Donohue and his counterpart at the second-largest state-employee union, Ken Brynien of the Public Employees Federation, were unwilling to call his bluff. The PEF deal, also made under the shadow of hundreds of looming layoffs a month ago, was reached just six days before the CSEA mailed ballots to its members. The timing was exquisite for Mr. Cuomo: nothing can nip an up-from-the-grassroots insurrection against a one-sided contract like the hard reality that even if you don't accept the terms, your neighbors are likely to, leaving you in an untenable spot.

"Seventeen thousand people voted for it, which is not exactly a mandate," said Kitty Lerin, noting that this was just 25 percent of the CSEA's state membership, and that just slightly more than 40 percent of the rank and file had bothered to return the mail ballots. "I don't know why more people didn't vote," said the veteran Lottery Marketing Executive 1, who was outspoken against both the terms and the length of the contract.

She chalked up the relatively low return—more than 60 percent of city transit workers typically cast mail ballots on their wage pacts—to "apathy," but said she understood why many union members were reluctant to vote no and risk major job losses.

'Many Have Nowhere to Go'

"It's a different thing," Ms. Lerin said, "when many people are working for slightly above minimum wage and they don't have anywhere to go. A lot of people I think are just happy to have a job, and they're not willing to fight."

With more than 22 years of service, she had said last month that she was hoping to retire in three years, but on the day after the deal was ratified, she said the lost pension income that would result from the furloughs meant leaving even after five years might not be practical for her.

"I'm disappointed," she said about the contract. "I'll just have to live with it."

Even more revealing, her disappointment was apparently shared by many of those who voted for the contract. Among them was a co-worker, John O'Brien, a former CSEA elected official, who said that when he stopped into the State Lottery's Varick Street offices in lower Manhattan August 17, he found "a very somber mood. The younger people didn't seem relieved that their jobs had been saved. The older people were very distressed about the contract being passed."

And more than a few were mystified, he continued, about how the union wound up giving Mr. Cuomo the full savings he had demanded at the outset of talks, despite the claim by some CSEA negotiating team members that they had beaten back some of the more-unappetizing demands from the state.

'Did They Really Negotiate?'

"Some people said they never really negotiated that deal; it was cut months ago," Mr. O'Brien said. There was some additional cynicism over the fact that rather than using an outside party to tally the ballots, the count was conducted by what he described as the same officials who negotiated the deal.

"Even though I voted for the contract," he said, "there was so much mixed emotion I had about it and the methodology for the way it happened."

Yet how much less-severe would the union concessions have needed to be if Mr. Cuomo had agreed to a modified extension of the income-tax surcharge along the lines proposed by Mr. Silver? His claim that the state needed to send a signal that it was easing the tax burden before it could generate greater economic activity was indirectly contradicted by Mr. Buffett, who wrote, "And to those who argue that higher rates hurt job creation, I would note that a net of nearly 40 million jobs were added between 1980 and 2000. You know what's happened since then: lower tax rates and far lower job creation."

Soak Rich, Dampen Ambitions

The Oracle of Omaha went on to propose that the Federal Government raise tax rates on those making in excess of $1 million in taxable income, with an increase in the taxes they paid on dividends and capital gains as well. Mr. Cuomo, perhaps correctly, perceives that taking such positions is not the best way to advance a political future that he clearly hopes will land him in the White House after the 2016 presidential election.

Better than most people, he is able to appreciate the political price that can be paid for taking unpopular stands rooted in principle, even when you do so by appealing to people's better natures.

One such elected official many years ago criticized a president for a philosophy he described as "Make the rich richer, and what falls from the table will be enough for the middle class and those who are trying desperately to work their way into the middle class."

This official argued that to be a Democrat meant embracing a constituency that at its heart included "the middle class, the people not rich enough to be worry-free, but not poor enough to be on welfare . . . we believe in a government that is characterized by fairness and reasonableness . . . the sharing of benefits and burdens for the good of all . . ."

That speech did not help elect as president the candidate on whose behalf it was given. Nor, for all the plaudits it earned, did it lead the man who gave that keynote address at the 1984 Democratic National Convention to run and win, as some thought he was capable of doing, eight years later. But it enunciated ideals and a vision that our current governor seems to lack, even on those days when the cadences and throbbing intensity of his voice remind us of that speaker.

Then again, maybe Andrew Cuomo believes his father could have gotten a lot further politically if he'd strong-armed public employee unions and their members a few times to gain approval from those higher up on the income ladder.

In December 2011, after being dubbed "Governor 1 Percent" by Occupy Wall Street and amid mounting public sentiment for requiring the richest New Yorkers to pay more, Mr. Cuomo steered into law a variation of Sheldon Silver's proposal that slightly reduced the surcharge for those with taxable income above $1 million—while making that rate a permanent part of the income tax—but restored individuals earning between $200,000 *and $1 million to the old tax rate and offered a small reduction to those earning less than that. Any notion that this marked a lasting shift in his sentiments was quelled when, less than six weeks later, he proposed sharply reducing pension rights for future city and state workers.*

Staring Down the Barrel of Reagan's Legacy

(March 4, 2011)

"Why does it always fall on the backs of workers?" Jimmy Conigliaro, the head of the New York/New Jersey branch of the International Association of Machinists, asked the crowd of labor activists gathered on the steps of City Hall February 23 in support of the public employee unions in Wisconsin.

"Labor has to stand up," he said insistently to the cheers of the couple of hundred people gathered. "We first went through this with Reagan . . . we can't sit back anymore."

Earlier in the month, the centennial of Ronald Reagan's birth was celebrated amid drives to memorialize the 40th president on everything from public buildings to the $50 bill. For more than a few union members, however, the Gipper's winning smile and sunny personality were the tools that offered right-wing forces in this country the opening for a full-scale attack not only on the power of unions but on the benefits and job protections granted to working people here.

The most-notorious example, of course, was Mr. Reagan's decision to fire the entire cadre of Air Traffic Controllers while decertifying their union in response to their strike in 1981, his first year in office. It sent a signal to private employers that it was open season on unions that stood up aggressively on behalf of their members, one that was accompanied by changes at the National Labor Relations Board that made it more difficult to bring unscrupulous employers to justice and to organize employees who lacked representation. Cutbacks in staffing and enforcement at the Occupational Safety and Health Administration meant that workers who didn't belong to unions found it especially hard to have job hazards even inspected, never mind corrected.

Chipped Away at 50 Years of Gains
As amiable as he could seem, that is a large part of the Great Communicator's legacy: he served as a front man for those seeking their own version of a claw-back of the gains made on behalf of ordinary Americans starting with the New Deal legislation of the 1930s and continuing with the rise of the American labor movement, as well as the civil rights struggles of the 1960s. As was noted in Eugene Jarecki's recently released documentary, *Reagan*, his subject, who as a teenager had been an idealistic but nearsighted lifeguard, in office seemed blind to the ways in which government programs had allowed his own family to survive the Great Depression despite a less-than-conscientious father and promoted policies that reopened the income gap between the well-off and ordinary Americans to something like what had existed during his early boyhood.

Small wonder, then, that the other primary engine behind the hard-right swing of the 1980s, the media empire of Rupert Murdoch, has strived so hard over the past couple of weeks to cast Wisconsin Governor Scott Walker as a modern-day Reagan tilting against the greedy public employee unions dragging his state toward insolvency. That narrative got a bit of a jolt on the same day as the City Hall rally, however, when a blogger impersonated David Koch—a billionaire who along with his brother Charles was a major financial backer of Mr. Walker's election victory last November—and engaged the governor in a lengthy colloquy about his tactics in dealing with the protesting state workers. Mr. Walker confided to "Mr. Koch" his plans to trick State Senate Democrats who had left the state to delay a vote on his bill to end collective bargaining for public workers into returning to the state capital in Madison on the pretext of negotiating with them. He also said he had considered planting "troublemakers" among the protesters.

At one point the Wisconsin governor said he was looking into whether the unions were paying the hotel bills of the state senators who had holed up in Illinois to prevent a quorum that would have allowed his bill to pass, suggesting that would be a serious ethical violation. But when the phony Koch later in the conversation said, "Well, I tell you what, Scott: once you crush these bastards I'll fly you out to Cali and really show you a good time," Mr. Walker replied, "All right, that would be outstanding. Thanks for all the support."

The Billionaire's Club

When the governor explained that he had offered to meet with the Democratic senators as a ruse to lure them back inside the state so that they could be forced to allow a vote to proceed, the faux Koch told him, "Bring a baseball bat. That's what I'd do."

Mr. Walker replied, "I have one in my office; you'd be happy with that."

He went on to say that he had showed his staff a photo of President Reagan and likened what he was attempting to do to the firing of the Air Traffic Controllers. "That was the first crack in the Berlin Wall, because the Communists then knew Reagan wasn't a pushover," the governor said.

Their conversation, the kind Mr. Murdoch's media outlets reveled in when those taken in were unsophisticated employees at ACORN and Planned Parenthood (not surprisingly, this episode was disposed of in a 100-word brief in the next day's *New York Post*), ripped the veneer off the Wisconsin governor as someone just trying to cope with serious budget problems to show him serving the interests of a billionaire whose twin bogeymen are unions and government regulation. Rather than the kind of crusading reformer Frank Capra immortalized in *Mr. Smith Goes to Washington*, Mr. Walker now resembled a mash-up of the protagonists of two later Capra films—*Meet John Doe*, in which Gary Cooper played an ordinary guy being manipulated by a wealthy man trying to use his populist patsy to bring fascism to America, and *State of the Union*, in which a candidate for the Republican presidential nomination played by Spencer Tracy denounces Big Labor as a threat to the country at the behest of a wealthy newspaper publisher. The modern-day real-life parallels are striking enough that the night before the Walker hoax was revealed, protesters massed outside Mr. Murdoch's News Corporation, which they called the driving force behind the Tea Party movement.

Even before Mr. Walker's unctuous display in conversation with the man he believed to be David Koch, it should have been clear that his crusade against the unions was one rooted in ideology rather than economics, since the American Federation of State, County and Municipal Employees chapter in Wisconsin had by then agreed to significant benefit concessions that were equal to a pay cut of 7 percent for their members.

A Pass for Union Supporters

Givebacks are an unfortunate part of collective bargaining in recent years for both public- and private-sector unions. Mr. Walker has pushed beyond that with his bill—also supported by the Republican majorities in both houses of the Wisconsin State Legislature—seeking to strip the public employee unions of collective-bargaining rights on all matters besides wages. Any doubt that this was a political push was swept aside by the fact that he exempted the police and firefighter unions—which both endorsed him last year—from the bill's provisions.

"If he was really a purist, he wouldn't have made those exemptions," Hector Figueroa, the secretary-treasurer of Local 32BJ of the Service Employees International Union, said during an interview at the News Corporation protest. "If you ask the rank-and-file police and fire, I think they would say they overwhelmingly support the right of other public workers to organize and collectively bargain."

International Association of Firefighters General President Harold Schaitberger delivered a fiery speech during a rally in Madison at which he declared, "This is about the heart of America . . . You fought for the right to have collective bargaining, and there's no goddamn state legislature gonna take it away from you now." But it was notable that neither the Patrolmen's Benevolent Association (PBA) nor the Uniformed Firefighters Association (UFA), both of which have traditionally been more conservative than the IAFF, had their leaders at last week's City Hall rally.

Not Burning GOP Bridges

Two weeks earlier, UFA President Steve Cassidy and his PBA counterpart, Pat Lynch, stood on those same steps denouncing Mayor Bloomberg for trying to strip their members of the $12,000 annual Variable Supplements Fund benefit, starting a campaign that forced the mayor to scale back his legislative effort to deny it only to those who weren't already eligible. Spokesmen for the two union heads did not return calls about why they didn't attend last week's rally, on an issue that doesn't directly affect their rank and files, although most labor leaders believe that what happens in Wisconsin will wind up affecting labor unions both public and private all over the country. But both union presidents have maintained strong ties with Republicans throughout the state, and Mr. Cassidy provided a crucial endorsement to President George W. Bush's 2004 reelection campaign at the same time that the rest of the labor movement was protesting his policies outside Madison Square Garden during the Republican National Convention.

Ed Ott, the former executive director of the AFL-CIO New York City Central Labor Council, said February 22, "It seems to get more plain than anything that the Republican Party doesn't want unions to have collective-bargaining rights. The big surprise is the Democratic Party showed some spine for a few days. It's finally dawning on people that [Republicans and their financial backers] don't want any organized group bargaining for working people. It's either the beginning of something very important or a very, very, very bad moment."

61 Percent Oppose Rights Loss

One official from a national union pointed to a Gallup Poll showing that 61 percent of Americans surveyed opposed the stripping of collective-bargaining rights for Wisconsin public employees. But that was also the percentage that told Fox News on Election Day that they favored discontinuing the Bush tax cuts that disproportionately benefit the wealthy, only to see President Obama a month later bow to the political reality that Congressional Republicans would not act on any legislation he championed unless he extended the cuts.

And one obstacle to translating sentiments expressed to a pollster into real political force is that, as Mr. Figueroa noted, less than 7 percent of private-sector workers are union members. Even in New York, just 16 percent of private-sector employees are unionized. That lack of representation, he said, means "you have lost the base of support for public workers." It was why the chants at both of last week's rallies here of "nationwide strike!" stirred apprehension among those in the crowd who were a bit more realistic about the mood in the country and the ability of the forces aligned against them to shape it.

It is why Kathryn Nocerino, a retired Administrative Staff Analyst from the Human Resources Administration, was out of step with most people outside the union movement when she lamented, "Instead of going after the super-rich to pay their fair share of taxes, they go after the workers, the poor. Corporate and bank profits and bonuses are the highest ever recorded—Bernie Madoff isn't the only crook."

That is not part of the prevailing national dialogue, however, at least not judging by the coverage in the *Post* and the *Daily News*. Actually, the pension and health-benefit rights government employees enjoy are so superior to what most other workers receive that it has been used against them by chief executives and editorialists to stir up resentment among those employed outside the public sector. Mr. Figueroa told the crowd outside Mr. Murdoch's corporate headquarters, "The lack of pensions and health care in the private sector is what we have to fix." During the City Hall rally the following morning, Communications Workers of America Local 1180 President Arthur Cheliotes declared, "After they get rid of us, there's no stopping the race to the bottom."

'30 Years of Wage Suppression'

Mr. Ott, who is a labor historian, said the growing disparity in benefit rights between the public and private sectors was traceable to the Reagan era, when companies walked away from unions by relocating to right-to-work states or moving their operations overseas, two trends that still continue.

"You've gone through almost 30 years of wage suppression in the private sector," he said. "The unions have to figure out a way to get wages up in the private sector."

He also said the unions had to do a better job of communicating the benefits to ordinary citizens of having an orderly collective-bargaining process for public workers. It allows for their grievances and demands to be addressed without resorting to the strikes that were prevalent in the days before key rights were granted, starting in, ironically enough, Wisconsin in 1959 and then spreading to New York. While right-wing critics here have blistered then-Governor Nelson Rockefeller for approving the Taylor Law locking in those rights for state workers, he was moved to do so in part because the previous law prohibiting public employee strikes, the Condon-Wadlin Act, was ineffective because it required that strikers be fired. Mr. Reagan had an entire nation to choose among in replacing the Air Traffic Controllers, a luxury state and local governments don't have in dealing with strikes by large employee groups like the transit workers, and so the Taylor

Law offered a far more practical, and therefore daunting, penalty of deducting two days' pay for each day of a job action.

Tax Cut As Good As a Raise?

The wave of primarily Republican governors (with Governor Cuomo one notable Democrat who has taken the same tack) elected in recent years after vowing to get tough on public employee unions while refusing to use taxes to help cope with serious budget deficits has been aided by the peculiar logic planted in citizens' minds as they cope with their own financial problems.

"In the absences of anything else," Mr. Ott remarked, "the tax cut is a form of wage increase."

He thought Governor Walker "overplayed his hand" by seeking to strip public workers of virtually all their collective-bargaining rights. But later in the week, governors in swing states like Ohio and solidly Republican ones like Oklahoma pushed for similar legislation, hoping to ride momentum that Mr. Schaitberger said was generated by political pundits whom he called the modern version of strike-breaking Pinkerton guards.

"The financial elites and their political mercenaries are waging class warfare against working people and the middle class," Stuart Appelbaum, the president of the Retail, Wholesale and Department Store Union, told those gathered at the City Hall rally.

Chris Shelton of the CWA turned the rhetorical flame even higher, saying, "What this is about is not even collective bargaining and unions. It's about two things: power and greed. They wanna take away our democracy and let corporations rule this country. They will destroy the middle class if we let them."

For the moment, however, the unions are having trouble making that sale to the American public, and in some cases, even communicating the urgency of the situation to some of their colleagues.

'They're Out for Blood'

One official whose national union is heavily involved in the battle in Wisconsin expressed optimism about Mr. Walker's gaffe, the decision by Indiana Governor Mitch Daniels—who stripped public workers in his state of bargaining rights shortly after taking office six years ago—not to press legislation that would have made Indiana a "right-to-work" state, and the resistance to Ohio Governor John Kasich's anti-union efforts.

"These bad guys are out there pushing class warfare, and they're out for blood," he said. "If we can keep demonizing Kasich and Walker . . ."

Then again, as Mr. Conigliaro said ruefully, unions "first went through this with Reagan." It's been downhill ever since for the labor movement, and a bill is finally being presented to the public sector unions that have weathered the onslaught better than others.

The only reason for optimism is that those leading the charge against them lack someone who projects likability as well as Mr. Reagan. And with Governor Walker's duping, the public got some insight into who makes people like him dance by pulling the strings from behind the curtain.

Even before the economic crisis of the past few years brought public employees and their compensation to the fore as a target for savings, right-wingers were beating the drums for privatization as part of their crusade against Big Government.

One of the early supporters of this approach who held local public office was Mayor Rudy Giuliani, sometimes for tactical reasons, sometimes for what cynical people thought were financial enrichment, as well as in cases that seemed overtly political or ideological. When he took office in 1994, armed with the suspicion that New York City was no longer reaping the full productivity gains intended from a 1981 program that cut staffing on Sanitation Department trucks from three workers to two, he briefly flirted with the idea of contracting out some collection work until he gained a new agreement with the Uniformed Sanitationmen's Association that lengthened routes and strengthened language on recycling duties.

He turned most of his focus, however, to contracting out in areas like social services and education where he did not seem to have much expertise but could advance his political career by placing himself more in step with the conservative wing of the national Republican Party.

Giuliani had run for election promising to "reinvent government," arguing that a string of Democratic mayors had let patronage hirings turn municipal agencies into jobs programs. The subtext of this claim was that many of the employees in the agencies he was talking about were black and

Latino and were using their positions as generations of white workers had before them as a passport into lower-middle-class life. They were doing so in agencies that were known for bureaucratic sclerosis, making them low-hanging fruit for attack.

At one of those agencies, the Department of Employment, he began his second term in 1998 by appointing a supportive city councilman, Antonio Pagan, as commissioner, fleshing out his thin list of minority appointees to ranking positions in his administration. But he then set about phasing out the agency's duties in favor of using private-sector firms to prepare the city's welfare recipients for the world of work.

Perhaps his most-ambitious foray involved a 1999 $104-million job-training contract awarded to a firm called Maximus that was given a five-month head start over other potential bidders. Among the interesting aspects of the deal was that $30 million of this money was supposed to go to a firm known as Opportunity America, which was headed by Richard Schwartz, who prior to striking out on his own in the private sector had been Mr. Giuliani's key adviser on welfare-to-work issues.

A contretemps arose the following year over the cozy arrangement and the bidding advantage that the firm had been given, with some wondering whether, if Mr. Giuliani was out of public office when his term as mayor ended at the beginning of 2002, he might land nicely on his feet with a position as special counsel to Opportunity America at the kind of retainer befitting a man of his stature.

The controversial contract award wound up in the courts, where so many of his privatization efforts played out and eventually faded into obscurity: by the time in 2001 that a lower-court ruling was reversed and the contract was allowed to stand, Maximus had lost interest in the project.

Mr. Giuliani by that point had forged ahead with efforts to privatize some city hospitals and, when that move was stymied in the courts, hospital services, ranging from food to security. There generally were several political elements to each of these moves—beyond the currency they earned him in national Republican circles as he looked beyond the city for a career that was supposed to be launched with a 2000 run for U.S. Senate—they tended to come at the expense of unions that had either been political antagonists of his or had simply not supported his 1997 reelection run at a point when many normally Democratic labor leaders had crossed over as a matter of self-preservation. He knew he couldn't count on those unions for future political contributions, while private firms that gained city business were inclined to be generous to their benefactors.

The 'Evil Genius' Loses One

(March 9, 2001)

There were three dozen Health and Hospitals Corporation (HHC) Special Officers sitting in Manhattan Supreme Court Justice Charles J. Tejada's courtroom February 28 when he began reading his decision granting their union an injunction blocking city efforts to privatize hospital security.

They sat silently, some in uniform, others in civilian clothes but with their badges displayed, as Justice Tejada made clear what his decision was going to be by mentioning contract language requiring that Teamsters Local 237 be allowed to make a counterproposal to that presented by the private contractor.

"An injunction is warranted here," the judge said, "because the court finds likelihood of success on the merits of the improper practice charge [and] irreparable harm" to the employees if the contracting out began before the improper practice case was decided by the city Board of Collective Bargaining (BCB).

'City Won't Suffer More'

"Neither the city nor the HHC will suffer harm which will be proportionately greater than the harm suffered by petitioners if not afforded their rights under the collective-bargaining process," he said.

"There is a great public interest in maintaining labor peace through the use of collective-bargaining mechanisms. There is the public interest of maintaining proper security for these [hospitals] pending the resolution of these issues before" the BCB.

It was only when Justice Tejada said what he had already made obvious, that he was "granting the injunction," that the rapt silence was broken by the exclamation of "Yes!" by a hospital cop in the second row, while others raised their arms triumphantly. And then a dozen of them applauded, a celebration so restrained that neither the judge nor the court officers saw any need to quiet them.

"That was the most monumental victory in our history," one of the Special Officers said as he stepped into the 15th-floor elevator with his jubilant colleagues. "If we lost, this would have been the end of the Taylor Law."

His words might have seemed hyperbolic, since their union president, Carl Haynes, had not regarded the hearing as worth killing a morning to attend. ("His lawyers told him his presence wasn't necessary," Mr. Haynes's spokeswoman said the following day.)

But the symbolism behind this confrontation should have made clear what was at stake for even those municipal employees who weren't directly affected: HHC, with the encouragement of the city, was ready to cast off a well-regarded workforce of 850 unionized employees to save money on less-qualified personnel—who will be paid roughly half as much—provided by a private contractor.

"They talk about a $313-million shortfall," said Special Officer George Roache of Lincoln Hospital, referring to the budgetary problems HHC President Luis A. Marcos has cited to justify privatization. "The state government has a surplus and the city government has a surplus. If the state and the city really cared about poor people and funded HHC, there wouldn't be a shortfall. I think the mayor feels the city shouldn't be in the hospital business, and that's why he shortfunded HHC and hasn't supported the hospital police."

Hoped for 'Kinder, Gentler Mayor'

Mr. Giuliani in the past had peaceful if not always joyous relations with Local 237. Mr. Haynes was able to gain rank-and-file approval of the same onerous 1995 wage contract containing a two-year freeze that District Council 37 got past its members only by stealing their votes. His argument at the time was that job security was his first contract priority, and that he had gained it with a provision guaranteeing against layoffs through mid-1998.

"They were probably hoping to get a kinder, gentler mayor in upcoming negotiations," Mr. Roache said when asked if he was surprised that Mr. Haynes pushed approval of that deal.

Dwayne Webb, an 11-year veteran of the hospital police who works at Kings County Hospital, shared the view that Mr. Haynes thought he had improved his future bargaining position when he agreed to the contract at a time when the mayor was coping with serious budget problems. Now, well after those problems have been solved, Mr. Giuliani has continued underfunding HHC, paving the way for it to try to cut corners by laying off a sizable contingent of Local 237's membership. The administration has offered school security jobs to the hospital cops, but accepting them would require taking a pay cut.

But unlike some of his colleagues, including the then-heads of DC 37 and Transport Workers Union Local 100, Stanley Hill and Willie James, who cast aside their doubts about Mr. Giuliani's intentions and endorsed his reelection, Mr. Haynes remained neutral during the 1997 mayoral run.

Asked why, Mr. Haynes's spokeswoman, Moronke Oshin, said of the mayor, "I don't think he was being particularly kind to labor at that point. Carl didn't feel comfortable giving him our endorsement."

Not a Stealth Mayor
It's telling that Mr. Haynes is still in office while Mr. James and Mr. Hill have both been forced out, with their problems in coping with nonpolitical issues the primary reason for their ousters.

It's not as if Mr. Giuliani ever concealed his intentions—one prominent union official early on paid grudging tribute to the mayor's skill in overpowering key labor leaders without having to go to war by dubbing him "that evil genius."

From the outset of his administration, Mr. Giuliani eviscerated the city's subsidy to HHC, and by the time of his reelection campaign he had already tried to privatize Coney Island Hospital and been thwarted in court, in no small measure by the City Council and its Speaker, Peter Vallone. Mr. Vallone also intervened in the security privatization fight by steering through a bill that would make it impossible for a contractor to take over hospital policing.

Amid all the mayor's sweet talk to labor leaders during his first term, there was little effort to conceal his intent of chipping away at their memberships, unless they were cops—and the hospital police clearly don't count in Mr. Giuliani's reckoning. His first labor negotiator, Randy Levine, six years ago described the mayor's vision of "a smaller, better-paid workforce." It's doubtful any labor leader believes the mayor has made good on the "better-paid" part of that pledge but, except for adding thousands of NYPD cops while keeping their salaries low, he has certainly pursued the "smaller" part of that vision with enthusiasm.

"We don't have our wages up to par," said Marilyn Jarrels, who has spent the last 25 years of her 29-year career as a Special Officer working at Kings County. "Their bringing in per-diems and wanting to privatize is not right."

"People aren't as well-trained; I doubt whether they're going to take the risks we take," remarked Leona Wilson, a 30-year veteran of Kings County. "They'll just be security; they're not allowed to arrest."

That distinction is at the heart of the council bill that is currently pending before the mayor: contract security personnel would not have the peace officer powers enjoyed by the Special Officers.

'First Line of Defense'

That is a huge difference, said Goldie Ack, another Kings County Special Officer who has 15 years on the job. "You have a lot of violent crimes in hospitals," she noted. "The [nearest police] precinct is a while away; we're the first line of defense when patients' safety is at risk."

Crime in the hospital system has dropped sharply over the past two decades because of improvements in training and the dedication of employees, said Steve Green, who retired not long ago as a Hospital Police Captain after spending 30 years working at Harlem, Morrisania, and Metropolitan Hospitals.

If the public wants a preview of the troubles that await if hospital security is privatized, Mr. Green said, "You don't need to look any further than what's happened in HRA, where violence has increased in the welfare centers. Private security could never do what these trained peace officers do."

The mayor and Dr. Marcos have chosen to ignore the problems encountered by the Human Resources Administration (HRA), not the least of which is the reluctance of contractors to have their employees intervene in violent incidents because of concern about liability suits. HRA and its sister agency, the Administration for Children's Services, have a long history of not acting to correct dangerous situations until tragedy strikes because they serve primarily poor citizens who lack the ability to attract attention until they become victims of truly horrendous crimes. Their inaction has been tolerated and thus enabled by the news media, which also tends to zone out on safety issues affecting the poor until somebody dies.

Self-Fulfilling Prophecy?

The defunding of HHC by the city can have a similarly corrosive effect, since any decline in service and hospital safety is likely to drive away patients who can afford treatment at private facilities. This makes ex-patients of those constituents who are most capable of rallying political support for public hospitals, while creating in their minds doubts about those institutions' worth. It also makes the municipal hospital system increasingly the province of the poor and the voiceless.

And so unions like Local 237 and DC 37 have had to take up the cudgel along with community activists and have used their clout in the Council and the power of the law—whether interpreted by judges or, in this case, the Board of Collective Bargaining—to protect municipal hospital services and their members' jobs.

The BCB late last month ruled that there was reasonable cause to find that HHC had not bargained in good faith with Local 237 before moving ahead with its plan to privatize security in the hospitals. It was that decision that was the linchpin of Justice Tejada's ruling, which blocks privatization for up to two months until the BCB makes a final decision in the case.

Making the Law Work

And so once again, the mayor's orchestration of HHC's withdrawal from the hospital business has been stymied, not by a public outcry but by the legal safeguards meant to keep even evil geniuses in check.

Four years ago at this time, former Mayor Ed Koch correctly forecast DC 37's endorsement of Mr. Giuliani, predicting it would back him despite the deep philosophical divide between its members' needs and the mayor's desires because "unions are now engaged in saving unions more than saving the world."

Labor leaders, some quicker than others, have come to understand that "saving" their unions by embracing Mr. Giuliani is often just a temporary reprieve. More-lasting survival depends on being ready to fight him.

Giuliani was succeeded in 2002 by another Republican, the billionaire Michael Bloomberg, whose financial status placed him beyond the lure of well-heeled corporate contributors. His primary interest in privatization was in the area of charter schools, having become convinced that the union-ized workforce in the city school system was too well protected by contract rules governing everything from job security to discipline to achieve to his standards. Despite that belief, he cultivated a solid relationship with the then-president of the United Federation of Teachers, Randi Weingarten, with whom Giuliani had constantly warred, and eventually made peace with most of the city's major unions.

But Bloomberg was convinced that the city was paying more than was reasonable toward employee health-care and pension costs, and as municipal finances worsened during his second term, he began taking aim at curtail-ing those benefits. State law guaranteed that pension rights could not be reduced for those already on the payroll, leading him to push to cut benefits in that area for future city workers, while he also made the case that the lack of basic health-care out-of-pocket costs for city workers was not only unique but a luxury that could no longer be afforded.

His strongest offensive initially involved a benefit extended only to cops, firefighters, and correction officers known as a variable supplement, which was derived from the profits of their pension funds but was not considered a pension benefit, making it subject to reduction if he could gain the consent of the City Council and the state legislature. Bloomberg was not averse to stretching the facts to help bolster his case with the aid of a compliant and sometimes uninformed media.

'Christmas Bonuses' and Other Wicked Fables

(March 20, 2009)

"Let me tell you about the very rich," Scott Fitzgerald wrote in his short story "The Rich Boy." "They are different from you and me."

To which Ernest Hemingway later wrote in response, "Yes, they have more money."

This explains the phenomenon of Mayor Bloomberg, seeking reelection after antagonizing much of the population by getting the Term Limits Law amended for his own benefit without using a voter referendum, striving mightily to reduce compensation for future cops and firefighters at the same time that he is lobbying against tax increases on wealthy New Yorkers.

On his March 6 radio show, Mr. Bloomberg, who has proposed a sales tax increase that would most affect poorer residents, argued that it was bad policy to raise taxes on the wealthy because it would prompt some of them to leave the city and dissuade those who may be considering coming to live here.

Please Don't Annoy the Affluent

"The first rule of taxation is," he said, "You can't tax too much those that can move."

He did not say who wrote that rule, but Marie Antoinette wouldn't be a bad guess.

It's the sort of thinking that has helped bring our national economy to the state it's in: don't do anything that might upset the most privileged in our society, no matter how much the alternatives work to the detriment of those further down the pecking order.

Yet it also runs counter to something the mayor has said more than once during his seven-plus years in office, and sometimes to well-to-do audiences: that even if the cost of living is higher here, there's an energy and a unique climate for ideas that argue strongly for the city being the place you would want to settle and start a business if you're a person of ambition.

Which raises the question as to whether, if the city or state were to impose income-tax hikes aimed at those making $250,000 or more a year, he's primarily worried that we might drive out those getting paid well but not really earning it. Which ultimately wouldn't be quite the drag on the economy he fears, since it's entirely possible that persons with more drive will move into the luxury homes and apartments they vacate in search of a low-tax haven.

Two days after Mr. Bloomberg voiced his concerns that those persons of means more fickle than he is about the city's virtues might abandon it, the *New York Post* began a three-day crusade against its version of undeserving slackers: retired cops and firefighters.

A Sunday feature on the sizable disability pensions some firefighters were receiving was followed the next day by an article on what the paper called "Christmas bonuses" for police and fire retirees in the form of $12,000-a-year Variable Supplements Fund (VSF) payments each December. And the lead editorial in Tuesday's *Post* tied it all together under the headline "Five-Alarm Payouts."

It referred to the VSF payments as "the legacy of a decades-old sweetheart deal," noted the mayor was battling grimly in Albany to discontinue the practice for future cops and firefighters, and concluded by hoping "it's not too late to stop the coming pension tsunami from swamping the city *completely*."

Partly Based on a True Story

It was a remarkable performance in the service of Mr. Bloomberg, although as is sometimes the case with the *Post*, it was also at odds with the facts. Which brought to mind the observation by a fellow alumnus of the paper, Rob Polner, that, "If journalism is the first rough draft of history, the *Post* is the first rough draft of journalism."

Start with the first two paragraphs of the March 9 VSF story: "So-called 'Christmas bonuses' given to NYPD and FDNY retirees as pension 'sweeteners' topped $450 million last year and are poised to be an extra-sour burden on recession-shocked city coffers.

"Deft bargaining by union officials 40 years ago won their retirees a share of the returns of their pension funds' investments—and in a later amendment to the deal, the unions masterfully negotiated a fixed-cash payment whether the funds experienced a boom or a bust."

It's an interesting concept: take a well-known situation—the city's not in great shape and police and fire retirees receive cash payments in addition to the pensions—sprinkle in some likely sounding but utterly false claims about the history of the VSF, and stir, hopefully bringing public discontent to a boil.

The truth, as is invariably the case, is quite a bit more complicated.

For one thing, the implication in those paragraphs is that the unions snookered the city to get the original benefit and then played a second mayoral administration for chumps so that their members got all the gravy while the only ones at risk were the taxpayers. It relies in part on caricatures of Mayor John Lindsay—under whose administration the VSF originated—as too generous to the unions, and of Ed Koch—who was there when the conversion to a defined benefit occurred—as a softie when it came to police and fire bargaining. Neither of those stereotypes has much relevance to what actually happened.

The original deal came about at the city's urging because the Lindsay administration wanted to be able to invest money from the Police and Fire Pension Funds in the stock market and needed the approval of the unions. The unions wanted an improvement in the formula used to calculate what percentage of salary would determine pension allowances for their members.

City Actuary Proposed VSF

The matter went before an arbitrator, former United Nations Ambassador Arthur Goldberg, and during the discussions, the Chief City Actuary at the time, Jesse Feld, proposed as an alternative that the VSF be created, with funding to be provided only in years when the performance of stock investments topped that of the city's bond holdings by a specified percentage. The unions decided this was acceptable, and Mr. Goldberg incorporated it in his award. The funds were created by a state law passed in 1970 that made them retroactive to October 1, 1968.

So much for the "sweetheart deal" described in the *Post* editorial. In fact, while profits were good enough to provide "skim" into the VSF for the first two years of the funds' existence and an initial benefit of $40 per month for "service" retirees (those who receive disability pensions are ineligible for the VSFs, even if they worked the 20 years mandated to qualify for a full regular pension), an 11-year dry spell followed.

A Mutual Desire for Change
The lack of growth in the funds brought some restlessness within the police and fire ranks, which intensified when at one point fire officers were unable to receive benefits because there wasn't enough money in their union's fund in the early 1980s. Then a five-year stretch of robust stock-market performance swelled the VSF coffers, producing a climate in which both sides were looking to make a change.

By the time the Patrolmen's Benevolent Association was negotiating for a contract that would take effect retroactive to July 1, 1987, the VSF payouts had risen to $150 a month, but retirees and some active members were convinced that much more could be paid. The city and union trustees who oversaw the police and fire VSFs were constrained by the recommendations of the City Actuary, who had to be certain that the funds would not have their reserves exhausted if the stock market suddenly tanked.

While this was frustrating to recipients, Mayor Koch found it exasperating that when the skims came, the retirees did well but the city could not take advantage of the boom times to pull out excess funds to improve services. He instructed his chief negotiator, Bob Linn, to seek a deal with the PBA that would pave the way for the city to have predetermined costs in return for set payments, limiting what it would have to share during bull markets.

'Traded Uncertainty for Certainty'
A reminder of the way the market could turn came with the October 1987 crash and probably helped convince the PBA that there was something to be said for a defined benefit payment, even if it potentially surrendered a bigger share if the boom times came again. Then-union President Phil Caruso reached an agreement in May 1988

under which the city gained control of the PBA fund by agreeing to raise the annual benefit from $1,800 to $2,500, with $500 increases in each year to follow until a peak was reached of $12,000 in 2007. Mr. Linn said, "We were both willing to trade uncertainty for certainty."

Some other police and fire union leaders had reservations about the trade-in, for reasons that went beyond the city placing a different value on the shift for the PBA than for their members. Within the Uniformed Firefighters Association, a vocal group sprang up in a Bronx firehouse that laid out in detail why it believed the deal did not make financial sense for firefighters.

Mr. Linn predicted at the time that the city would realize its greatest savings from the trade-in over the long haul, and a decade later that prediction seemed to have been borne out with a vengeance. During Rudy Giuliani's second term as mayor, it was estimated that the city's share of the pension funds' profits during the stock-market boom of the late 1990s was $4 billion greater than it would have been had the unions refused to make the conversion to a defined-benefit payment. There were those who joked that the city ought to erect statues of Mr. Linn and former Deputy Budget Director Howard Green—who put together the calculations for the trade-in—alongside Nathan Hale's at the west entrance of City Hall.

No Skim if Funds Were Flush
Mr. Green also had the foresight to get a key component into the VSF legislation that maximized city profits during the boom: a "sluice-gate" provision under which it was only required to skim off profits from stock investments if the funds' liabilities exceeded their assets at the time.

Then the market cooled off at the beginning of this decade and reached what Mr. Bloomberg has described as meltdown status over the past year. No longer does it seem that the unions got taken and the city made out like bandits, and the swing of the pendulum has served as a reminder that union leaders' decision "to trade uncertainty for certainty" was a pretty good one. Nobody would argue, however, that this amounts to a bonanza, unless they were trying to create a straw man for the legislature to knock down by passing the Tier 5 pension proposal Governor Paterson put forward largely at the mayor's request. And Mr. Bloomberg has found a willing accomplice in the *Post*. "They have so much misinformation," UFA President Steve Cassidy said during a March 11 interview. "They're lumping apples and oranges."

'That's Scoppetta's Team'

The story about firefighters retiring with huge disability pensions, he contended, created a false impression that his members were winding up with retirement allowances that exceeded their salaries. The top five people on the list of disability pensions, Mr. Cassidy noted, were among the department's most-senior people, not only in terms of service but by rank. "The *Post* is referring to staff chiefs as firefighters," he said. "They're [Commissioner] Nick Scoppetta's management team."

And that article and one last month about a rise in the percentage of fire retirees who qualified for disability pensions between 2004 and 2007 made it sound like the system was being gamed when the actual cause was what the UFA leader called "hopefully a once-in-a-lifetime catastrophic event."

"The *Post* and those at City Hall seem to want to pretend that 9/11 never happened," Mr. Cassidy said. "It seems clear that City Hall is interested in a new pension tier system and the mayor has tried to demonize firefighters to help get it."

In addition to the verified lung damage suffered by 10,000 firefighters who were part of the response teams during the post-9/11 recovery and clean-up operation at the World Trade Center site, he noted, "We responded to more emergencies in the last five years than ever before. This is an incredibly physical job."

That helps explain why even prior to 9/11, better than 60 percent of the firefighting force was retiring on disability pensions, reflecting both the physical grind and the accumulation of toxins in their lungs from fighting fires and the build-up of diesel fumes from their trucks inside the firehouses.

Warns of Aging Force

The situation will worsen, Mr. Cassidy said, if the Tier 5 bill is passed, requiring future firefighters to serve 25 years before qualifying for a full pension and leaving them unable to collect at that point if they are younger than 50.

The great majority of those who spend more than 20 years on the job, he said, are officers, and even those among them who are still responding to fire scenes are not carrying the 100-plus pounds of gear borne by line firefighters. "The roofman carries 130 pounds of gear, and in many situations they are required to go up aerial ladders doing it," he said. "It is and remains a young man's job, but a lot of the realities have disappeared as City Hall pushes for a new pension tier."

His counterpart at the PBA, Pat Lynch, didn't even mention the physical liabilities of the potential change, instead focusing on how it would hurt the Police Department's ability to recruit. (Mr. Bloomberg, whose agreement with the union last summer brought starting salary—which had been $25,100 at the start of 2008—to slightly more than $40,000, is clearly hoping that would-be cops are unaware of the money they would lose if the VSF was eliminated for future hires.)

'Not Source of City's Problem'

"Furthermore," Mr. Lynch said in a statement, "the Variable Supplements Fund has long been self-funded and still is today. It does not cost the city a dime. Our pension is not the source of the city's fiscal problems and should not be looked to as the solution."

Mr. Cassidy is concerned enough about the impact that a steady stream of stories in the tabloids and editorials in all three city dailies have had on Albany legislators that last week he placed a full-page ad in the *Capitol*, a newspaper distributed there, pointing out the hazards of firefighting and defending the pensions his members receive. He also noted that his retirees who qualify for pension cost-of-living adjustments have them reduced by the amount they receive in VSF payments.

"I am very concerned," he said about the prospect that the bill could get caught up in a tidal wave of Bloomberg-orchestrated publicity about the drawbacks of the current pension and VSF systems. "I believe that many of the elected officials don't fully understand what firefighters do day in and day out."

Given the desire of both the *Post* and the mayor to highlight the city's hundreds of millions in annual costs resulting from the VSF, last week's article had one curious omission: the fact that firefighters who retired last year could have received payments worth several times the $12,000 maximum.

A DROP from Mayor's Narrative

That little sweetener resulted from Deferred Retirement Option Plan (DROP) legislation passed in 2002 under which firefighters from that point on who continued working after marking their 20th year on the job could "bank" the VSF payment for each year they would have received it had they retired. In other words, someone who would have been eligible to collect the bonus in December 2002, when it was $9,500, but continued working, by last December would have accumulated $76,500 in his VSF "DROP" account.

It would have been a bit awkward for the administration to point this out to the *Post*, however. For one thing, the DROP program was set up because Mr. Scoppetta was concerned about retaining experienced staff after the FDNY's top command under his predecessor was devastated by the loss of veteran officers on 9/11.

For another, this "Christmas bonus" that multiplies for as long as the affected 20-year veterans stay active was ushered through the legislature at Mr. Bloomberg's request.

He would undoubtedly agree with Mr. Fitzgerald and Mr. Hemingway that what you leave out of a story is as important as what you put in.

Unions Finally Aroused
by Mayor's Distortions

(February 18, 2011)

The Citizens Budget Commission (CBC), according to its president, Carol Kellermann, focuses on "whether the taxpayers' dollars are wisely spent."

She made this remark February 9 at a conference called "Rethinking the Rules of Public Employment" as a prelude to pointing out that the city's pension-benefit costs now account for more than 10 percent of the city budget and "almost as much as we spend for police, fire and sanitation combined. There's a similar problem with health insurance for retirees."

These are old, familiar refrains for the CBC, so much so that the pamphlet it distributed at the conference sponsored by the conservative organization Common Good, entitled "The Explosion in Pension Costs: Ten Things New Yorkers Should Know about Retirement Benefits for New York City Employees," was actually published in April 2009 and relied on pension-fund data that only went through June 2007. This was okay, because some things never change for the CBC, which was founded by business interests during the Great Depression and seemingly has just one reason for being: to make the case that city employees are getting too much.

Blinkers on for CityTime

If the focus were broader than that, Ms. Kellermann's presentation might have touched on the more-than $700 million that has been spent on the CityTime payroll system that was originally expected to cost $63 million, with numerous glitches still to be ironed out and the meter clicking merrily away. Or the $1.8 billion the Bloomberg administration has spent on an emergency-response communications system that the unions contend is less efficient than the old procedure.

Not to mention why, if Joel Klein was such a whiz-bang chancellor despite lacking any background in education before Mayor Bloomberg anointed him, he had at the time his departure was announced last November eight deputy chancellors to prop him up when traditionally no more than three had been needed. Or even why the mayor himself has seven deputy mayors, a number Ed Koch started with and cut down to three before he'd completed a year in office because he'd discovered bigger didn't necessarily mean better.

But that's not why the CBC is here. Some might accuse it of being misnamed, but a more-accurate moniker, say the Anti-Municipal-Worker Budget Commission, would not have the nonpartisan ring that serves its purposes so well.

The Manhattan Institute, at least, makes no pretense about being an even-handed good-government organization. It is a right-wing think tank that regards much of city government's history prior to the Giuliani administration as a calamity. E. J. McMahon, the senior fellow who heads the Institute's Empire Center for New York State Policy, is an amiable and quotable man who knows his stuff, although it may not be a coincidence that in assigning blame last week to various mayors and governors for allegedly giving away the store to the unions, he left out both Mr. Giuliani and then-Governor George Pataki, whose pension deals a bit more than a decade ago are responsible for many of the benefits Mr. Bloomberg is trying to roll back today.

Mr. McMahon also gets a kick out of hyperbole. A study he co-authored two months ago entitled "New York's Exploding Pension Costs" featured a cover photo of a mushroom cloud above a pile of rubble, and in talking about what he regards as Governor Rockefeller's policy of appeasing public employee unions in return for political support, he invoked Neville Chamberlain's "peace in our time" remark following his Munich capitulation to Adolf Hitler.

The CBC and the Manhattan Institute, along with the editorial pages of the *Daily News* and every part of the *New York Post* besides the sports section, have proved useful allies in the mayor's crusade to strip the municipal unions of key employee benefits and rights at a time when the strapped fiscal condition of both the city and state has created a climate in which the only question regarding cutbacks is how deep they have to be.

Unions Slow to Grasp Mayor's Aim

The unions, on the other hand, have seemed slower to grasp the urgency of the battle before them, perhaps because they are convinced that the city's financial problems are less grave than Mr. Bloomberg claims. But while the crisis is the product of a money shortage, the real issues are power and control, and the mayor's belief that the unions are a hindrance to his exercising both.

It's hard to imagine that a man who has staked a big chunk of his legacy on education intends to lay off massive numbers of teachers; Mr. Bloomberg himself floated the number of 21,000 a couple of weeks ago and then swiftly yanked it in favor of "thousands," as if he couldn't believe his own threat. Nor would a big reduction in pension rights for future employees save the city significant money in the short term, notwithstanding his questionable claim that up to $200 million could be carved out this year alone. The preposterousness of imagining that the legislature, or even the City Council, would approve stripping police and fire retirees of their Variable Supplements Fund rights gives rise to the thought that the mayor only threw that out there—after just two weeks earlier targeting only those who weren't yet collecting the benefit—because it was the one benefit cut that he could claim would produce a billion dollars in immediate savings. (The police and fire unions are skeptical of that projection, but that's another story.)

But the VSF proposal, and the mix of outrage and fear it generated among police and fire retirees, had the effect of propelling their two largest unions out of the shell from which they previously issued press releases and into the breach in front of City Hall last Wednesday, where Patrolmen's Benevolent Association President Pat Lynch stated loudly that Mr. Bloomberg was full of what he called misinformation.

The PBA leader accused the mayor of lying about the VSF being a "Christmas bonus" "to make the public mad and confuse legislators." Uniformed Firefighters Association leader Steve Cassidy was even more blunt, saying Mr. Bloomberg was essentially telling retirees, "I'm gonna steal money from your pocket."

They pointed out that the city benefited greatly from the 1988 VSF trade-in when the stock market was booming a decade later, and it had $4 billion more available for general spending than it would have if the deal had not been made. Part of the agreement, under which the unions had immediately surrendered $150 million from their funds, was that, as Mr. Cassidy put it, the benefit "goes on forever."

'Telling One Lie after Another'

The UFA leader grew angrier as he spoke in the biting cold. "No mayor has conducted himself like this," he said. "To go to Albany and sit before the legislature and tell one lie after another."

Mr. Lynch called it "insulting" to pit workers against each other by saying, as Mr. Bloomberg had, that he would have to lay off 10,000 teachers if legislators did not do the right thing by wringing the money out of the police and fire retirees who had the bad taste to go on living and collecting their "Christmas bonuses," not to mention their unspeakable pensions.

"What's next," Mr. Cassidy interjected: "he's not gonna pick up your garbage unless he gets the VSF?"

Something interesting happened: local television stations besides NY1 covered a story that was too complicated to be reduced to easily digestible sound bites. The daily papers reported the story in some depth, with even the *Post*—which started the ball rolling on the mayor's VSF crusade two years ago with a spectacularly distorted story about its history—presenting the unions' positions fairly.

Perhaps most remarkably, two days after the rally—and following a meeting with Mr. Cassidy—the *Post* editorial board urged the mayor to focus his VSF efforts strictly on denying the benefit to future hires and chided him for "almost sneeringly dismiss[ing] the payment as a 'Christmas bonus.'" You would have thought it wasn't the same paper that two years ago popularized that phrase during a three-day series, culminating with an editorial entitled "Five-Alarm Payouts" that called the VSF "the legacy of a decades-old sweetheart deal."

Tough to Get Labor's Side Out

Numerous union leaders have lamented that it is increasingly difficult to get their story out on issues that involve conflict with city and state government. State AFL-CIO President Denis Hughes last year wrote an op-ed piece to rebut editorials in the *Post* about the cost of city employee pensions, and the paper refused to publish it. Communications Workers of America Local 1180 President Arthur Cheliotes, speaking at the same Common Good forum last week where Ms. Kellermann made her remarks, said that when it comes to issues like employee benefits and seniority protections, "much of what we read in the media comes from a corporate-run media."

And until the unions launched last week's offensive, it seemed unrealistic to expect the owners of many of those media organs to be brought up short by the idea of depriving retired cops and firefighters in their 70s and 80s of a $12,000-a-year payment that in some cases eclipses their basic pension allowances. Rupert Murdoch, who owns the *Post*, the *Wall Street Journal*, and two local TV stations in addition to the Fox News Network, 18 years ago reveled in using the bankruptcy laws to deprive some longtime employees of more than $100,000 in severance pay when he busted out the Newspaper Guild at the *Post*; for those workers, the severance money *was* their pension.

The unions in recent years have generally been content to play the inside game to achieve their objectives, counting on longstanding relationships with legislators on both sides of the aisle in Albany to protect their turf and to occasionally win benefit improvements. That may not be good enough in the current climate, with Governor Cuomo seemingly reluctant to blow his extended honeymoon with many of the conservative media forces that have aligned with the mayor in his anti-union campaign, and Senate Majority Leader Dean Skelos at the very least talking the talk Mr. Bloomberg wants to hear after donating $650,000 to help Republicans regain control of the Senate last year.

Chance to Win Over Public

But labor leaders, like their counterparts upstate, have begun to realize that much of the public is not dazzled by the rhetoric suggesting that they should take government workers down a notch by stripping them of benefits not available to many of those in the private sector. Those representing city workers have the added advantage that Mr. Bloomberg's mishandling of the CityTime boondoggle followed quickly by his blizzard fiasco have turned public opinion against him at a time when he was already on probation with many residents because of the manipulations that gave him the chance to seek a third term. His slimmer ration of good will has been further eaten away by Cathie Black's less-than-endearing public persona as Mr. Klein's successor.

And so union leaders, despite Mr. Bloomberg's edge in off-payroll advocates to buttress his case, possess an advantage if, rather than simply responding to his offensive, they aggressively but reasonably make their own case. They are not trying to carve out more benefit gains at a time when their affordability is in doubt but rather preserve what they have as the product of fair negotiations.

In that pursuit, they enjoy one clear advantage over Mr. Bloomberg: telling the truth does not hurt their cause.

Pensions a Beachhead for Class Warfare

(May 26, 2010)

The cover of *Barron's* last week featured a cop and a firefighter lounging on beach chairs and holding cocktails at some island resort beneath the headline "Investors Beware." Smaller type said, "States and cities are going broke. One reason: gold-plated pensions for police, firemen, teachers and bureaucrats."

The story by senior editor Jonathan Laing began, "Like a California wildfire, populist rage burns over bloated executive compensation and unrepentant avarice on Wall Street. Deserving as these targets may or may not be, most Americans have ignored at their own peril a far bigger pocket of privilege—the lush pensions that the 23 million active and retired state and local public employees, from cops and garbage collectors to city managers and teachers, have wangled from taxpayers."

Several cute concepts are test-driven in the passage. One is the attempt to equivocate about whether rage over "bloated executive compensation and unrepentant avarice on Wall Street" is justified; another is the move to downplay the drain on the economy by the greedy boys who created a national financial crisis by arguing that "a far bigger pocket of privilege" can be found in pensions that public workers "wangled," presumably by using something even more insidious than derivative swaps: the collective-bargaining process.

'Leave Seniors Eating Dog Food'

Mr. Laing builds momentum as he goes, arguing that while the defined-benefit pensions are not affected by economic turbulence, defined contribution plans that offer retirement income for others are, and so "maybe some seniors will have to switch from filet mignon to dog food."

And grandpa battling Fido for the daily meal isn't the only dire consequence of what the article headlines as "The $2 Trillion Hole." Cuts in public services are sure to bedevil local governments, Mr. Laing writes, some of which "don't even have the courage to switch new teachers, bureaucrats and police to a defined-contribution system, to prevent the funding problems from worsening as time rolls on."

He goes on to say, "Stories are rife around the country of various pension hijinks by public employees," citing a fire chief in California "who boosted his annual pension from $221,000 a year to $284,000 by getting credit in his final earnings for unused vacation and sick leave."

The unusually large pension allowance is supposed to leave readers so stunned that they don't ask why putting the unused leave time to an employee's advantage amounts to "hijinks" rather than a product of the bargaining process that acknowledges that an employer benefits by having workers whose attendance is so good that they retire with significant leave balances that can buttress the size of their monthly checks.

It would be easy to dismiss the piece as a screed against public workers disguised as a straightforward news report from a publication known for its hard-right ideology even before it came under the talons of Rupert Murdoch's media empire. But a day after it appeared, New Jersey Governor Chris Christie used his budget speech to offer a ringing denunciation of public employee unions for having played a lead role in creating his state's $10.7-billion budget deficit.

He vowed to veto any proposal to increase taxes to cover that hole, instead proposing a 9-percent cut in state spending that would include 1,300 layoffs—from a state workforce of 65,000—next January, and pension-system reductions that would include the repeal of "an unwarranted 9-percent pension increase" that his fellow Republicans approved in 2001.

"Is it fair to have any public employees getting 4.5-percent salary increases every year, even when inflation is zero percent, paid for by citizens struggling to survive?" Mr. Christie demanded. "Is it fair to have New Jersey taxpayers foot the bill for 100 percent of the health insurance costs of teachers and their families from the day they are hired until the day they die?"

Praise the Workers, Damn Union Bosses

He tried to draw a distinction between "rank-and-file teachers [who] know this is not fair" and their "union bosses," as if those teachers were imploring their union to give up hard-won benefits and forsake pay raises in the best interests of the state, only to be rebuffed by their greedy leaders. Governor Christie went on to demand changes to limit contract arbitration awards and to allow local governments "the option of opting out of civil service."

Given that he campaigned against incumbent Jon Corzine's past coziness with labor, including a Communications Workers of America local whose president at one point was romantically involved with the former governor, last week's diatribe was not shocking. But taken together with the *Barron's* piece and the attempt by Republicans in Washington to hammer President Obama for his ties to labor, a trend begins to emerge of a bare-knuckle assault on working people.

Sometimes it's cloaked in arguments like those in the *Barron's* piece that public employee pensioners are the real fat cats who are gaming the system. State Attorney General Andrew Cuomo March 18 joined the pile-on by using precisely that term in announcing that his office would investigate cases of excessive overtime meant to pad pensions of employees at the end of their careers. He at least acknowledged that lack of management oversight rather than employee cupidity might be the root of the problem.

Whacking the City

A variation on Mr. Christie's claim that the "union bosses" are the cause of this milking of the public by their members occurred last week where the straw man taking the whacks was the city in which they worked. Indiana Congressman Steve Buyer derided a bill to aid workers who became seriously ill as a result of their work at the World Trade Center site on and after 9/11 as "Congress only acting for the benefit of New York City." Yes, New York, home of all those undeserving cops and firefighters and construction workers who irretrievably compromised their health by looking for survivors and then trying to recover bodies at the site and now have the gall to ask that their own medical problems be covered by the nation that was symbolically attacked when the terrorists drove their planes into the Twin Towers.

Mr. Buyer suffers from a pernicious strain of the malady that afflicts other government officials and editorial writers who put a more civil tone on their arguments: they love waving the flag on behalf of first-responders who die in the line of duty but have a tougher time reconciling themselves to the fact that generous health-care and pension provisions for those who survive the risks they face might be part of the reason those employees take dangerous jobs.

Mayor's War on VSFs

Mayor Bloomberg, aided more than a bit by Mr. Murdoch's *New York Post*, has been making the case for more than a year that those fringe benefits have become unaffordable, particularly for cops and firefighters, and must be scaled back. Last year, they collaborated in a campaign to stir public fury against the Variable Supplements Funds for cops and firefighters that give retirees $12,000 annually beyond their basic pension allowances, and given the worsening economies of both the city and the state and the fact that the VSF is unique to the city forces, it is likely another legislative push against them—certainly for future members of the NYPD and FDNY—will begin later this spring.

The mayor two weeks ago presented a list of 14 demands to the Municipal Labor Committee (MLC) aimed at reducing the city's health-benefits costs. They include eliminating the HIP HMO rate as the benchmark for all health-plan reimbursements and imposing co-payments and deductibles for all members of that plan, as well as cutting city welfare-fund contributions. Mr. Bloomberg wants to eliminate the annual $35 million the city provides to the Health Insurance Stabilization Fund, require employees to work for at least 15 years to qualify for health benefits once they retire, and cut Medicare Part B reimbursement in two key areas.

However unpalatable most of these changes are to the MLC, there will be growing public pressure for concessions once the media campaign is cranked up that such givebacks are preferable to the kind of service cuts that might be forced by city and state budget problems.

Another Wall Street Con?

But State AFL-CIO President Denis Hughes argued that the building frenzy is the result of clever manipulation not unlike what the

Wall Street wheeler-dealers exercised first for their massive rip-offs and then to return to old routines with their bonus compensation not only intact but fervently defended by Mr. Bloomberg and Governor Paterson.

"We're in a fiscal situation that was based on the inability of investment bankers and other financial experts to properly manage risk," Mr. Hughes said in a March 18 phone interview. "But the people who are responsible for this economic downturn walk away unscathed. And the only real tangible effect is the assault on the economic security of working men and women. To go after the pensions of people who in many cases have risked their lives and are in high-stress public jobs is really outrageous."

Uniformed Firefighters Association President Steve Cassidy strongly concurred with that sentiment. "I don't have to make an excuse for the pension system we have—not at all," he said. "It is a backstop for the families of firefighters who are seriously injured or killed. I don't think a system that would have firefighters standing outside a burning building wondering whether their families will be taken care of if they're killed or seriously injured would serve the public's interest."

He acknowledged concern, however, that a climate could develop in which the demand for reduced benefits placed intense pressure on the unions to resist. "I think there's clearly a movement afoot to try to take the fiscal crisis and use it to demonize public employees," he said.

Patrolmen's Benevolent Association President Pat Lynch, who noted that the city's pension systems—in contrast to New Jersey's, where Mr. Corzine held back nearly $1 billion of a scheduled contribution last year—are more than adequately funded, called the *Barron's* piece "just one more volley in a misinformation campaign designed to deflect attention away from Wall Street's role in our recent financial collapse. The fact is that the pension benefit for New York City police officers is part of an overall compensation package that is modest in comparison to other police officers, locally and nationally."

'Blaming the Victim'

Mr. Hughes said that while it is difficult for labor to get its side heard by the media in such situations, "We have to make that case. It's a classic example of blaming the victim."

One longtime government official with a healthy respect for both capitalism and the pension system said the campaign against public employee benefits was freighted with irony, as the barons of the business world practiced a kind of class warfare that turned private-sector workers against their public-sector counterparts.

"A very real problem that civil servants have these days is pension envy," said this official, who spoke conditioned on anonymity. "To give the moneyed class credit, they have succeeded in getting many people angry that civil servants have these pensions, rather than that *they* don't."

Uniformed Sanitationmen's Association President Harry Nespoli sees a hypocrisy in the demand to reduce the cost of public employee benefits at a time when Wall Street firms that created the problem are back to doling out seven-figure bonuses as if they hadn't been kept afloat with Federal bailout money.

Referring to the sentiments voiced by the *Barron's* piece and Governor Christie, he said, "Isn't that the reaction all the time? Let's turn around and kill Main Street and the middle-class."

Don't Punish Unions' Foresight

Public workers shouldn't be punished, he continued, because they and their leaders had the foresight to recognize the importance of good pensions and health benefits long before they popped up as national issues because of an extended Wall Street slump that required local governments to spend more to cover those benefits.

"We gave up [portions of] raises for benefits many years ago," Mr. Nespoli said. "Now they're complaining about the benefits being too good. But I don't see how you can compare a civil-service pension to what people like Rupert Murdoch get. All we have is a piece of the American dream that we got for saying we're going to dedicate our lives to the city. I don't think that's asking much."

Over the past two decades, a municipal labor movement that had previously been seen as notably more honest than some private-sector union leaders in New York representing carpenters, longshoremen, and painters who at some point wound up in Federal court facing charges of organized-crime infiltration was discovered to have its share of rogues and thieves representing everyone from clerical workers to transit cops.

Yet based on the complaints of some top officials of two consecutive mayoral administrations and their supporters at New York's tabloid newspapers, the greatest threat to civilization among them was posed by a diminutive woman never accused of financial wrongdoing named Randi Weingarten, who spent a dozen years as president of the United Federation of Teachers before moving on to head its national union, the American Federation of Teachers.

The daughter of a public school teacher, her first affiliation with the UFT was as a lawyer for its outside labor-negotiations firm, and she wound up on the losing end of a 1985 wage-contract arbitration battle. She survived that setback, which came toward the end of the tenure of legendary UFT President Al Shanker, and was brought in house by his successor, Sandra Feldman, first to be her chief negotiator and eventually, in 1997, to succeed her when she took over the national union.

As president, Weingarten was a soft-spoken but tenacious advocate for her rank and file. She feuded with Rudy Giuliani, who denied her members a long-overdue contract largely from spite, but cultivated a friendly relationship with Michael Bloomberg, even as she often wound up clashing with his Schools Chancellor, Joel Klein.

Giuliani, Klein, and their tabloid allies accused her of looking to protect incompetent or morally deficient teachers at the expense of the system's 1.1 million pupils and of using her alliances in the state legislature to block much-needed reforms. Weingarten countered that she was merely offering her members the vigorous representation to which they were entitled and that many of the changes being sought at the top of city government were ideological in nature and would actually harm education.

Despite her occasional dust-ups with Bloomberg, she persuaded him to raise teachers' pay 43 percent over a six-year period. She also won added benefits from him for agreeing to a plan for merit-pay awards on her own terms and a revised pension plan for future workers that, although less generous than what existed for incumbent teachers, was decidedly more generous than the pension arrangements negotiated at the same time for state workers. There was little doubt that she was the best of the city's union leaders in a time of major transition.

The first of the following columns was written roughly halfway through her tenure as UFT president; the second one as she was winding down her time there in order to devote her full energies to the national union.

Tabs to Randi: Burn, Baby

(November 21, 2003)

It sometimes seems like the editorial pages of the *Post* and the *Daily News* believe that educational reform should begin with the building of a stake outside the Tweed Courthouse, the better to facilitate the burning of Randi Weingarten.

After the *Post* took the early lead in the battle to brand Ms. Weingarten a witch for performing her job as the president of the United Federation of Teachers, the *News* has been playing catch-up ball, apparently convinced that extremism in the pursuit of readers is no vice.

A week after one of its more-excitable columnists advocated provoking a transit strike to reform New York City work practices, the *News* published a November 12 editorial titled "Scurrying from Sunlight" that lambasted Ms. Weingarten for criticizing City Council Education Committee Chair Eva Moskowitz's plan to hold hearings on teacher work rules under the UFT contract. To make sure its audience grasped the image of a rodent that it was trying for, the editorial chortled, "How delightful her squealing is!"

Letting the Testosterone Flow

Imagine one of the city's tabloids using such language to describe the president of the Patrolmen's Benevolent Association over a similar dispute tied to a contract. You'd have to use your imagination, because it hasn't happened and is unlikely to in the future. It isn't necessarily sexism at work; the deep thinkers who write editorials at the two papers might show better control of their testosterone-fueled impulses where the PBA is concerned simply because they worry far more about being labeled anti-cop than anti-teacher. Or, for that matter, anti-labor.

It happened that a day prior to the *News* editorial, several stories ran in the dailies quoting Ms. Moskowitz as saying that teachers who had planned to testify about harmful provisions of the UFT contract had been scared off. She compared it to the atmosphere that existed when Frank Serpico was the one cop willing to talk about police corruption 30 years ago.

Confronted about the analogy, Ms. Moskowitz insisted she hadn't meant to imply there was the threat of violence of the kind that left Detective Serpico seriously wounded after fellow cops were slow to respond as back-up during a drug bust. She told reporters she hadn't really been talking about Mr. Serpico specifically, but rather about the climate during the Knapp Commission hearings where he was the star witness, when "there were many instances of intimidation of witnesses."

She was speaking following her November 13 hearing on the teacher contract, a few minutes after Ms. Weingarten had jolted the City Council Chambers with a sustained burst of fury that was initially directed at Council Member Moskowitz but soon turned to Schools Chancellor Joel Klein and, to a much lesser degree, Mayor Bloomberg.

Saying her union had blown the whistle on problems in the schools much as Mr. Serpico had on wrongdoing in the NYPD, Ms. Weingarten remarked, "And so, when I realized the implications of the chair's comment, I thought it was really strange for her to evoke his name in this context."

'We Expose, They Demonize'

Her voice rose in intensity as she made her case: "Forty percent more assaults on my members the last year, more overcrowding than we've ever seen before. My suspicion is that the more we talk about this, the more we will be demonized and the more my members will be demonized."

She had been preceded at the hearing by Anthony Lombardi, the principal of P.S. 49 in Queens, which was rated one of the 200 most-improved schools in the city. Mr. Lombardi testified that there were sections of the UFT contract that had the effect of saying "hands off to supervision." He claimed that it was too difficult and time-consuming to fire teachers, and so he instead often looked to persuade bad instructors to change schools.

When Council Member Robert Jackson asked whether the problem with the UFT contract didn't amount to poor management decisions in agreeing to some of its provisions, Mr. Lombardi responded that there was "a management vacuum that the UFT filled."

Ms. Weingarten fired back that if the UFT contract was so good at protecting teachers, "Why do they have no control or latitude in their classrooms?" With a teacher from P.S. 49 seated alongside her, she called Mr. Lombardi "tyrannical," then asked, "Is what Tony Lombardi does, is his style of leadership, the preferred style of leadership today? His definition of a qualified teacher is one who when he asks you to jump, you say, 'How high?'"

She continued, "Highly qualified teachers bristle at demands for blind obedience to dumb directives. If teaching under this contract is such a cushy job, why do one in four new teachers leave within a year, and 40 percent leave within three years? Even though retention rates throughout the country are bad, they are not as bad as this."

Ms. Weingarten said at least 200 new teachers had not yet received their first paycheck more than two months into the school term, and thousands had yet to receive health-insurance coverage.

An Offer He Can Refuse

She pointed out that in September she had offered to waive the contract rules in up to 150 schools, conditioned on teachers being given a say in setting the working conditions at the pilot schools. She still has not gotten a response from Chancellor Klein, Ms. Weingarten said, nor a set of contract demands from him nearly six months after the old agreement expired.

She made it clear that she objected to Ms. Moskowitz's hearing because the media coverage it attracted colored the atmosphere in which she and the Bloomberg administration bargain. "Forcing participants in collective bargaining to make public commitments up front makes great headlines, but we've seen in the past few days that it also makes the participants' positions far more rigid," she said.

Ms. Moskowitz said following the hearing, "If the timing is bad, when do parents and the general public get to say what they feel?"

Ms. Weingarten, however, pointed out that until she raised a fuss about the hearings, the Education Committee had not planned to give the public a chance to testify.

She accused Mr. Klein of scrapping successful programs that produced recent gains in student achievement—including the chancellor's district under which underachieving schools went under the direct control of him and his predecessor—arguing that his main gripe was that he couldn't claim credit for implementing them. There was little question about her target when she said, her voice rising to a crescendo, that veteran teachers disliked being condescended to and told "'just do it my way and don't ask questions,' especially by people who have never walked in their shoes."

She said of her members, "They want change. They don't want parts of the contract that are in now. But what they don't want is to be defamed and demonized."

Citing one portion of the contract that school officials have attacked, a provision that exempts teachers from having to monitor students in school cafeterias or hallways, Ms. Weingarten said the prime mover behind the contract language was then-Mayor Rudy Giuliani.

She told the committee what is widely accepted as the genesis of the provision: freeing teachers from those chores created the need to hire more school aides, giving the mayor the happy circumstance of being able to reward one of his key labor allies, Charlie Hughes of Board of Education Workers Local 372 of District Council 37, with thousands of additional dues-paying members. She and her members, Ms. Weingarten said, would have been much happier with a pay raise, although she noted that the discontinuation of monitoring duty allowed teachers to spend more time in the classroom.

Cutting Peer Program

She pointed out that the chancellor was looking to eliminate the Peer Intervention Program, which was created under the UFT's 1987 contract to allow tenured teachers who were performing unsatisfactorily to get help from their colleagues in a school, despite the fact that it costs just $500,000 a year.

She clashed with Ms. Moskowitz over the seniority provisions of the UFT contract, which she said existed to guard against the kind of favoritism that was rampant when Tammany Hall–style patronage controlled government jobs and assignments. When she asked Ms. Moskowitz whether she believed any teacher invoking seniority transfer rights to claim a desirable vacancy was automatically a bad teacher, Ms. Moskowitz shot back, "Of course not. You have a very good way of twisting words."

In the days preceding the hearing, UFT officials had cited the rumors that Ms. Moskowitz planned to run for Manhattan Borough president in 2005, suggesting she was using the hearings to raise her political profile. Ms. Weingarten said during the hearing that Mr. Klein, too, had an ulterior motive, contending he was happier posturing as an educational purist being thwarted by an evil union than negotiating changes that would leave him "responsible for the results."

She said, following more than two and a half hours of sparring with Ms. Moskowitz, that she believed Mr. Klein's caustic comments about the contract to a *Post* reporter several months ago "created the environment" for last week's hearings.

'Doesn't Consult Us'

"There's no consultation," she said in reference to the chancellor's management style. "There's nothing other than a peripheral conversation about any of those things . . . but the rhetoric about the contract has gotten more and more heated."

Ms. Moskowitz, asked about Mr. Klein, responded, "I don't know that much about his vision." She made clear, however, that she'd gotten a bit more than she'd bargained for from Ms. Weingarten.

"Randi's a very good street-fighter," she said. "I hope to acquire those skills." She asserted that the UFT leader, while accusing others of demonizing her members, was "demonizing anyone who wants to examine" the UFT contract and its impact on the school system.

One city official who's no fan of Ms. Moskowitz said following the hearing that he wondered whether Ms. Weingarten's coming on so strong had really helped her cause.

If the tabloid editorials are the gauge, he had a point. The *Post* the following day said that all she did at the hearing was "Rant. And carp. And whine about being 'demonized.'" The *News* said Ms. Weingarten had "[gone] batty trying to defend the indefensible."

A Phony Populism

But all she had really done was stand up for her members and poke holes in many of the arguments that the UFT contract was a prime impediment to students learning. Pointing out that this is what a labor leader is supposed to do would be wasted on the *News* and the *Post*. Their owners both take a certain pride in having busted out the Newspaper Guild a decade ago while accommodating the two unions that even management officials acknowledged were the ones most responsible for unreasonable costs: those representing the drivers and pressmen.

If the chancellor and Mr. Bloomberg are sincere about making significant educational improvements, sooner or later they're going to have to deal seriously with the UFT. The union has outlived a decentralized system that some pundits claimed would diminish its power. Instead, UFT leaders figured out how to leverage that system through activism in school board elections, until finally, as Ms. Weingarten noted, the union used its muscle to help Mr. Bloomberg get Albany approval for the system to be restored to City Hall's control.

That's one pretty good sign that the UFT is too smart and too tough to shrivel up just because some blowhards break wind in the public prints.

Sister Randi Explains It All

(December 21, 2007)

Randi Weingarten's 50th year was an eventful one.

The United Federation of Teachers leader, who celebrated a landmark birthday December 18, was elected to her fourth full term as president in March with 87 percent of the vote, a mandate that was expected after the early wage contract she negotiated was ratified by 90 percent of her members a year ago.

In April, Mayor Bloomberg compared the UFT to the National Rifle Association while complaining about the disproportionate power it was wielding in thwarting the implementation of another school reorganization plan. Ten days later, the plan had been restructured to win the UFT's blessing, eliminating language that would have reduced teachers' tenure rights and committing money to reduce class size.

Merit Pay and Pension Gains

In October, Ms. Weingarten reached a deal with the mayor under which a school-based merit-pay program was agreed to, granting bonuses to every teacher in struggling schools that showed marked improvement. Not incidentally, the initiative was linked to the city's support for two measures that improved pension rights for union members and retirees, one of which allowed them to qualify for a full pension at age 55 if they had 25 years' service.

Later that month, the UFT won the right to represent 28,000 home day-care workers, expanding its active membership by nearly 25 percent, to roughly 150,000—allowing it to surpass District Council

37, which had been the largest municipal-employees union for the previous 40 years.

It was almost enough to overshadow the fact that a couple of weeks earlier, Ms. Weingarten had publicly disclosed that she was gay while accepting an award from Empire State Pride Agenda.

All this, and sweating out the serious illness of a close family member who has since taken a turn for the better, might have seemed quite enough for one year. But Ms. Weingarten, whose admitted flaw—"Unless it's perfect, I'm not satisfied"—gives her away as a compulsive overachiever, lived up to type in a less-welcome way when an early birthday roast December 4 nearly turned into the site of a carpenters' union picket featuring the inflatable rat that strikes terror into the heart of any labor leader at whom it's grinning.

It turned out that another of Ms. Weingarten's activist moves— using $28 million of teachers' pension funds to build affordable housing for union members—had become a good deed punished because the developer opted not to use union labor, contrary, the UFT leader said during a December 11 interview, to the assurances she received when the deal was announced two months ago. She believed those assurances enough, she said, that trades-union officials were "legitimately" furious about her insistence that the developer intended to honor prevailing-wage regulations for union jobs.

"It was unfortunate that it took so long to realize what was going on," said Ms. Weingarten, who ended the UFT's involvement in the project. "I desperately want affordable housing for our members. But you can't accomplish that at the expense of other union members."

National Union on Her Horizon?

It was one of the rare embarrassments she has endured in the decade since she stepped up on an acting basis to replace the late Sandy Feldman, who left the UFT in mid-1997 to run the American Federation of Teachers following the death of Al Shanker. Ms. Weingarten is the third member of that troika that since 1964 has built the UFT into the model of a local labor union, and for much of the past year there has been speculation that if AFT President Ed McElroy did not seek another term next spring, Ms. Weingarten would follow her predecessors in leading the national union.

"All I've said thus far for the record is I won't rule out anything," she said. "I think my national president has done a fantastic job. His focus has been on organizing and politics—we've been out there doing the work we ought to do. My personal preference is for him to stay on. If and when he makes a different decision, I'll decide what my next steps are."

It is not as if she'll be idling until then. Ms. Weingarten, an avid and longtime backer of Hillary Clinton, will be more than a bit engaged by the Democratic presidential primaries, particularly New York's February 5 vote. And her roller-coaster relationships with Mr. Bloomberg and Schools Chancellor Joel Klein almost inevitably will produce some additional dips, curves, and shrieks in the coming months.

In mid-November, less than a month after the mayor lauded the UFT for being intrepid enough to agree to the school-based merit pay program, Mr. Klein resumed his role as the administration's educational Bad Cop by announcing that he had retained a team of lawyers to get rid of teachers faster. Ms. Weingarten decried the firing squad as inflammatory and overkill, and soon after questioned whether the Department of Education was engaging in age bias by not placing older teachers from schools that had been closed or contracted into permanent new assignments.

'Infantilizing Teachers'

"The most frustrating and infuriating thing is the infantilizing and disrespecting of teachers, both in New York City and across America," she said. Her "biggest anger" regarding Mr. Klein was his refusal to create an educational culture "that deeply respects the work that teachers do. Instead, I think he took the easy way out to be able to say he's the change agent, rather than the teacher being the change agent, or the school."

Mr. Bloomberg had parried such criticisms in the past by pointing out that during his administration teacher salaries have risen by 43 percent. Under the current contract, top pay for a teacher will reach $100,000 in May.

Ms. Weingarten, who began her career with the UFT more than 20 years ago as its outside negotiating counsel, isn't about to deprecate what she's been able to achieve at the bargaining table. She also knows the difference between Mr. Bloomberg's demanding and sometimes mercurial personality and the constant vituperation she faced from Rudy Giuliani, whose rudeness was compounded by a determination during his final year in office not to make a contract deal that would have benefited the city as much as the union. The pact was signed off on by Mr. Bloomberg less than six months after he took office.

'Raised Living Standard'

"On an economic basis," the UFT president said, "we've accomplished a lot with Mayor Bloomberg, even in the context of pattern bargaining, even with my objections to pattern bargaining. We've been able to change the standard of living for teachers [and] maintain health benefits and improve pension benefits in ways that members needed. One thing I admire about Mayor Bloomberg is that he will take the risk to make a deal. The other thing is, he supports education."

But, she added, the reluctance of the mayor and Mr. Klein to work more closely with the union on improving education has led to a system that has yet to strike the right balance "between tests and teaching" and a mistrust among her members of the administration's motives as it tries to expand its success in the lower grades to middle and high schools.

"I see some signs of turning corners," Ms. Weingarten said. "The level of teacher quality these days is huge; walking into classrooms, it's definitely better than it was in the '80s. But I don't see the esprit de corps that ought to be happening. There's still too much looking over people's shoulders. The mayor constantly cheerleads teachers, but there's the little ditty, 'Actions speak louder than words.'"

Mr. Bloomberg's success as a businessman has sharpened his belief in concrete results being the definitive proof of whether something works. Ms. Weingarten said she too is a believer in the value of standardized tests, but that they are overrated as a measure of how much students are really learning.

'Test Prep Not Life Prep'

"The focus on outcomes has probably been somewhat of a motivator," she said. "There's not a question that people know they're there to teach; nobody thinks they're just treading water. But the dilemma is that there's more time spent on assessing kids and what they've learned as determined by state standardized tests than on whether we're preparing them for college, whether we're preparing them for life.

"Can Johnny critically think? Can he engage in a debate about search and seizures? Can kids work as a team, and if they lose, come back and rally next time? That's not part of the conversation, at least on a macro level, and that's disheartening to me."

She continued, "I think they're gonna do everything in their power to get the highest test scores they can in the 2008–2009 school year," the final full one of Mr. Bloomberg's term. "But even if they get that, what will happen to the kids three or four years later? I've always been one who believes in incremental but sustainable results. The third-grade teacher builds on the second-grade teacher."

The incremental approach has served her well at the bargaining table. Ms. Weingarten's success in improving teacher salaries at both the entry and upper levels, and doing so with timely and even early contracts, has stood in marked contrast to the city union leader who most shares the struggle to keep pay competitive with what's offered in the suburbs: Patrolmen's Benevolent Association leader Pat Lynch. His contentious relationship with Mr. Bloomberg has not been interrupted by periodic happy endings, and the PBA is currently in arbitration to replace a contract that expired in August 2004.

Mastered Give-and-Take

Both union leaders have demanding rank and files, but Ms. Weingarten has fared better in breaking through members' expectations when they grew too high and in giving up some rights—on matters ranging from work time to transfer rights to discipline—as the price that had to be paid for better wages without alienating her members. Her 2005 contract, even though it was approved by 70 percent of her members, provoked significant grumbling because of concessions in all those areas. But, she noted pointedly last week, besides the tangible economic gains it produced, there was an agreement in that pact to explore a 25/55 pension bill that came to fruition in the deal reached two months ago.

And the hard feelings expressed two years ago by some delegates and rank-and-file members, she noted, spurred her to create the 300-person negotiating committee that proved a major help in formulating demands and reaching a solid successor contract last fall, nearly a year before the October 2007 expiration date of the previous one.

Reflecting on her 10 years running the union, she said, "What surprised me is how much I've learned since then. It shows the value of experience. I actually take more risks now than I did then."

That has carried over to her personal life, which gets crammed into a schedule that typically features 14-hour workdays. Many of those who deal with her regularly knew that Ms. Weingarten was gay; when she was together with her partner at union events, she would sometimes quietly introduce her to longtime acquaintances.

But until six months ago, she had never spoken openly about it, despite the urging of the rabbi at her synagogue, Sharon Kleinbaum. When she finally did so, during a service at Congregation Beth Simchat Torah in June, Ms. Weingarten said, nearly a dozen attendees profusely thanked her, with several uttering variations on "You gave me a will to live."

"That struck me," the UFT leader said. "It's 2007 and people are still afraid of the ramifications." A *New York Times* story about gay senior citizens who were "vilified in their assisted living facilities" because of their sexual orientation, she said, pushed her further toward a decision to make a speech in a larger forum.

'Not a Spectator Sport'

"If you want to speak truth to power, you have to make it personal," Ms. Weingarten contended. "Also, I tease about it, but when you reach a marker like 50, and 10 years as president of the UFT, you start thinking about whether you've done the things you want to do when it comes to things like social justice and economic opportunity. If you care about those things, it's not a spectator sport."

And so she made her public declaration while receiving the award from ESPA. After initial, straightforward news coverage, it became clear that she had not triggered a media sensation.

"I had a flurry of reactions [from union members] that were extremely positive," Ms. Weingarten said, "but mostly it was, 'Never mind. Let's talk about my grievance now.' Or class size."

As if energized by the response, she completed the deal combining school-based merit pay with the pension gains less than a week later, and the following week won the right to represent the home daycare workers. It proved, she said, that in its middle age the UFT had reinvented itself—"we tried to undertake this culture of organizing." In recent years, the union has expanded the number of nurses it represents and gained the right to bargain for administrative law judges, and she noted that during her tenure "we started calling ourselves a union of professionals, not just teachers."

'Salt of the Earth'

The home day-care providers, Ms. Weingarten said, are essentially the first level of education for the children they serve. "They're really the salt of the earth; they work so hard. This is a group of people who are incredibly exploited," referring to their low salaries and lack of benefits—even with the bargaining certificate, the UFT does not have the right to negotiate pensions for them. "They need the collective strength that a union gives them. They get the connection between being in a teachers union and the professional opportunities that may be created for them."

Ms. Weingarten wasn't even a teenager when the UFT under Mr. Shanker won the right to represent paraprofessionals in 1969, prevailing over DC 37 in a close vote. She is steeped enough in the union's history, however, to know that many teachers at the time opposed the organizing drive, either because of lingering resentments from the racially charged battle over community control of schools that fueled the lengthy UFT strike a year earlier or because they viewed the paras as less-qualified intruders in their classrooms.

'Like Night and Day'

This time, she said, there was none of that resistance. Some veteran teachers got involved in the organizing drive, and "most of them gave us permission to do it. The difference between what happened when para organizing started and what happened when we started with family day-care was really night and day."

Even as she welcomes a new group of employees to the union, she argues that their needs merely represent a more-acute version of what teachers face.

"Teachers are more respected than they've been at any time since I've been in education," Ms. Weingarten said. "It's still not enough." Whatever she's been able to achieve for them economically, she said, there remains the challenge of making "every school a school where parents want to send their kids and educators want to work."

Back in her mid-30s, this daughter of a teacher began reconstructing her career track, spending six years teaching in Brooklyn even as she went from being the UFT's outside attorney to its in-house counsel and later an officer who was groomed by Ms. Feldman to succeed her.

"The one thing that's never gone away is the idealism," Ms. Weingarten said. "I've become more practical and thick-skinned, but what's never gone away is the passion."

One of the sadder indicators of public labor's plight was the shutdown of the New York City Off-Track Betting Corporation after 40 years of existence at the end of 2010. A couple of months earlier, after surviving several doomsday scenarios, the unions representing both line workers and managers voted to accept sizable concessions, including the loss of more than half the 1,000-plus jobs in the betting operation, so that 400 or so could survive in a pared-down structure.

OTB had been plagued by political machinations—not the least of them, patronage hiring for numerous top jobs—from its outset and miscalculations that harmed its bottom line as the convenience it initially represented to those unable or disinclined to go to the track gradually ebbed as technological advances and legislative changes made it possible for customers to bet first over the phone and then through their home or work computers. The employee givebacks were part of a plan to rescue OTB from bankruptcy, but party-line infighting within the New York State Senate doomed the bill that would have enacted it when three Democratic legislators were unavailable on the day the vote was scheduled. There was some suspicion that the scheduling was orchestrated by the man in charge of OTB at that point, Lawrence Schwartz, despite the wishes of then-Governor David Paterson to save the jobs, because the man who succeeded him less than a month later, Andrew Cuomo, wanted to take office free of the headache OTB had become, and Mr. Schwartz was hoping to keep his primary position of secretary to the governor in the new administration.

OTB Workers Unwilling to Gamble on Defiance

(October 15, 2010)

At 9:43 p.m. October 6, Maria Gonzalez of the American Arbitration Association (AAA) announced that members of Off-Track Betting Local 2021 of District Council 37 had voted 271 to 139 in favor of a deal that would cut the union's membership in half, eliminate double-pay for Sunday work, and transfer OTB's phone-betting and Internet operations to another entity.

Shouts of "yes!" came from a few people among the hundreds scattered throughout the meeting room in DC 37's headquarters. There were no audible groans from the dissenters, but for most of those on hand, the emotional range did not run much beyond relief or resignation. In the end, the union members had taken a cue from their leaders and opted to limit their losses rather than taking a plunge on their future in a company rooted in gambling.

The biggest winner appeared to be OTB CEO Greg Rayburn, the turnaround specialist who was playing with house money beyond the $125,000 a month he was being paid to salvage OTB even while selling off the parts that have the greatest potential, its Internet and phone-betting operations. Local 2021 and DC 37 were unwilling to call his bluff about going into court to void the union's contract unless it agreed to his terms, despite their ties to Mr. Rayburn's boss, Governor Paterson, and Assembly Speaker Sheldon Silver, who can be a more-formidable obstacle than many governors once he takes a position.

As one official familiar with the situation put it, "They were willing to settle at any cost. Management realized that and pounced."

Stars Aligned Against Unions

Maybe they had made inquiries of the two state leaders and weren't encouraged by the responses at a time when the state has major fiscal problems. Mr. Silver has to be wary of taking on new battles while girding for the arrival of Andrew Cuomo as governor, and the media attitude toward unions in general and OTB itself would politely be described as unsympathetic. Whatever the case, what they presented to the rank and file last week was a blueprint for survival that would actually translate to no better than a few thousand dollars in severance money for a good percentage of them.

But Mr. Rayburn's strategy succeeded in part because he wasn't too greedy or ideological. He backed off the one demand that no union could accept—the right to lay off workers without regard to seniority—and offered just enough money in the severance package to make it palatable, particularly to those who had decided to retire anyway.

And he gave both Local 2021 and Teamsters Local 858 one more safety valve that served as an incentive for them to push their members to ratify the deal. Two days prior to the vote, Mike Riggio, DC 37's White-Collar Division director, asked Mr. Rayburn what would happen if one union accepted the deal and the other voted it down. He said Mr. Rayburn replied that he would immediately go into court seeking to vacate the dissenting union's contract and then lay off all its members "without severance." The one that ratified would be spared.

Less than half an hour before the Local 2021 ballot-tallying was completed, Vice President Paulette Sher announced that Local 858 members had ratified the deal, by what turned out to be a 70 to 37 count, virtually the same percentage in favor as at the larger union.

Principles vs. Pragmatism

Reasons for and against backing the deal fluctuated wildly, judging by interviews with about a dozen union members. One employee who doesn't work in telephone betting said she voted no because she thought it was wrong to give away what employees regard as the most valuable part of the franchise simply to settle about $65 million of OTB's debts; Communications Specialist Bruce Borovoy also questioned the wisdom of the swap but voted in favor of the deal "because I believed they would be able to null and void the union contract."

It figured that the strongest resistance to the terms would come from the phone-betting division and the per-diem and less-senior full-time workers who were more vulnerable to layoffs, but two such employees, including Mr. Borovoy's wife, Jessica, said they voted yes both because of the severance money and their feeling that they were young enough that it wouldn't be that hard to find another job or even change professions.

The other man in that category, who spoke conditioned on anonymity, cited another factor: he lacked the seniority to be given Sunday work, and so the loss of double-time pay on that day had no impact on him. "So why vote no and risk everyone being out of a job and you can't even collect unemployment?" he said. "Most of the younger people I know voted yes. A lot of the older people and the managers were going to vote no because they're counting that money for Sunday."

Cuomo the Dark Horse

There were those who doubted that the racing industry, led by the New York Racing Association (NYRA), which figures to pick up the phone-betting and Internet operations, could have afforded to have OTB go down in flames had the unions dug in their heels, because the money generated at its parlors would not be easily made up. That theory, however, ignores the possibility that Mr. Rayburn could have looked to wipe out the union contracts, laid off the employees, and then either hired them or people off the street at reduced salaries and negligible fringe benefits.

It's hard to imagine that Mr. Paterson, who for all his quirky unpredictability is the man who saved New York City OTB two years ago and the son of a well-respected labor lawyer, would have allowed that sort of union-busting. But if the process dragged on through the end of the year, Mr. Cuomo—whose father while in office made clear his disdain for the horse-racing industry and the wealthy people at the top of its management—might not have been as squeamish, particularly since he would have scored points with the tabloid editorial boards by letting the carnage go forth.

No Phone-Worker Assurances

But questions still remained as to whether Local 2021 and DC 37 couldn't have done more for the phone-betting workers in the form of gaining some commitments from NYRA about bringing many of them over when the operation changed hands. Mr. Riggio tried to reassure the several hundred people attending last week's meeting that enough members were retiring or taking the severance buy-out that layoffs wouldn't be necessary beyond the per-diem staff. That didn't mean they went away convinced. Some members with as much as 15 years on the job but less than five of them as regular employees were worried that they would be vulnerable to layoffs.

'Major Score' for NYRA

One older employee who said he planned to retire argued that the fact that just 410 of the union's roughly 1,050 members showed up to vote on a deal to decide their future reflected the distaste many had for a situation he likened to having "a gun pointed at your head." (A different perspective was offered by Ms. Gonzalez, AAA's associate director, who called it a remarkably high turnout for a walk-in election.)

In the end, though, faced with a choice between biting the bullet or dealing with anxieties many times beyond what they had experienced for much of this year, the union's members swallowed the concessions forced upon them. NYRA and Mr. Rayburn both made what at the racetrack is called a "major score," while the workers, like the smaller horseplayers who are their bread-and-butter customers, lived to fight another day.

'The Prince' Incarnate in a Cuomovellian Gambit

(March 23, 2012)

The simplest explanation for why the state legislators the public employee unions regarded as their firewall against Governor Cuomo's Tier 6 plan stepped aside and let them get burned was offered 30 years ago by Norman Adler, then the chief lobbyist for District Council 37 at a point when it was still a major player in Albany.

Addressing 300 union members who had taken buses to the capital to lobby for, of all things, an improved pension tier, Mr. Adler told them that when approaching their legislators, they should keep in mind that "the two goals of every senator and assembly member are: One, get reelected; two, never forget goal number one."

Governor Cuomo, who apparently shares Mr. Adler's read on the denizens of the legislature, played on that weakness masterfully in getting the pension changes enacted in return for going along with the new district lines designed by legislators to maximize their chances of perpetuating their time in office.

It required the governor to break one campaign pledge—to ensure nonpartisan legislative districts—to achieve another, but he certainly knew which one mattered most to the People Who Count in the media and business communities. You didn't even have to tune in to the bulletins from Rupert Murdoch's eavesdropping empire to confirm that judgment; you just had to speak to former Mayor Ed Koch.

Subverted to the Greater Good?

Mr. Koch devoted much of 2010 to getting honest district lines, signing up legislators throughout the state in support of his plan and declaring those who balked to be "enemies of reform." Yet when what had initially seemed a remarkably successful effort got tunneled in favor of a see-us-in-10-years plan to have nonpartisan districts drawn up by a commission that would actually have to report back to the legislature, Mr. Koch was not raging at how his ideal had been corrupted by Senate Republicans or sold down the river by the governor.

Instead he said he was sad but that he understood Mr. Cuomo's reasoning: "what he got in return was enormous. Pensions are breaking the back of this city."

And that is what passed for conventional wisdom, as Mr. Cuomo and Mayor Bloomberg ride a ballooning of pension payments over the past decade that is the result of abnormally poor stock-market performance and a screw-the-future decision by a previous governor and mayor that depleted the retirement funds of a cushion for the time when the stock boom would fizzle.

Uniformed Fire Officers Association President Al Hagan marveled at how those at the top of city and state government had diverted attention from Wall Street's long Lost Weekend to the temporary spike in pension costs, saying, "They got to drink all the whiskey, and we're gonna pay the tab."

But why would fairness matter to the governor? As much as any action during his administration, the pension/redistricting swap symbolized an ethos that it's more important to get a deal done than to examine the results of what you're doing. It's the essence of the skilled political player and sets him apart from his two Democratic predecessors. One union official described the frenetic lobbying to line up the votes and the outcome of those efforts this way: "The governor's people were on the floor of the Senate and the Assembly twisting arms like there was no tomorrow. Spitzer was a toy steamroller; this guy's a mega-steamroller."

Some Got Haircut, Others Scalped

But Mr. Cuomo also showed the ability to shift gears when the moment demanded it. A backlash was created in the hours before the deal was struck when *Daily News* Albany bureau chief Ken Lovett wrote a column saying that the city police and fire unions would be spared any of the hardships of Tier 6. State Senator Diane Savino, noting that 46 percent of the city's projected $30 billion in long-term savings under the bill hinged on it applying to cops and firefighters, said late Wednesday afternoon that if they got a pass, "then there's no savings; all you've done is stick it to some low-wage workers."

In the final negotiations, future cops and firefighters were included under one element of the bill: their pensions will be based on final average salary over a five-year period rather than the three years that has been standard. The police and fire unions were also unhappy that the Tier 3 disability provision that took effect in 2010 remained intact, leaving those hired since then who qualify with pensions worth 50 percent of their final salary.

This isn't nearly as good as the 75-percent tax-free disability pension that those hired earlier in those jobs are entitled to, and Uniformed Firefighters Association President Steve Cassidy expressed disappointment about that. But he didn't fault the governor, noting that the Bloomberg administration has been unwilling to negotiate on that issue since Stephen Goldsmith left as deputy mayor for operations last summer and made clear it would not try to cobble together a deal—even when Mr. Cassidy and Patrolmen's Benevolent Association President Pat Lynch offered savings in other areas—on short notice when aides to Mr. Cuomo broached the possibility of a compromise in late February.

To address the police and fire unions' complaint about Tier 3 requiring new members to work 22 years rather than 20 to qualify for full pensions, Mr. Cuomo saddled new correction officers and sanitation workers with the 22-year obligation as well, apparently on the notion that if you can't make somebody happy, they might be consoled by someone else's misery.

None of the city unions, of course, can appreciate misery the way the state unions have come to under the gentle ministrations of this governor. The CSEA's relationship with Mr. Cuomo is so far beyond redemption that union President Danny Donohue's spokesman, Steve Madarasz, wasn't even attempting to conceal his outrage.

"It was just a disgustingly naked political deal," he said of the redistricting/Tier 6 package. "What the governor did during this whole fight was really reprehensible. Telling localities they were going to go bankrupt [without Tier 6] was outrageous. Actually Tier 6 isn't going to save them that much—at least not for the next 20 years. It was just a bogus scare tactic."

'Played Us Against Each Other'

He accused the governor of altering his message depending on which labor leader he was addressing while "burning every bridge and strong-arming. He was playing everybody against everybody else."

Perhaps the union leader who was most stung was United Federation of Teachers President Mike Mulgrew. His future members will be paying a higher contribution rate to the pension system virtually from the time they start, since the first trigger point is $45,000. And because the most-recent UFT members under a Tier 5 deal reached with Mr. Bloomberg three years ago were able to retire at age 55 with 27 years' service and collect a full pension, the raising of the eligible retirement age to 63 hits those who came after them in 2010 or later far harder than state workers, who would have had to work until 62 to collect full pensions even without the change.

"It's another win for the 1 percent," Mr. Mulgrew said, a harsher assessment of a gubernatorial policy than has been customary, as he has in recent months praised Mr. Cuomo as the voice of reason in the UFT's battles with the mayor over teacher evaluations. "The redistrict-ing lines," he continued, "are a disgrace, so I think the governor and the mayor wanted so badly to get the pensions of the workers that they were willing to make a pretty disgusting deal on the [legisla-tive] lines."

Those comments were echoed by his predecessor, American Federation of Teachers President Randi Weingarten, as she joined him at an anti-Bloomberg rally in Foley Square less than 12 hours after the Tier 6 plan was adopted. "It's clear the governor's first priority is Wall Street, the mayor's first priority is Wall Street," she said. "I think it's a terrible mistake on Governor Cuomo's part."

Silver Didn't Ride to Rescue

It has always been presumed that Assembly Speaker Sheldon Silver would be the UFT's last line of defense against the governor, the mayor, and the business-funded groups that have railed against the union's power over the years.

Ms. Savino speculated that Mr. Silver, seeing the way the politi-cal tide was rolling, decided it was more important to protect his members—and by extension, his standing as Speaker—by locking in the district lines of their preference. "You can fix pension bills; you can't fix district lines," she explained.

Peter Abbate, the chair of the Assembly's Government Employees Committee, offered a stronger defense, saying, "What does Shelly do in a situation like that other than to negotiate the best deal that he could?" He contended that some of the key scale-backs, which included taking the retirement age down from the proposed 65; improving the percentage by which pension allowances are determined so that employees after 30 years will collect 55 percent of final average salary, splitting the difference between the 60 percent current workers receive and the 50 percent Mr. Cuomo had proposed; and eliminating the 401(k)-style option from the portion of the bill covering unionized workers, were Mr. Silver's doing.

"Those are things Shelly worked hard on doing when his back was against the wall," he said. "And there were a lot of members saying, 'What can we get now rather than something worse two weeks from now?'"

Shutdown Threat Worked

Mr. Silver and other Assembly Democrats were not willing to risk a government shutdown, which Mr. Cuomo had threatened if Tier 6 wasn't part of a budget agreement by April 1. "Even if it was a couple of days and workers didn't get paid, that would've been how he would've gotten his savings," Mr. Abbate said of the governor.

Ms. Savino said concerns about that were secondary in the minds of most legislators to the redistricting issue. "If [approval of the legislature's lines] was contingent on the passage of Tier 6, that was a very dangerous place for the labor movement to find itself in," she said. "The governor very artfully handled this; he ran the table on them. He gets the politics of the moment the way very few governors do."

The outcome left several union officials muttering about the politics of the future: Mr. Cuomo's reelection run in 2014 and an expected bid for the White House in 2016 (one even said, not altogether jokingly, that he would make an ideal running mate this year for Mitt Romney).

Mr. Mulgrew, asked whether this episode soured labor leaders on backing Mr. Cuomo in a presidential run four years from now, said, "You'd have to talk to Rich Trumka and the AFL-CIO. I think their opinion pretty much is he's anti-union and anti-worker."

Ms. Weingarten added, "You never say never, but right now it's pretty clear whose side he's on."

And Mr. Madarasz contended, "For the governor, there will be damage for a long time. There will be repercussions for his relationship with labor, and especially with us."

Not Reckoning with Adaptability

Others weren't so sure. Mr. Hagan recalled that when Mr. Cuomo sought the State AFL-CIO's endorsement in 2010, he told union officials, "The first two years are gonna be tough, and after that it's gonna be good."

Senator Savino said it was important to consider that just as Mr. Cuomo has been able to adapt to changing circumstances, from remaking himself after he seemed to bomb out of politics a decade ago to the adjustments he made to get the Tier 6 bill through, he is likely to do what's necessary to shore up his support among unions.

"For New York State, having a governor in control is a big thing—we haven't had that for a while," she noted. "He's got a 70-percent approval rating, and he understands it's a bad economy. He plays the fiscal conservative, then he does the good lefty/liberal things like gay marriage. Now he's gonna look to do nice things with the unions. He'll probably start with the building trades and put their people back to work."

In an interview with *New York Times* reporters shortly after Tier 6 was approved, Mr. Cuomo compared state government to the Knicks, saying, "I don't think we have a Jeremy Lin in Albany, but I think the team is having a much better season than they've had in many, many years."

A 'Melo' Kind of Player

A day earlier, Mike D'Antoni had resigned as Knicks' coach after losing a power struggle with Carmelo Anthony, who is far more successful at scoring than he is at making his team a winner.

Like Mr. Anthony, Mr. Cuomo is very good at wearing down opponents and getting his points, even if he alienates those around him in the process. It's possible, however, that scoring the way he did last week weakened the state in two critical areas.

With Leaders Like These . . .

Brian McLaughlin (*left*), who as leader of the umbrella group for New York City labor unions stole $3 million, heads into Federal District Court in Manhattan with one of his lawyers on the day he was sentenced to 10 years in prison for his crimes. Photo reprinted courtesy of the *Chief-Leader*.

During the 1960s and 1970s, the AFL-CIO New York City Central Labor Council (CLC), an umbrella group for both public- and private-sector unions, was a major force in city government under the dynamic leadership of Harry van Arsdale Jr., who had come out of Local 3 of the International Brotherhood of Electrical Workers. As his health declined, however, the influence of the CLC diminished, and it continued to do so following his death in 1986 when he was succeeded by his son, Thomas van Arsdale, who one former union official said was as suited to running the city labor movement as he was to being a runway model in the garment district.

The younger van Arsdale had gained election against Victor Gotbaum, the far-more engaged leader of District Council 37, through a combination of strong support from the building trades unions and the backing of a few public employee unions, most conspicuous among them the United Federation of Teachers, which had felt the sting of Gotbaum's comments on issues it considered beyond his purview. But van Arsdale lived up to expectations, taking no action against the heads of unions representing carpenters, painters, and building service workers who were either under the sway of organized crime or independently corrupt. Yet he moved to expel from the CLC the president of Hospital Workers Local 1199 of the Service Employees International Union, Dennis Rivera, for having the bad taste to get so involved in supporting striking employees of the New York Daily News during a nine-month walkout that began in 1990 that the CLC's feeble efforts in the conflict looked embarrassing.

Later in the decade, van Arsdale mercifully stepped down and was succeeded by his longtime top aide, Brian McLaughlin, who also had come out of Local 3. McLaughlin was more ambitious and seemed like a spiritual descendant of Harry van Arsdale, getting the CLC involved on wider labor issues including the battle to keep Walmart out of New York City because of its anti-union practices and shoddy treatment of employees. Not content to be a behind-the-scenes powerbroker, McLaughlin was elected to a state assembly seat representing the district covering Electchester, the Queens housing complex Local 3 had created for its members. There was talk during the late 1990s that he might run for citywide office, although nothing came of it.

By 2006 it became apparent why. McLaughlin was under investigation for allegedly stealing money from every sphere in which he traveled, from his union posts to his campaign fund to the Electchester Little League. He stepped down from the CLC post while the probe was being conducted; when an indictment was handed up by the U.S. Attorney's Office in Man-

hattan, it charged that he had misappropriated millions of dollars to support a lavish lifestyle including a Long Island home that while within easy driving distance was light years removed from Electchester.

All of this had gone either unnoticed or unremarked upon by other union officials. The lack of vigilance was not an isolated case; around that time the same U.S. Attorney's Office brought indictments charging that the Genovese Crime Family had controlled an Amalgamated Transit Union local representing New York City school bus drivers and escorts through its top two leaders, with the corruption including collaborations with school officials in the awarding of bus routes to companies that made payoffs of hundreds of thousands of dollars each year.

It was not just the unions that were asleep at the switch for this one. The suspicions about mob control of the industry dated back to the late 1970s, when a school bus strike was marked by violence, with some drivers pulled from their buses and beaten as horrified pupils looked on. Yet mayoral administrations had continued to award the bus contracts to the same firms without putting them out for competitive bids. Top city and education officials seemed willing to look the other way, in part because corrupt unions generally are not terribly militant about securing benefits for their members. Salaries for the school bus drivers lagged behind those of city drivers represented by other ATU locals, and the gap was even greater when it came to pension benefits. Nor was ATU Local 1181 terribly diligent about defending members who were hit with disciplinary penalties, some on decidedly flimsy grounds, by their employers.

Judge Speaks Loud for McLaughlin's Victims

(May 29, 2009)

Over a career that's included stints as a Federal prosecutor, Queens district attorney, and counsel to the Knapp Commission investigating police corruption, Michael Armstrong has seen more than his share of human cupidity that landed the culprits in the criminal dock, from white-collared fraud merchants to blue-collared cops.

No doubt those experiences helped immunize him against any feelings of shock about the transgressions of his latest client, Brian McLaughlin, as he argued for leniency on behalf of the former president of the AFL-CIO New York City Central Labor Council at his sentencing hearing May 20 before U.S. District Judge Richard Sullivan.

He noted that Mr. McLaughlin's contrition could be seen from the fact that he informed the U.S. Attorney's Office of sums from ill-gotten gains it hadn't been aware of, bringing his restitution up to $3 million from the $2.2 million he was originally charged with stealing.

'Small Amounts from Different Pots'

And, Mr. Armstrong said, while what his client had done was clearly wrong, it was not as bad as defrauding a single individual of his life's savings. Rather, the former union leader and Queens Assemblyman had committed "thefts from different pots but in small amounts."

That last description seemed remarkable in its understatement given the very large amount Mr. McLaughlin admitted to pilfering, but Mr. Armstrong had not yet taken his home-run swing in that area. That came when he added, "There are no real victims in this case, Your Honor."

"No real victims?" Judge Sullivan repeated incredulously.

"Individual victims," Mr. Armstrong clarified.

It was at that point that the Judge began a discourse that was as inspiring as the conduct that provoked it was soul-deadening. Where Mr. Armstrong suggested it would have been surprising had Mr. McLaughlin confined his illegal activities to just one corner of his life as a State Assemblyman and labor leader, Judge Sullivan condemned him for dipping into every pot those multiple roles placed at his disposal, as if living by a policy of No Bribe Left Behind.

The breadth of the thievery was "mind-boggling," he said, so much so that he believed a departure from normal sentencing guidelines was warranted that could have gotten Mr. McLaughlin as much as 15 years behind bars, rather than the prescribed eight to 10 years. It was only what Assistant U.S. Attorney Daniel Braun called his "substantial assistance" in other Federal corruption probes that led him to scale back the sentence to 10 years, the Judge said.

Those who wrote asking for leniency on Mr. McLaughlin's behalf included AFL-CIO President John J. Sweeney, who cited Mr. McLaughlin's "long record of service to the working men and women of New York City." It was not the first time that Mr. Sweeney seemed overly tolerant of a union leader abusing his power for his own benefit; as president of the Service Employees International Union two decades ago, he overlooked the outlandish salary and opulent living quarters inside the offices of Building Workers Local 32BJ enjoyed by then-President Gus Bevona until the excesses became a well-publicized embarrassment.

Courage or Chutzpah?

Father Brian Jordan also wrote a letter on Mr. McLaughlin's behalf, stating that "he truly cares about the working-class people and the dignity of labor," and that he "stood tall" on behalf of immigrant workers when it was not terribly popular to do so. Father Jordan went on to say that "Labor has not adequately replaced Brian with someone who has as much intestinal fortitude."

Judge Sullivan viewed that fortitude as pure brass, however, decrying how Mr. McLaughlin perverted the qualities that elevated him to positions of leadership and "squandered" the opportunities he had gotten.

He said the favorable portrayals of Mr. McLaughlin conveyed in the letters sent on his behalf were "difficult to reconcile" with the crimes of "a man who so abused the trust of institutions and people who depended upon him that it staggers the mind."

And in setting an appropriate sentence, he said, the lack of previous blemishes on Mr. McLaughlin's record and the likelihood that he had learned from his misdeeds and would "never commit another crime" were overridden by the need for "sending a message that certain kinds of crimes cannot and will not be tolerated."

Even given the magnitude of the offenses and the amount of money involved, the sentence seemed high when compared to other cases involving corruption by union leaders during the past decade.

Charlie Hughes, who headed Local 372 of District Council 37, embezzled more than $2 million but was sentenced to three to nine years in jail; Al Diop as head of DC 37's Local 1549 got two to six years for stealing more than $1 million and helping to rig a DC 37 wage contract vote. They were both subject to the more-flexible guidelines for plea bargains in the state judicial system, but Ron Reale, the former transit police union leader who both stole from his members and tried to defraud the Campaign Finance Board, got his seven-year Federal sentence primarily because he insisted on going to trial rather than negotiating a plea for a lesser sentence.

Made CLC Relevant Again

In comparison to Mr. McLaughlin, however, all of them were minor figures, and despite Mr. Reale's run for Public Advocate, none would have ever been regarded as a serious candidate for major elected office. A decade ago, Mr. McLaughlin was considered a potential contender for mayor or city comptroller, and as head of the CLC he spoke for the entire city labor movement. One of his primary achievements during his decade in that post was in rescuing the umbrella group for both public- and private-sector unions from the moribund state into which it fell under his predecessor.

But that added visibility, Judge Sullivan seemed to say, conferred upon him a greater responsibility, and his illegal activities shined a harsher light on the labor movement than the sins of officials like Mr. Hughes, Mr. Diop, and Mr. Reale, none of whom was recognizable by the general public.

Likening his plundering to that of Boss Tweed 140 years earlier, Judge Sullivan said, "The cause of unions and of working people has been terribly undermined by your behavior." It confirmed the image presented by "the harshest critics of organized labor who accuse the leadership of corruption, and point to you as an example of that corruption."

An Offense Against All Workers
With those words, he rebutted Mr. Armstrong's argument that there had been no "individual victims" in the scheme. It wasn't just the members of the International Brotherhood of Electrical Workers whose bank account Mr. McLaughlin took $100,000 from, or the $185,000 in CLC funds he pocketed that was not available on behalf of the causes of its member unions.

It was the cause of those employees in contract battles who could see public opinion turn against them due to editorials from labor-bashing newspapers eager to capitalize on any hint of corruption by union leaders. It was also that of unions in general as they seek to organize underpaid workers who lack benefits in areas ranging from overtime and holiday pay to pension and grievance rights. One of Mr. McLaughlin's last public appearances before he was indicted nearly three years ago was as part of a rally against a Walmart in the city because of the company's exploitation of its nonunionized workers.

His conduct, Judge Sullivan said, "has encouraged a cynicism and a despair that is so counterproductive."

Those qualities could be seen in a description by one union official of the reaction of many of those who worked with Mr. McLaughlin in the past. Some of them wanted to see him do serious prison time, this official said, but others just wanted him to figuratively go away and allow them to wipe the stains he left behind off the pavement.

Mr. McLaughlin had a close-up view of the DC 37 scandal that resulted in more than two dozen union officials being convicted and a significant number of them doing some jail time. But no one served more than the three years done by Mr. Hughes. A remark said to have been made by another of the miscreants in that union, Mark Shaplo, lingers: when the Manhattan district attorney was closing in, he declared, "I can do the two years if I can keep my money."

A Lot More than Two Years

Mr. McLaughlin, even if he gets some time off credited to him for undergoing treatment for alcoholism, is likely to serve eight years of his sentence. As for keeping his money, Judge Sullivan ordered that as part of his restitution, he pay 10 percent of whatever he earns when he is finally discharged from prison.

Mr. Armstrong pressed for him to reduce the assessment to 5 percent, noting that the 57-year-old Mr. McLaughlin was unlikely to be able to work as an electrician by the time he completed his sentence, but Judge Sullivan stood firm.

Mr. McLaughlin had sat stoically throughout the proceedings and offered no visible reaction when the judge ordered the 10-year term. He had gotten his first inkling of how hard he might be hit when the *New York Post* reported a week earlier that Judge Sullivan was considering going beyond the eight to 10 years that Mr. Armstrong and the U.S. Attorney's Office agreed was the appropriate range before considering his cooperation in other corruption investigations.

Even in a relatively tame prison like Allenwood, where he is likely to be sent, eight or more years behind bars is hardly easy time. Judge Sullivan had served two purposes with the sentence: mirroring the outrage felt by the workers whose hopes had been compromised by Mr. McLaughlin's thievery and providing a deterrent scary enough for all but the hard-core outlaws who may lurk in union positions to think twice about following his path.

A School Bus Frame-Up DOE Won't Talk About

(October 8, 2010)

The brand of justice employed by the Department of Education to fire school bus driver John Bisbano is the reason for Article 78 of the state's civil-practice law, which governs decisions that are so arbitrary and capricious as to be "shocking to the conscience."

Mr. Bisbano and the escort with whom he worked, Maxima Alba, were accused of having abandoned two teenage boys in front of the Hawthorne Country Day School in Westchester, where DOE sends some developmentally disabled pupils, on May 18. Usually abandonment charges lead to the immediate suspension of the accused personnel, who are also generally arrested; in this case Mr. Bisbano and Ms. Alba were permitted to continue their regular duties until June 16, four weeks after the alleged transgression, which was eventually amended from "abandoned" to "left unattended."

Mr. Bisbano said in an interview September 28 that school officials claimed there was a delay in charging and removing him because of "a heavy caseload, but these cases of abandonment, they deal with them on the spot."

Reina Martinez, a 25-year veteran driver, put in, "Usually, you're in handcuffs right away."

Sole Witness's Changing Story
The woman who accused Mr. Bisbano and Ms. Alba, a Hawthorne Country Day employee named Julia Bates, originally claimed that Ms.

79

Alba left the two boys unattended and that Mr. Bisbano drove the bus to another school on the Country Day campus, leading her to pursue and berate him after one of the boys urinated against a school wall because he was upset at being left alone.

During the disciplinary hearing for Mr. Bisbano, however, Ms. Bates first testified that she had not spoken to Mr. Bisbano until later in the day, then said she had merely asked "the classroom staff" to speak to him about the incident and wasn't sure whether any of them actually had. When she was asked how far he had driven the bus away from her school's entrance, she initially said "maybe five, 600 feet," according to the trial transcript, but later acknowledged the distance traveled was "a few buses long," something Mr. Bisbano said he had done so as not to block any other buses entering the complex.

The most peculiar aspect of her testimony may have been that DOE officials allowed her to present it by phone, meaning that neither Mr. Bisbano's counsel nor the hearing officer could observe her as she amended or contradicted her previous statements.

The parents of both boys who had supposedly been abandoned wrote letters in support of Mr. Bisbano and Ms. Alba, saying they were both considerate of their children's needs. One child, his father said, had accused the officials who charged them of lying and the other, who is unable to speak, had been "experiencing tremendous emotional problems" because he was upset that they were no longer the ones bringing him to and from school.

The father of one of the boys, David Benitez, testified that when he had expressed unhappiness to the school's principal at not having been informed that his son was left alone, the principal responded, "No, I can assure you your son was never left alone."

DOE's Own Policy Not Followed

In fact, the first time that anyone publicly stated that the two boys had been left unsupervised was when Mr. Bisbano and Ms. Alba learned of the charges against them three weeks after the alleged incident, even though DOE policy in any case involving abandonment is to immediately notify the parents. When I asked a DOE spokeswoman back in June about the lack of notification, she said, "You'd have to talk to the school," but the school's executive director, Tina Covington, said she had no details of the case and that everything had gone through DOE's Office of Pupil Transportation.

Mr. Bisbano claims that officials at the school had been angered by his advocacy on behalf of some of the children he drove, including the boy who allegedly urinated against the school wall. He said that on June 21, five days after he was stripped of his driving duties, an administrator at the school, Junia Octobre, had called DOE to accuse him of abandoning another pupil. When it was discovered that someone else was driving his route, one Bisbano supporter said, the complaint was "quashed."

It is the lack of logical explanations for everything that transpired, not least of that being no action taken to remove Mr. Bisbano and Ms. Alba from working with children for a full four weeks after their alleged dereliction of duty took place, that gives credence to Mr. Bisbano's claim that he is the victim of a politically motivated hit engineered by a division of DOE that not long ago was a rat's nest of corruption. Inspectors in the Office of Pupil Transportation (OPT) in 2007 were found to have conspired with union officials—who themselves were controlled by the Genovese Crime Family—to protect bus-company owners who paid bribes; now Mr. Bisbano alleges a similar collaboration has occurred to keep him from running for president of the union next year.

In 2009, running at the top of the reform slate known as Members for Change, Mr. Bisbano narrowly missed winning the presidency of Local 1181 of the Amalgamated Transit Union after two former comrades broke away to run their own campaigns and splintered the opposition vote. Ms. Alba, he said, became a nonpolitical victim for having the bad luck to be working with him.

He cited the fact that during their combined 25 years of service, both had unblemished records. He also said there had been far more egregious cases of abandonment, involving small children being left sleeping in the backs of buses for as much as eight hours because the drivers took them back to garages believing they were empty, in which the penalty was no more than a six-month suspension.

Reformers' Lawyers Filing Suit

He said the union, headed by Michael Cordiello, who was close to his since-jailed predecessor, Sal Battaglia, had offered only perfunctory resistance to DOE's efforts to remove him, and that he had not even considered asking it to file a lawsuit on his behalf both because of the political hostility he engenders and previous cases in which the union's leadership had declined to file Article 78 petitions because "it's too expensive." Instead, lawyers working with Members for Change are about to file suit on his behalf.

Eddie Kay, a veteran union organizer who is an adviser to the reformers, noted it wouldn't be the first time that Local 1181's leadership and OPT had engaged in corrupt chicanery. He referred to the guilty pleas last year of three OPT supervisors to taking payoffs from school-bus companies to overlook violations or give them advance warnings of inspections, a Federal case that alleged that other unidentified OPT employees engaged in corrupt behavior. The case grew out of the Federal probe of the corrupt activities involving Local 1181 that led to the convictions of the union's two top officers, Mr. Battaglia and the late Julius "Spike" Bernstein, as well as Matty "The Horse" Ianniello, whom law-enforcement officials have identified as a boss of the Genovese Family.

'Union, OPT in Cahoots'

"The union and OPT were in total cahoots in telling the companies when there would be an inspection," Mr. Kay said. "What we see is a total conspiracy between the union, OPT, and the bosses. What they're doing to John is a smart move because he proved he was a viable candidate. They're very afraid the whole sweetheart arrangement among them would end if he was elected. They've attempted to destroy our movement, and they've done a pretty good job of cutting up a human being."

But continued collusion between OPT and Local 1181 would not be enough to get Mr. Bisbano railroaded. Ultimately, the decision to uphold removal of his certification to drive a school bus and fire him along with Ms. Alba needed final approval from Deputy Schools Chancellor Kathleen Grimm, acting on behalf of Chancellor Joel Klein. In identical letters to both employees, she stated, "After careful consideration of your case, I concur with the decision of the Office of Pupil Transportation . . . The penalty appears to be wholly appropriate."

'Didn't Read the Transcripts'

Mr. Bisbano, asked what could have led a well-respected career civil servant like Ms. Grimm to reach such a conclusion, responded, "I don't think anybody really read the transcripts" that made clear the shakiness of the testimony of the one witness against him and that the parents of the boys involved supported him and Ms. Alba.

Ms. Grimm did not return calls seeking an explanation for her decision in the face of those facts. An e-mail message to the mayor's press office seeking an interview with Deputy Mayor Dennis Walcott, Mr. Bloomberg's top education aide, also drew no response, although it's known that at least one elected official sympathetic to Mr. Bisbano had briefed Mr. Walcott on the case.

Members for Change has contended that one offshoot of the mob-orchestrated corruption within Local 1181 has been a passive approach to representing the union's 15,000 members, most of whom are school bus drivers and escorts. At the same time that the past leadership was taking bribes from bus-company owners for matters that included not looking to organize workers at some companies and assisting them in getting additional routes approved by OPT, it negotiated pensions for the rank and file that are only half as generous as those paid to New York City Transit drivers, including those represented by two other ATU locals based in Queens and Staten Island.

Only Dislike Aggressive Unions?
Mr. Kay and Mr. Bisbano said they believed DOE would prefer to deal with Mr. Cordiello despite his ties to the disgraced past leadership, rather than be confronted by someone who would aggressively bargain on behalf of Local 1181's members. They said Mr. Cordiello had permitted DOE and the bus companies with which it contracts to reduce health-benefit coverage, not pay drivers for some hours they worked, and replace laid-off employees with casual hires receiving reduced salaries and benefits, in violation of the union contract.

Mr. Kay said that DOE had been "against us ever since we demonstrated outside OPT in 2008. They don't want that kind of disruption."

He contrasted the harsh treatment of Mr. Bisbano with the special consideration afforded to Domenic Gatto, the school-bus company operator and Staten Island Republican activist who had managed the neat trick of becoming wealthy while being shaken down by the Genovese Family for payoffs that eventually totaled hundreds of thousands of dollars a year. Earlier this year, during a negotiation on renewal of his school-bus contracts, Mr. Gatto took out a gun, disturbing one DOE official enough that the police were called. But although DOE no longer permitted Mr. Gatto to be at the bargaining table, he wound up having all his contracts—worth a reported $200 million—renewed.

Mayor Bloomberg, while never touched by the whiff of personal corruption, at times has displayed a somewhat-disquieting "we're men of the world" attitude toward officials accused in bribery cases. He attended a fundraiser during his first term for State Senator Guy Velella meant to pay the lawyers defending him against charges of shaking down private companies to help steer state contracts their way. His close friend and investment adviser Steve Rattner has been accused of making questionable payments to middle men to obtain city pension-fund business, leading his own firm to disown his actions, but Mr. Bloomberg responded by giving Mr. Rattner greater responsibility for managing his private fortune.

In Mr. Velella's case the mayor was undoubtedly repaying past political favors; in Mr. Rattner's it seems more likely that he believed his friend was a victim of corrupt practices that had become entrenched at both the city and state levels, although nothing precluded Mr. Rattner from going to the authorities other than fear of losing out financially for doing the honest thing.

Imbalance on Scales of Justice

But it's hard to reconcile doing business with the likes of Mr. Gatto while standing by as Mr. Bisbano at age 65 becomes stigmatized as well as unemployed after a judicial process that couldn't pass muster in any self-respecting government body. It's not surprising that Mr. Walcott and Ms. Grimm decided to duck inquiries rather than step any deeper into the swamp.

At some point, Mr. Bisbano is bound to get justice through the courts. That will not occur before the next Local 1181 election, however, and so Mr. Kay said the Members for Change nominating committee will decide on another candidate for president sometime in the next couple of months.

"They got away with murder," he said of DOE and the union, "but we feel invigorated by this."

In April 2011, a Brooklyn Supreme Court Justice found Bisbano's termination to be arbitrary, capricious, and "shocking to the conscience" and ordered his reinstatement. Eleven months later, after a Local 1181 election in which he was barred from running because the Department of Education had not acted on the judge's order, Bisbano, with his penalty modified from a lifetime ban to a three-month suspension, returned to work.

Let's Not Strike for Spike

(July 7, 2006)

The threat of a school bus strike when summer school began July 5 was not taken seriously enough by private bus company owners to ask those doing the bargaining for them to forsake long holiday weekends.

Steve Mangione, a spokesman for Local 1181 of the Amalgamated Transit Union, said June 29 that at a bargaining session two days earlier, union officials renewed a request that marathon talks begin to work out a deal as the old pact headed for its June 30 expiration, "and again they were refused. Inexplicably, a couple of the chief negotiators said they couldn't do it because they were taking off for the Fourth of July weekend."

The lack of urgency may not be so hard to explain, however, in the context of the latest Spike Bernstein indictment.

May 'The Horse' Be with Him

Mr. Bernstein, birth name Julius, until two weeks ago held the title of secretary-treasurer of Local 1181, but his real power within the union stemmed from his less-official status as Matty "The Horse" Ianniello's man at the union. Mr. Ianniello, whom Federal investigators have linked to Mr. Bernstein for at least three decades, during that time matriculated to the position of boss of the Genovese Crime Family.

The two men were indicted last year, along with Local 1181 President Sal Battaglia and Ann Chiarovano, another union officer who is also Mr. Bernstein's girlfriend, on charges that Mr. Ianniello, Genovese capo Ciro Perrone, and others had infiltrated the local and controlled its activities and those of its pension and welfare funds.

Two weeks ago, Mr. Bernstein was indicted a second time on a charge that, if true, would demolish any credibility that Local 1181 has had on the issue of standing up for its members. According to a deposition submitted by FBI Special Agent Michael Gaeta, a bus company operator who was given immunity from prosecution stated that for nearly 25 years he had been paying Mr. Bernstein to ensure that Local 1181 did not seek to organize the nonunion drivers working his firm's routes under its contract with the city school system.

Mr. Gaeta stated that the bus company executive estimated that he had paid Mr. Bernstein between $200,000 and $300,000 under a system in which he was not charged for the first five routes under his contract but had to pay $1,000 for every additional route. He began making the payoffs, according to Agent Gaeta, after incidents in 1981 when members of the local—including some of its officials— "caused damage to his buses, made threats to him, and beat up one of his drivers." Initially, the company owner got police protection, but he eventually concluded there was greater security in paying off Mr. Bernstein, according to the deposition.

Agent Gaeta said the owner claimed to have made the payments to Mr. Bernstein early each school year. The indictment stems from the fact that his previous arrest last July apparently did not instill much caution in the 83-year-old union official: according to the owner, two months later he made his regularly scheduled payment to Mr. Bernstein, this time for $23,000.

Jobs for the Mob
The FBI Agent's deposition cited two other cooperating witnesses who said that more than one bus company had similar arrangements with Local 1181 officials dating back to the 1970s, and that, "As part of the Genovese Crime Family's control of Local 1181, they have, among other things, enlisted favors from Local 1181, including obtaining jobs for friends and relatives," some of them mob associates.

At the time of last September's alleged shakedown, Mr. Bernstein was free under a judge's order following his arrest July 27, 2005. This time it wasn't enough to post bail of $100,000 and agree to limit his traveling to the boundaries of New York State; Mr. Bernstein was forced to take a leave of absence from his position at Local 1181 as a condition of his release.

This meant that he was not at the bargaining table for the final negotiations before the contract expired, playing his longtime role as a belligerent kibitzer who made up in volume what his remarks lacked in substance. "Spike will speak up occasionally," was how Jeffrey Pollack, the chief negotiator for the coalition of school bus companies, put it.

It wasn't Mr. Bernstein's absence from the proceedings that gave management a lesser sense of urgency than Mr. Mangione said the local possessed about going 'round the clock. "I have no reason to doubt the union threats" about a walkout, Mr. Pollack said in a June 29 phone interview, a few minutes after the Local 1181 spokesman had acknowledged that "the likelihood of [a strike] happening before the 5th is very low because they want to see what happens in the next negotiating session." (Because they are employed by private bus companies, the Department of Education drivers and escorts are not subject to the Taylor Law, which prohibits strikes by public employees.)

Mr. Pollack said the eight-day gap in formal talks had as much to do with needing to present data supporting management's health-benefits demands as it did the holiday weekend.

'Need Health Deal First'

While wage and pension matters are also undecided, he explained, "We can't really talk about other issues until we have an agreement on health costs." The day after the last bargaining session, he said, management presented data to the union and was awaiting a response, and the lines of communication remained open despite the lack of further sit-downs.

A week earlier, Mr. Pollack was considerably less diplomatic in a statement that alluded to one of the areas that both the Federal government and union dissidents have asserted is a prime source of enrichment for Local 1181's leadership and Mr. Bernstein's alleged masters in the Genovese Family.

"The union continues to insist on maintaining the status quo of running its outdated, inefficient and ineffective self-insured welfare fund," Mr. Pollack said then. "The bottom line is health-care costs are

skyrocketing, the union is overspending for benefits, and our employees are not receiving state-of-the-art medical coverage or a larger
network of doctors."

Shook Down Doctors?

One of the charges against Mr. Bernstein in last year's Federal indictment was that he extorted a $100,000 payoff (which he shared with
Mr. Ianniello) from the union's medical provider to extend its lease
at Local 1181's Ozone Park headquarters.

The new charge of taking payoffs to forego increasing the union's
membership, against a man Mr. Mangione previously described as "a
valuable asset" on the Local 1181 board, could serve as a rallying cry
for dissidents who previously questioned the logic of threatening to
walk off the job at a time when most of them are already off for the
summer. Something along the lines of, "Let's not strike for Spike."

Hard to Feel Solidarity

Because seriously, why would any other labor leader honor a picket
line or otherwise support an organization whose leaders ran it like a
vehicle for extortion rather than a trade union?

That was why Simon Jean-Baptiste, one of the veteran Local 1181
members who has challenged the incumbent leadership, said of Mr.
Bernstein's latest indictment, "This is a situation that is going from
bad to worse for the entire membership. You can imagine what kind
of effect [the charge] has on the entire workforce."

At a time when "the contractors are in a more-powerful position
than ourselves," Mr. Jean-Baptiste said, the charge that Mr. Bernstein
extorted money not to organize nonunion bus companies would further undermine Local 1181 from a public relations standpoint if it
called a strike. That was one of the reasons he and other dissidents
had demanded that Mr. Bernstein, Mr. Battaglia, and Ms. Chiarovano
step down following last summer's indictments, and when they refused
to do so, urged the International ATU to take control of the local.

"I believe when you have personal problems, how are you going
to deal with the problems of 15,000 other people?" Mr. Jean-Baptiste
said, referring to Local 1181's total membership rather than the 8,400
drivers and escorts employed by the Department of Education. "Are
you going to take the time and energy needed to negotiate a contract,

or are Sal and Spike going to be more concerned with defending themselves in court?"

International Silent

The International ATU has continued to remain mute on the subject. Benetta Mansfield, the chief of staff to ATU President Warren George, did not return calls last week about whether Mr. Bernstein's latest indictment made the international more inclined to put Local 1181 in trusteeship. (Mr. Mangione said Local 1181 would have no comment on Mr. Bernstein's new legal troubles.)

Eddie Kay, a veteran union organizer with long tenures at Local 1199 of the Service Employees International Union and Transport Workers Union Local 100, said the only plausible explanation for the ATU's hesitance to act is its leaders' fears of the mob guys who have had their hooks in the local, according to Federal prosecutors, since the 1970s.

'Destroying the Local'

"It's just another example of the international sitting back from a know-nothing policy that is just destroying this local," said Mr. Kay, who has been assisting the Local 1181 dissidents for the past year. "They should have done exactly what the Feds did to Spike: throw him out immediately after [last year's] indictment. The international has given in to its own fears, their inability to understand the full problem, and the fact that the union, which is its largest local, has bestowed many favors upon the international."

He continued, "It's a wonderful thing to have a union run by the Mafia—it can destroy a union quicker than anything. It's a shame, and it's embarrassing to the entire labor movement."

Just as disturbing, Mr. Kay said, is the way in which the legal problems of Mr. Battaglia and Mr. Bernstein, and the negative publicity they have attracted, have weakened Local 1181 at the bargaining table. "The bosses are taking advantage of this," referring to a bargaining position that Mr. Mangione described as "a series of demands that is basically nothing but givebacks."

The Local 1181 spokesman differed with Mr. Kay, however, on the intent of the bus-owners' coalition. He contended that rather than looking to decimate the union contract, "it's almost as if they're welcoming a strike. It's as if the companies are hoping the city will come in and bail them out."

'City to the Rescue'

Citing the Bloomberg administration's decision following a strike early last year to assume responsibility for paying bus escorts, Mr. Mangione speculated that the owners were "hoping the city will come to the rescue by maybe taking over responsibility for some of the health benefits."

Mr. Jean-Baptiste contended that management might be counting on the reluctance of union members to walk off the job now, claiming the timing would be counterproductive. "I have not talked to anybody who's willing to go on strike in the summer, when most of our members are on unemployment," he said. "Most of the children are on vacation, so if you call a strike in the summer, you're putting pressure on what? It doesn't make any sense."

Unless, of course, the union leadership is figuring that a walkout would shift the members' anger toward their employers and away from the signs of rampant internal corruption.

Busfellas' Past Helped
Mayor to Break Strike

(March 1, 2013)

School bus workers returned to their jobs February 20, a day after the *Daily News* editorial cartoonist Bramhall depicted a bus driven by Mayor Bloomberg smashing into a union picket sign while he and his student passengers yelled "Road kill!"

Tabloid editorial cartoonists often strive to express the basest feelings of their bosses, but this would have seemed a tin-eared comment from a newspaper that has always portrayed itself as the voice of working New Yorkers even before the first post-strike stone was fired by a bus company owner named Joseph Fazzia, whose operations include an entity known as Jofaz Transportation. Offering yet another reminder that those who name enterprises after themselves sometimes are immune to the feelings of others, he welcomed back to work 109 matrons employed by his company Canal Escorts by firing them.

Mr. Fazzia, declaring that he had lost hundreds of thousands of dollars because of the 30-day strike, was quoted by the *Post* as shouting at the matrons, "This union thinks they can tell me what to do—they can go f--- themselves."

Proof 'Horse' Is Not with Them
The matrons might be excused for thinking that they were the ones, rather than Local 1181 of the Amalgamated Transit Union, bearing the brunt of his bile. But in one respect, he may have performed a

public service by clearing up the question posed by journalists of my acquaintance and officials from other unions as to whether Local 1181 was still mobbed up. Because it seems highly unlikely that Mr. Fazzia, who five years ago was acquitted after being charged along with several other bus-company owners with making payoffs to union officials, would have been so vocally asserting his First Amendment rights if the Genovese Crime Family still held sway over Local 1181.

That likelihood informed a tweet by Tom Robbins, the former *Village Voice* columnist who exposed much of the rot within Local 1181 when it was controlled by the recently deceased Matty "The Horse" Ianniello, on the first day of the walkout January 16: "Bus strike irony: City Hall tolerated mob-run school bus union and contractors for years. Now most mobsters are gone and suddenly it's war."

His implication was that Mayor Bloomberg would not have figured the coast was clear enough to attract serious bidders from outside the entrenched network of companies while Matty and his longtime man inside the local, the equally late Spike Bernstein, were still pounding the pavement.

Outlaw Rep Caught Up
Several officials on both sides of the bargaining table, most of whom were unwilling to be quoted by name, said last week they believed that while Local 1181 President Michael Cordiello, who served on the union's board when its unofficial chairman was Mr. Ianniello, may be operating with none of those old strings that were attached to his predecessor, the ex-Federal inmate known as Sal Battaglia, the baggage of its outlaw days had doomed the union's chances of a successful strike.

Victor Gotbaum more than 30 years ago summed up a failed strike by the Committee of Interns and Residents against city hospitals by remarking, "If you want to go to war, you'd better have some tanks and planes."

The union didn't have those, and aside from its own troops, it didn't have much in the way of reinforcements from other labor leaders. ATU International President Larry Hanley did what he could, and AFL-CIO New York City Central Labor Council President Vinnie Alvarez was steadfast in support, but one official said that the only other major New York union head standing with Mr. Cordiello at his rallies was John Samuelsen, president of Transport Workers Union

Local 100, a union that is no stranger to walking the picket lines or battling Mr. Bloomberg.

Doubt Savings Was Motive

On the one hand, union officials said, they believe Mr. Bloomberg was whistling in the wind when he characterized his decision to do away with the Employee Protection Provision—the action that led to the walkout—as motivated by the expectation that this would encourage new bidders for the Special Education bus contracts and save the city tens of millions of dollars.

Uniformed Fire Officers Association President Al Hagan argued that Bloomberg administration estimates that it saved $80 million on transportation costs during the strike even while paying for Metro-Cards and car services for families with disabled students "may be a product of the same kind of faulty number-keeping they've been doing with the tax obligations of hotels." He was referring to *News* columnist Juan Gonzalez's report of Yotel paying nearly eight times less in property taxes than it should have because of what a Finance Department spokesman called "an oversight."

Another union official scoffed at the likelihood of future savings through the expanded field of bus-route bidders. "This was about breaking the union," he said, a way for Mr. Bloomberg to claim a labor scalp on his way out the door.

Asked why, then, more labor leaders hadn't rallied to the cause, he responded that Local 1181 "was a mob outfit for a long time and didn't have many friends."

Flexed Wrong Muscles

Since the sometimes-violent strike in 1979, there had been occasional rumbles that might have threatened the Genovese Family's interests at Local 1181, but no mayor—including Rudy Giuliani, who feinted at taking on the local before the old racket-buster got a few concessions at workers' expense and declared victory—had posed a challenge similar to what it faced from Mr. Bloomberg. And mob-run locals are not known for encouraging member activism, since that could lead to an engaged rank and file asking questions about, for instance, why their pension plan was so inferior to those of city transit workers, including those belonging to ATU locals representing Bus Operators in Queens and Staten Island.

And so a local that often had corrupt relationships with bus-company owners and relied on the aura of mob muscle to keep matters under control had done painfully little, even after the worst of the rogues were driven out by Federal prosecutors, to develop the kind of organizing muscles that are so valuable when it comes time to mobilize for a potential strike. Local 1181 proved ill-suited, either at the bargaining table or through street rallies, to head off the transfer in recent years of city para-transit operations for the disabled and prekindergarten transportation contracts to nonunion companies.

In the school bus strike, the union didn't do enough to avail itself of rank-and-file members like John Bisbano and Anika Nugent, who were capable of framing the issues in terms that could have rallied public support, particularly since they were ordinary workers struggling to make do who could not be written off as "labor bosses," or, worse yet, union leaders with ties to the discredited old guard. The local's public relations firm, Sunshine Sachs, spends more time representing celebrity clients than unions, which one official said may have led to a diminished attention span for a strike that coincided with Academy Award season.

Blame They Didn't Deserve

Listen to Mr. Bisbano, a union dissident who previously ran against Mr. Cordiello but supported him throughout the strike and beyond, critique the argument made by Mr. Bloomberg and Schools Chancellor Dennis Walcott that the city had to rein in runaway school-bus costs and ending the seniority protection for workers was the best way to do it: "Walcott is saying we have to economize, we can't have two or three kids on a bus. Well, the companies don't make up the runs, the members don't make up the runs."

One management official said the biggest source of the ballooning costs was the city's inclination to allow the families of Special Ed children to pick the school their child was going to, even if that meant long-distance commutes with a driver and matron assigned to three or fewer children in more than a few cases. If Mr. Bloomberg acknowledged that, though, he would have sounded like he was picking on the disabled; whacking away at employees whose average salary is $34,000 has become a much-easier public relations tack to take in the mayor's gilded version of New York.

Mr. Bisbano, voicing a sentiment other union officials have expressed privately, pointed to the transformation in recent years of the workforce so that a majority of it is people of color, with Haitian immigrants making up the biggest cohort. "Now that the industry is 70 or 75 percent minority, it seems they want to pull away the economic ladder they're trying to climb," he said.

Will Pledge Become Action?

That story wasn't being told in the coverage of the strike, however. It may have been one of the reasons that the five Democratic candidates for mayor, at Mr. Hanley's urging, on February 14 issued a letter urging union members to return to work rather than suffer the slings of Mr. Bloomberg's intransigence. They pledged that if one of them was elected to succeed him, they would revisit the Employee Protection Provision upon taking office in January, which gave Local 1181 a face-saving justification for ending the strike before the trickle of workers crossing its picket lines became a flood.

Ms. Nugent, a Brooklyn driver for Reliant Transportation who two days before the strike ended said that even prior to the walkout she was struggling to pay the mortgage on her home in Canarsie, noted of that promise, "They're going to revisit, but they aren't necessarily going to do anything."

But at least the five, including the three with the best shot of actually becoming mayor—Chris Quinn, Bill Thompson, and Bill de Blasio—will approach the issue from a different ideological spot than Mr. Bloomberg.

Ms. Nugent, asked whether she felt the strike had been the right move even though it fizzled out with just the hope of a better future once the incumbent leaves City Hall, said, "Right now I'm in between; I'm not really sure."

'Had to Go Out'

But Mr. Bisbano said of his old rival, Mr. Cordiello, "I felt Michael had to do it," given Mr. Bloomberg's assault on employee job security.

I found myself thinking about what is arguably the one really successful strike in the city over the past quarter-century, the walkout of nearly six months by employees of the *Daily News* that began in October 1990. Mr. Robbins, a reporter there at the time who was one of the key activists in the strike, noted several assets they enjoyed that weren't in play for the Local 1181 members.

"Some of us," he said by phone February 21, "were reporters and we knew how to get our story out. That helped us get some big names: John Cardinal O'Connor. The governor [Mario Cuomo] spoke at our rally."

There were also some labor leaders who took it upon themselves to get heavily involved even as the Central Labor Council's leadership back then largely sat on the sidelines, he noted. "Dennis Rivera [of Health Care Workers Local 1199] was absolutely vital in getting support out there—I don't think there is anyone who's his equivalent out there for the unions now. And [then-Teamsters Local 237 president] Barry Feinstein got a lot of troops out to our rallies."

Euphoria Didn't Last

Yet even that victory was short-lived: less than two years after the strike ended, a new publisher at the *News*, Mort Zuckerman, busted out its Newspaper Guild chapter while firing 187 of its members, even while leaving largely undisturbed a drivers' union that was then in bed with organized crime.

Ms. Nugent, asked how her return to work had been, said, "A little bit hectic, but we're just happy we were able to get back to school."

She had been unaware of the firing of the 109 matrons by Mr. Fazzia. "Wow," she said softly. "And this is legal? That's sad."

Police Unions in All Their Complexities

Patrolmen's Benevolent Association President Patrick Lynch at a June 2000 union rally excoriated Bruce Springsteen for writing a song about the fatal shooting of Amadou Diallo by city cops that he and his members believed was unsympathetic to the officers involved. His predecessor at the union, however, shortly after the February 1999 incident had blamed what he called the overly aggressive enforcement policies of Mayor Rudy Giuliani and his police commissioner, Howard Safir. Photo reprinted courtesy of the *Chief-Leader*.

It is not insignificant that the organizations that negotiate on behalf of cops rarely include the word "union" in their names, instead being known as "benevolent associations" or "endowment associations." Unions took root in the United States to challenge the established order in the name of workers; cops by the nature of their jobs uphold that established order, and at times less than a century ago were deployed as strike-breakers in some New York City disputes. Some old-time labor organizers recall occasions when police officers would try to discourage them from doing their jobs by heaving them down the steps of the subway; one of them adopted the preemptive tactic of carrying a test-tube filled with water that he hoped the cops would mistake for acid as a way of getting them to maintain a respectful distance.

Aside from their roles in negotiating wages and working conditions just as other labor groups do, the police unions strive to protect their members from adverse disciplinary action. More often than for most workers, such cases involve alleged violations of the law or their authority. That job is made more complex by the fact that they are advocating for people who wear badges and carry guns; other public workers take an oath to obey the law, but cops swear to uphold it as well, often in perilous and emotionally charged circumstances.

Sometimes union officials in their determination to protect their members cast aside that mandate, one notorious example being the attempt to coordinate testimony by cops involved in a 1997 incident that culminated with one Brooklyn officer pulling down the pants of a prisoner named Abner Louima and thrusting a jagged stick into his rectum. More frequently, though less noticeably, the police unions do what they are supposed to: vigorously represent the rights of accused members in controversial cases by making the public relations case for them and rebutting the charges of their accusers—often in the corridors or on the street outside the courtrooms where the trials are being conducted.

Enough Blame to Go Around

(July 3, 1998)

Francis Livoti was a cop in need of help who couldn't admit it. Instead of help, what he got was a bunch of cops doing him favors, from his fellow officers in the 46th Precinct to the very top of the NYPD's uniformed ranks. By indulging him, they let him bury himself—and cause the death of another man.

Years before Mr. Livoti decided an errant football was reason enough to start a one-man riot, he gave indications that he lacked the maturity and judgment to be a good cop. His commanding officer at the 46th, William Casey, in 1991 recommended that Mr. Livoti undergo psychological counseling and that he be transferred to a less-stressful assignment, perhaps in a quieter precinct.

Anemone Blocked Transfer
Effecting such a transfer was difficult anytime the officer involved happened to be a Patrolmen's Benevolent Association delegate, Chief Casey would later testify in a court deposition. And Mr. Livoti had managed to ingratiate himself with the then-president of the PBA, Phil Caruso, and with Louis Anemone, at the time a Bronx commander on his way to becoming the NYPD's chief of department. Chief Anemone countermanded the transfer order.

There were subsequent signs that Mr. Livoti's knack for racking up civilian complaints for using excessive force amounted to something other than what such complaints sometimes reflect: an active cop being sandbagged by felons. On one occasion, he got into an argument with a Lieutenant and shoved him.

It was this incident that made so ironic the argument by Mr. Livoti's defense attorney, Stuart London, last week that the fatal confrontation with Anthony Baez could have been avoided if one of Mr. Baez's brothers, a military veteran, had remembered that when you are given an order, you comply, whether you agree with it or not.

The shoving incident was a particularly alarming indication that Mr. Livoti believed himself immune from a paramilitary chain of command. It would have been bad enough if he was simply a Police Officer, but his status as a delegate—someone who had been chosen by his fellow officers for a position of leadership—made it that much more egregious.

This anointed leader had demonstrated that he could not command even himself, but this loss of self-control brought no action more serious than the requirement that he ride with a Sergeant, William Monahan.

'Sleeping at the Wheel'

In his summation to the jury in U.S. District Court Judge Shira Scheindlin's courtroom June 25, Assistant U.S. Attorney Andrew Dember was nearly as caustic regarding Sergeant Monahan's conduct on December 22, 1994 as he was about Mr. Livoti's. While Mr. Livoti charged out of their patrol car after it was struck by the Baez brothers' football, Mr. Dember said of Sergeant Monahan, "He's oblivious. He was sleeping at the wheel that night."

"This defendant," he said of Mr. Livoti, "was told by the commander of the 46th Precinct to avoid using excessive force in making arrests. He was also told to avoid any unnecessary confrontations with civilians."

And the Sergeant who was riding with him specifically to make sure Mr. Livoti heeded that warning, Mr. Dember suggested, was acting like Sergeant Schultz: seeing nothing, knowing nothing. But the prosecutor also offered up one explanation why: Sergeant Monahan had been promoted just nine months earlier. He was still in his probationary period, making him easy to demote.

And so Sergeant Monahan was in a decidedly precarious position: as surely as he could hurt his career by failing to supervise properly, he would also be running a risk if he antagonized a PBA delegate powerful enough to shove someone two ranks above him and draw no more severe a punishment than the assignment of a babysitter. Given a tough choice, he chose badly, not jumping out to intercede until things were out of hand.

Yet the reactions of other cops in the aftermath of Anthony Baez's death were just as stunning. There were meetings among the officers who were on the scene to discuss what had happened on as many as three occasions: at the PBA offices, in the 46th Precinct stationhouse parking lot, and at the Bronx district attorney's office.

The PBA is sometimes criticized for aggressive and vocal representation of its officers. Such criticism is often misplaced: the union is giving its members what their dues money entitles them to. But the PBA differs from, say, the steelworkers union in one important respect: both its leadership and its rank-and-file are sworn to uphold and obey the law.

Justice Comes Second

The convening of a meeting at union headquarters to make sure stories are in order is about as cynical a response to that duty as you can get, because it proclaims that allowing a criminal investigation to unravel the truth of an incident is irrelevant when weighed alongside protecting a fellow cop.

"Incredibly unprofessional" was how Mr. Dember described the meetings to the jury. Nor was there any clearer direction from higher up in the NYPD, as Chief Anemone defended Mr. Livoti in the immediate wake of the incident, calling him the type of active cop you needed in a tough precinct. Whatever personal fondness he had for him, Chief Anemone's placing the weight of his office behind Mr. Livoti after this incident and in light of his prior conduct was hardly good judgment.

In his first trial in the Bronx, Mr. Livoti was acquitted in a peculiar and at times self-contradictory ruling by Acting State Supreme Court Justice Gerald Sheindlin. That was where his luck ran out, however. In February 1997, after a departmental trial in which it was determined that, despite his denials, Officer Livoti had used a chokehold that had been outlawed more than a decade ago by the NYPD, Commissioner Howard Safir fired him. His power and his connections could not save him now—he had become a profound embarrassment to the department.

During his most recent trial, the union officials who turned out in solidarity for the first case up in the Bronx were not present, despite the short walk from the PBA's headquarters to the Federal courthouse. PBA President Lou Matarazzo's spokesman, Joe Mancini, when asked whether this was intended as a signal of a change in the union's position on Mr. Livoti, replied, "Nobody should read anything into it. He's supported by the PBA—witness the fact that he's got very able PBA lawyers defending him."

Yet among the 100-plus people packed into Judge Scheindlin's courtroom for the summations, only three of them were clearly recognizable as cops. When the jury looked out at spectators, what it was most likely to see, along with the Baez family seated in the last row, was a sea of overwhelmingly young faces. Some were prosecutors looking in on the trial, but many looked like students curious about whether the system would produce justice. Mr. Dember spoke of a "clear and bright line" separating the truth from lies and asserted that the cops who testified in Mr. Livoti's behalf were lying to protect him or themselves.

When Francis Livoti was choking Anthony Baez, Mr. Dember said, one of Mr. Baez's brothers had shouted to his wife, "Call the police!"

'They Weren't There'

Mr. Dember continued, "The police weren't there. This defendant wasn't a police officer. He was a bully, engaged in brutality."

It was a searing indictment, and not of Mr. Livoti alone. The jury's judgment that Mr. Livoti was guilty and jurors' statements afterward that they discounted as lies the testimony of his fellow officers, ought to be a sobering message to every cop. If it's not, the perjury indictments the continuing Federal investigation is likely to produce surely will be.

Mr. Livoti, who thought he had outsmarted a commander who wanted him to come in off the street and deal with his problems, is looking at a 10-year prison sentence, his life in ruins. It casts a very different light on the notion of taking care of your own.

A Tough Guy Gets Undressed

(April 11, 2008)

Joseph Guzman had just begun describing the shooting that left Sean Bell dead and himself seriously wounded when Queens Assistant District Attorney Charles Testagrossa asked him April 1 where he was struck by a bullet fired by Detective Gescard Isnora.

"Upper right shoulder," replied Mr. Guzman, who is big enough to play nose tackle for the Jets, and he took off his tie and unbuttoned his shirt to display the scar from the wound.

It would be nearly two hours later before he remembered to button up again. By then, Mr. Guzman was under heavy cross-examination by lawyers for the three Detectives on trial in the shooting of Mr. Bell, himself, and Trent Benefield outside a Queens nightclub on November 25, 2006. It was cold enough in Queens Supreme Court Justice Arthur Cooperman's courtroom that many in the audience were wearing their coats, but he was perspiring on the witness stand, frequently mopping his brow and close-shaved head with a blue handkerchief.

Provoking with a Purpose

The defense lawyers spent more than two hours during the morning session figuratively trying to get Mr. Guzman out of his suit and tie so his Inner Thug could be seen.

First James Culleton, the attorney for Detective Michael Oliver, poked and prodded, needled and badgered, and Mr. Guzman turned from a relaxed, street-savvy prosecution witness into someone

103

who could be as combative as he was confident on the stand. Then Anthony Ricco, Detective Isnora's Harlem lawyer with the Italian name, grabbed the baton and turned up the heat, their exchanges evolving into a noisy street dispute that brought reactions from Mr. Bell's supporters on the right side of the courtroom each time they thought Mr. Guzman got the best of their verbal flurries.

Then Mr. Ricco asked whether Mr. Guzman had told Fabio Coicou, the man in black with his hand in his pocket who quarreled with several members of Mr. Bell's bachelor party as they exited Kalua Cabaret, that he was going to get his gun to settle their dispute. "Where you from!" Mr. Guzman demanded. "Where you from!" He insisted he had no gun to retrieve and so, "Where I'm from, that's not a good bluff."

He didn't appear to realize it, but Mr. Ricco had him on the ropes and was methodically jabbing his credibility to pieces. In short order Mr. Guzman said he had no qualms about Mr. Bell getting behind the wheel of the car that was supposed to take them from Jamaica back to their homes in Far Rockaway, even though his friend's blood-alcohol level would later turn out to be nearly twice the standard for being considered legally drunk.

And where Mr. Guzman several times previously offered testimony that had deviated from statements he'd made to prosecutors or the grand jury, this time he reiterated what he'd told grand jurors about his brief conversation when a uniformed cop approached him after the shooting early that morning on a desolate street. "Officer, you just killed us for nothing," Mr. Guzman recounted to the courtroom. "There's no gun in this car."

In making those statements, he seemed to undercut his claims that he hadn't known that those who had confronted him, Mr. Bell and Mr. Benefield, were cops, or why they did so.

A Question of Justification

The case against the three Detectives hinges on whether they lacked justification for opening fire on the three men. Their attorneys have asserted that based on the dispute between Mr. Coicou and those in Mr. Bell's party—including Mr. Guzman's alleged remark about getting his gun—Detective Isnora had reason to believe they might be planning a drive-by shooting and sought to head them off. After he was struck by the car driven by Mr. Bell, which also collided with a minivan in which his backups were approaching, and Mr. Bell drove forward again, Mr. Isnora began firing his weapon, a decision that could be justified by either his belief that Mr. Guzman was reaching for a gun or that Mr. Bell was trying to do him serious harm using the car as a deadly weapon.

Five cops wound up firing 50 shots—11 by Mr. Isnora, 31 by Mr. Oliver, four by Detective Marc Cooper, and four by two other officers who weren't indicted. No gun was found on the three occupants of Mr. Bell's car, or in its vicinity. But the criminal case against the officers hinges on whether they had reason to fear for their lives unless they used deadly force.

Many of the witnesses called by the Queens DA's Office—which concluded its case the morning after Mr. Guzman testified—were friends of Mr. Bell's who had been with him inside Kalua. Some of them told different stories in court than they had related to prosecutors or grand jurors before the indictments were brought, and lawyers for the Detectives tried to make the case in their cross-examinations that the charges were concocted either out of loyalty to Mr. Bell or to improve the chances of the $50-million civil suit brought by Mr. Bell's family, Mr. Benefield, and Mr. Guzman.

Justice Cooperman, who at the Detectives' request is deciding the case without a jury, will have to wade through the inconsistencies, not least among them Mr. Coicou's statement to the Queens DA's Office in January 2007 that someone in the Bell party said, "We'll get the gat," something that on the witness stand last month he denied having heard.

Believed He Had Gun

Two of Mr. Bell's friends, Larenzo Kinred and Hugh Jensen, both said in court that they believed Mr. Coicou had been armed on that fateful night, based on the fact that he had just one hand in a coat pocket. And Mr. Guzman last week said he too thought that was possible, describing Mr. Coicou as "a short black male with a leather coat" standing by a black Ford Expedition SUV with chrome wheels outside Kalua, where he was waiting for his girlfriend, one of the club's dancers. "He was saying, 'I'll fight you,'" Mr. Guzman testified, adding that one member of their party, James Kollore, responded, "I'll take your gun."

Other witnesses who were with Mr. Bell have said that he also threatened to take the gun that Mr. Coicou had not in fact produced, even though Mr. Bell was supposed to get married later that day to his longtime girlfriend, Nicole Paultre. Among those who urged him to reconsider were Johnell Hankerson, a longtime friend and next-door neighbor of Mr. Guzman's who was married to the sister of the bride-to-be.

Another witness who said Mr. Bell argued with Mr. Coicou, Jean Nelson, testified that Mr. Coicou had threatened, "I'll shoot y'all." Mr. Nelson, who had been with Mr. Bell, also said that Detective Isnora had approached Mr. Bell and his two friends in their Altima and said, "I wanna holler at you" before Mr. Bell drove into him, a claim Mr. Guzman would later contradict on the witness stand when he said he never saw the cop approach them and first became aware of him when he started shooting.

The attorneys for the cops implied that Mr. Guzman invented details on the witness stand to aid his civil suit and create greater sympathy for himself and Mr. Bell.

Benefield Flounders

The day before Mr. Guzman's court appearance, Mr. Benefield was on the stand and like several previous witnesses appeared a bigger help to the defense case than to the prosecutors for whom he testified.

He denied hearing any conversation between Mr. Coicou and Mr. Guzman outside of their discovering that they both came from Far Rockaway, but he also said he believed Mr. Coicou might have been holding a gun inside his coat.

Mr. Benefield disputed what Detectives said he had told them after the fatal shooting about having drank a Long Island iced tea and five Hennessy cognacs at Kalua, claiming in court that he actually drank three Long Island iced teas and no cognac. He also denied having told doctors at Mary Immaculate Hospital, where he was taken to have his wounds treated, that he drank at least four beers every day— telling the courtroom that he did not drink beer—and had smoked marijuana every day for six years. His blood alcohol level when he was tested after the shooting indicated he was drunk at the time.

Rugged Grilling

When the lawyers for the Detectives weren't hammering Mr. Benefield over his consumption of drugs and alcohol, Mr. Ricco was prodding him to admit that he had revised earlier statements he'd made to cops about the confrontation between Mr. Bell and Mr. Coicou to improve the chances of winning his civil suit on the grounds that the cops had no reason to suspect violence might be imminent when they approached Mr. Bell's Altima.

Mr. Guzman, who at 32 is eight years older than Mr. Benefield (Mr. Bell was 23 when he died) was a considerably more self-assured witness when he limped to the witness stand shortly after 9 a.m. last Tuesday, walking with a cane as a result of some of his wounds, which damaged his intestines as well as his legs. Mr. Testagrossa, seeking to inoculate him against the cross-examination to come, early on had Mr. Guzman acknowledge that he had done two "bits" in prison for felonies, in 1995 for an armed robbery that eventually was reduced to a lesser charge and in 2002 for the sale of crack cocaine to an undercover cop within 1,000 feet of a school.

Mr. Guzman delivered the first, wrenching irony of his testimony when he told the court that originally Mr. Bell's friends had planned to hold his bachelor party in Mount Vernon, "but nobody wanted to drive."

He himself had confined his drinking to a single cocktail, explaining, "I'm a diabetic, so I don't really drink."

Claims He Cooled Beef
And he claimed to have sought to defuse the confrontation with Mr. Coicou, testifying, "I said, 'Listen, player, we're not gonna get into this.'"

He said as he and Mr. Bell walked to the Altima, Mr. Coicou drove past them slowly, and crossed into their path while making a turn onto Liverpool Street. "I told him, 'G'head,'" Mr. Guzman said. "He told me, 'G'ahead.'"

They got into their car, he testified, and Mr. Benefield came running up and jumped into the backseat on the driver's side.

Mr. Guzman made no mention of Detective Isnora approaching; rather, he said Mr. Bell started to drive and "a green minivan comes along and we hit it in the front."

The next thing he noticed, Mr. Guzman testified, was a "black male, silver gun . . . on the passenger side of the vehicle." He said the man was shouting but did not remember what he said; just that right after that, "He shot."

After displaying the wound, Mr. Guzman said, "When he shot me, everything to me slowed down . . . I'm looking at him. He kept shooting."

He said he told Mr. Bell, "Let's do it, let's do it! This is not a robbery; they're trying to kill us!"

Asked by Mr. Testagrossa to identify the man who had shot him, Mr. Guzman responded, "This kid right here, what's his name."

'Don't Got to Respect Him'

It would be the first of several times that he referred to Detective Isnora, who is 29, as a "kid." When Mr. Ricco asked him on cross-examination why he would not acknowledge him as an adult, Mr. Guzman retorted, "I don't got to respect nobody on that side and call him no man."

He said he never saw Detective Oliver fire his gun, explaining that after he was initially hit he tried to move away from the gunfire from Detective Isnora by climbing toward the window on the driver's side of the car.

There were clearly some mistaken details in his account. Detectives Endowment Association President Mike Palladino would note later that day that Mr. Isnora carried a black Glock, not the silver gun Mr. Guzman remembered, and he claimed to have been trying to crawl to safety while the car was still moving, a dubious proposition since it would have been virtually impossible for Mr. Bell to shift from "reverse" to "drive" in an attempt to get away while a man of Mr. Guzman's size was climbing over him.

'Shooting Didn't Stop'

Some of what he said rang true even in the areas where it was exaggerated. Mr. Guzman, asked whether there had been any pause during the shooting, testified that the gunfire "was continuous. It didn't stop. It seemed to me like it was going on for an hour."

And when it ended, he said of Mr. Bell, "There wasn't much left of him."

He testified that he told his friend, "S, I love you," and that Mr. Bell had replied, "I love you, too," although that didn't square with a doctor's testimony a week earlier that one of the bullets had pierced Mr. Bell's vocal cords and made him incapable of saying anything.

Assistant DA Testagrossa elicited from Mr. Guzman that he had not heard anyone say, "Police, don't move." Referring to a uniformed officer of higher rank who approached the car after the shooting ended, Mr. Guzman said, "The only time I knew he was police was when he came out of the car and said, 'Let me see your f------' hands.'"

He spent 18 days at Mary Immaculate Hospital, and then another six weeks at Jamaica Hospital. Mr. Guzman has "a dropped foot and nerve damage," a metal rod in one leg, "numerous holes in my intestines," and four bullets that remain in his body from the 16 that struck him.

The defense lawyers showed him no sympathy when they began cross-examination, and Mr. Guzman tried to match them. It would soon become clear that the attorneys were hoping to rile him, to bring the blustery street-tough side of him to the surface and transform him from victim to a not-altogether unwitting accomplice in the events that cost Mr. Bell his life.

Troubled Past Excavated

Mr. Culleton began by asking him about his relationship to Mr. Hankerson, who the defense attorneys believe may have had the gun—in the Mercedes that he had driven to Kalua—that Detective Isnora allegedly heard Mr. Guzman referring to.

After Mr. Guzman replied that he had lived next door to Mr. Hankerson his entire life, Mr. Culleton asked whether his 1995 criminal conviction had involved holding up someone at gunpoint. "I never possessed a gun," Mr. Guzman responded.

"Was someone you were with armed with a handgun?"

"That's what they were trying to say," he replied, his temper beginning to creep past the preparation he had received from the Queens DA's Office for what he would testify to and what he could anticipate on cross-examination.

Mr. Culleton moved on to the November 2002 bust for selling crack on 147th Street just off Rockaway Boulevard. Mr. Guzman bristled when the attorney asked where he got the crack, saying, "What difference does that make? It's in the neighborhood. It's all over the neighborhood."

Sentenced to two to four years in that case, he was released, Mr. Guzman testified, "almost exactly" a year before the shooting outside Kalua. While he had been employed as a mason by a construction firm "after my first bit," his return to Queens following his second imprisonment left him scrambling for work, going to a corner every day where a kind of shape-up was held by contractors looking for day-laborers.

Getting Under His Skin

Mr. Culleton brusquely pressed him on whether he had driven to Kalua in Johnell Hankerson's Mercedes, whether he had told friends that night to "take me to my bitch's house," and whether he had tried to pick up a female bartender in the club that night.

When Mr. Culleton asked him whether he was contradicting his grand jury testimony about when Mr. Benefield left the club that night to square it with Mr. Benefield's statements the day before, Mr. Guzman said with rising irritation, "I ain't trying to hide nothing, man. I ain't learned nothing from yesterday, and I been livin' this for 16 months."

He began responding to questions even before Mr. Culleton finished them, prompting Justice Cooperman to admonish him.

When Mr. Culleton, pursuing the defense's theory that Mr. Guzman on his way to the car might have called Mr. Hankerson about retrieving his gun, asked whether he had used his cell phone, the witness exclaimed angrily, "It's four o'clock in the morning, who am I talking to on the phone?"

To which Mr. Culleton sternly replied, "You tell me—I ask the questions." After an hour of doing so, he ceased his cross-examination, but Mr. Ricco took the same confrontational approach and added to it his penchant for addressing witnesses in the street language they employ.

Banter Gets Heated

At first, Mr. Guzman seemed to enjoy the give-and-take, telling Mr. Ricco after one question about his criminal past, "You did your homework."

But when he insisted that he didn't have a gun during the 1995 robbery, Mr. Ricco retorted that he made the same claim regarding the night at Kalua.

"Did you find a gun?" a no-longer-amused Mr. Guzman replied. "Did they find a gun?"

Mr. Ricco then shifted the focus to the 2002 arrest that he referred to as "your crack situation." "Who bagged the crack?" he asked.

"What difference does that make?" an exasperated Mr. Guzman replied. ". . . I bagged the crack."

"Who took care of your money?"

"That's obvious."

"Who took care of the protection?"

Mr. Guzman looked at him disdainfully and asked, "I look like I need protection?"

But the bluster was starting to wear on him, as he disputed statements by Detective Isnora's lawyer that a cooler witness would have ignored. He scoffed at Mr. Ricco's characterizing the bust as the culmination of a long-term probe, saying, "Two-to-four, it couldn't have been that long-term."

'Didn't Do Homework'

He corrected Mr. Ricco about the school near where he made the cocaine sale—"you didn't do your homework."

But when the attorney noted it took place in "the community where you spent your whole life," Mr. Guzman momentarily turned rueful. "You make bad choices," he said.

Mr. Ricco asked whether he had spoken to any other witnesses to make sure their accounts conformed, and Mr. Guzman replied, "Nobody wants to talk about this, man."

Contrasting him with Mr. Bell, who was legally blind in one eye, Mr. Ricco expressed incredulity that he claimed not to have seen Detective Isnora as he approached their car, saying, "You don't have an eye problem and you wasn't drunk."

"I just told you I didn't see him," Mr. Guzman retorted.

Referring to his urging to Mr. Bell, Mr. Ricco asked, "Does 'let's do it' mean 'run him over'?"

"No," Mr. Guzman said. "Let's do it means, we gotta go. They're shooting at the car, they're shootin' like crazy, they're killin' this kid. That's what y'all did."

'Doing What You Wanted'

A few minutes later, after another exchange in which Mr. Guzman angrily challenged the lawyer, Mr. Ricco diverged from Mr. Culleton's tactic of citing court protocol to establish that he was the one who was in charge in this setting. Instead, he stated, "I bet you were kind of tough out there at Club Kalua that night. I bet you weren't paying 'that kid' no mind when he said, 'Show your hands.' You was doing what you wanted to do, which is what you're doing right now."

With that flourish, which lacked only a question to justify it, he was framing for the Judge and those in the courtroom what he saw as the essence of Mr. Guzman's demeanor: that he wouldn't defer to a lawyer in a courtroom any more than he was likely to have just brushed off Mr. Coicou's posturing with a mere, "Listen, player, we're not gonna get into this."

If there were any doubts on this matter, Mr. Guzman dispelled them moments later with his, "Where you from? Where you from?" outburst.

That was the most dramatic moment in their battle, but Mr. Ricco may have sealed the case against trusting this witness when he then asked, "Were you concerned in any way, Mr. Guzman, that Sean Bell wasn't in the best condition to drive?"

"If I felt like he couldn't drive, I would've drove," Mr. Guzman replied.

A Matter of Judgment
In saying so, he further damaged his credibility by raising questions about his own judgment that night. One of the hazards of driving drunk is that being intoxicated slows a person's reflexes, but this is not the primary consideration—if it were, it's likely that we would license 14-year-olds to drive more readily than 60-year-olds given their superior reaction time. The greatest danger of getting behind the wheel while under the influence is that a person's judgment is impaired.

Mr. Bell had already proved he was operating at less than peak efficiency in that department by getting so drunk on the morning of his wedding, then becoming embroiled in an argument with a stranger at a time of day when the odds of it having unforeseen consequences were especially high, and finally looking to drive despite his inebriation. He certainly didn't deserve to die for those mistakes, but they were all contributing factors in what followed.

The Queens DA has argued that in the heat of the moment, the cops on the scene panicked and fired 50 bullets without having established that they were in real danger. It seems at least as possible, however, that it was Mr. Bell who panicked; that if he didn't realize immediately that Detective Isnora was a cop, then the collision with the green minivan would have filled in the blanks, and that he responded as he did not out of fear for his life but because he realized he might wind up spending his wedding day behind bars. At a time when he was inhibited from thinking clearly, that might indeed have seemed like a fate worse than risking death by driving at Mr. Isnora to try to escape the circumstances that macho bluster outside a nightclub had created.

'He Knew They Were Cops'

After court adjourned that afternoon, Mr. Palladino remarked, "Isnora [got] hit by the car and there's scientific evidence that proves that. [Mr. Guzman] knew damn well that they were the police, right from the start. I think we got a good look at the type of individual Joseph Guzman was by his demeanor on the stand. He's probably used to that type of behavior on the street."

At the start of the trial, the DEA leader said, the defense lawyers all believed it would be imperative to put the Detectives on the stand, placing their credibility up against that of the witnesses against them. But with the three cops' grand jury testimony having already been read into evidence by the prosecution and the DA's witnesses being so problematic on issues of consistency and believability, Mr. Palladino said, "The big dilemma now is whether you even put the three guys on the witness stand."

One feature of the defense case that began April 3 is likely to be the lawyers' belief that Johnell Hankerson had the gun Mr. Guzman allegedly referred to stashed in his Mercedes. Mr. Palladino claimed that he fled the scene on foot and did not return for his car until hours later.

Part of Later Shootout?

Less than five months after the Bell shooting, Mr. Hankerson was shot while eating a slice of pizza on Rockaway Boulevard. Detectives eventually recovered a gun near the scene that a witness claimed Mr. Hankerson had dropped during a shootout, but Mr. Palladino said ADA Testagrossa opted not to bring charges against him. During his own appearance on the witness stand, Mr. Hankerson denied that he had won an assurance that he wouldn't be prosecuted in return for giving testimony for the DA's Office.

It's only a theory, one that has some interesting circumstantial evidence to support it but nothing to prove it's valid. But then, the attorneys for the three Detectives don't have to make that case; they just need to establish reasonable doubt on behalf of their clients.

And that, with the help of the performances on the witness stand of the two men who were in the car with Mr. Bell, they seemed well on their way to doing.

All three of the Detectives were acquitted of all charges in the case. Following internal disciplinary trials, however, Detective Isnora was fired and stripped of his pension while his two colleagues retired. He has sued over the disciplinary penalty, and the case is pending.

The paramilitary nature of police departments makes it inevitable that more often than not when public outrage is directed beyond an individual officer's action and focuses on policies set out by the upper levels of the organization, the unions close ranks behind the commanders under fire, just as they expect them to do on behalf of their members. Occasionally, however, union leaders have stepped forward when they believe their members are unfairly being placed in bad spots by questionable decision-making at the top and lashed out at those calling the shots.

Two notable cases of that occurred in response to the hailstorm of criticism that descended on cops carrying out policies believed to have originated directly from then-Mayor Rudy Giuliani that resulted in the fatal shootings of two unarmed black men, Amadou Diallo in 1999 and Patrick Dorismond in 2000.

Savage Steps Out Boldly

(April 23, 1999)

With words that had echoes of Thomas Paine, James "Doc" Savage last week launched a revolution of his own at that most unlikely of places, the Patrolmen's Benevolent Association.

Speaking about the NYPD's intensified anti-crime effort, Mr. Savage told PBA delegates April 13, "If we don't strike a balance between aggressive enforcement and common sense, it becomes a blueprint for a police state and tyranny."

With a declaration like that, the action he prompted the delegates to take—a unanimous vote of "no confidence" in Police Commissioner Howard Safir—seemed almost superfluous. In a union where presidents under pressure have generally responded by making political turns to the right, Mr. Savage went left into traffic.

The effect was breathtaking. Looked at carefully, the cause seems logical.

Unconventional Wisdom?

Mayor Giuliani and Mr. Safir ascribed Mr. Savage's words and actions to the political struggle he finds himself in as he seeks a full term as PBA president. But his move seemed counterintuitive, something that might make perfect sense for a trade-union leader but not at a police union, where the tendency in situations like these has been to launch broadsides against "radicals" who don't have the NYPD's best interests at heart.

Mr. Savage stood the conventional wisdom on its ear, in essence saying that if radicalism is at work here, it is coming from City Hall and the top of the NYPD. "I don't think it's good for the citizenry or the police officers to set up roadblocks just to give people summonses," Mr. Savage said in an interview the day after he led the quiet rebellion that rocked the NYPD.

"I think we should get back to community policing, building up relationships with the communities we serve."

This kind of heresy would earn him the castigation of the mayor and his off-payroll publicists at the tabloids. But within the department, Mr. Savage said, "A lot of people of all ranks have called offering their support and saying I did the right thing."

It also paid an unexpected political dividend for him when Commissioner Safir, in criticizing Mr. Savage, said he agreed with PBA Recording Secretary Jim Higgins that the union president took the no-confidence vote as a "publicity move."

This put Mr. Higgins, who has vociferously criticized what he contended was an insufficient response by Mr. Savage to police critics, in an awkward position. Despite his pronouncement, Mr. Higgins himself voted yes on the no-confidence resolution, but he suddenly found himself thrust forward by Mr. Safir—the very object of the delegates' derision—as his preferred candidate in the four-way race. All he needs now is an endorsement from Mayor Giuliani and you can start making funeral arrangements for Mr. Higgins's candidacy.

The vote of no confidence in Mr. Safir had three roots. One, Mr. Savage said, was discontent with how the Police Commissioner has handled disciplinary cases. The PBA delegates resent some of Mr. Safir's rulings, as well as his inclination to defend himself against outside criticism by bragging about how many officers he's fired.

A second key factor is the Commissioner's recent knack for placing himself in compromising positions and a stunning lack of veracity on his part in dealing with some of those situations.

The Hollywood Shuffle

It would have been far easier for Mr. Safir to defend spending a Sunday at the Oscars if he hadn't previously indicated he had a scheduling conflict that would prevent him from testifying before the City Council the following day on the Diallo case and the Street Crime Unit. He compounded the knuckleheadedness of his conduct by initially putting out word that he had paid for the trip himself, when in fact a Revlon executive picked up the tab.

An even worse signal was sent to his troops by his behavior regarding his wife's fender-bender incident and lawsuit. Mr. Safir's claim that he had no idea what was alleged in the suit flies in the face of the standard procedure in such cases that plaintiffs sign contingency agreements with their lawyers that lay out exactly what is being sought. When he announced he was firing his lawyer and retaining his friend Raoul Felder to press the suit, it was hard to resist wondering whether cross-examination might be handled by Mr. Felder's associate, Jackie Mason.

Throw in the Palm Beach trip and Mr. Safir's use of eight Detectives to provide free security at his daughter's wedding and a picture starts to emerge of a Commissioner who wants the same perks as a high-powered corporate executive rather than having to pay for the better things in life the way lower-ranking cops must. Unfortunately for Mr. Safir, the NYPD is one of the few agencies the mayor has not considered privatizing.

Mr. Safir's credibility was not shored up, either, by his remarks following the PBA's no-confidence vote that he had tried to get cops raises during the first two years of their current contract but was thwarted by Mr. Savage's predecessor, Lou Matarazzo.

Not Based in Fact
The Commissioner's claim notwithstanding, the only known proposal to give cops more money in return for having new officers work 10 extra tours concerned the fourth year of the current deal and would have added a point to a 3-percent raise. Mr. Matarazzo balked at that contract proposal by city negotiators—which began with a two-year freeze that eventually was imposed—believing that the money offered was not good enough to compel new union members to work the extra tours.

Dissatisfaction with the contract that came out of the arbitration of that dispute hastened Mr. Matarazzo's retirement and is the source of much of the discontent within the PBA ranks.

But that dissatisfaction is also reflected in the rank and file's resentment of both Mr. Safir and Mr. Giuliani, because in both symbolic and tangible ways, their position in that negotiation indicated how little they believed the cops themselves deserved credit for the drop in crime.

Tale of Two Unions

While the arbitration case by the union's lawyers was not particularly well presented, Mr. Matarazzo frequently remarked upon how the surge in arrests and summonses issued demonstrated added productivity by his 26,700 members. In essence, the city replied that this extra activity could not be rewarded unless the arbitrators were also prepared to impose pay cuts in the future if crime surged upward.

Yet at virtually the same time, the Giuliani administration negotiated a new productivity deal with the Uniformed Sanitationmen's Association that boosted differentials paid to collection crews for meeting new tonnage targets. The deal constituted a reworking of the original two-worker truck agreement nearly two decades ago that gave employees a bonus in return for the union allowing collection crews to be reduced by one man with the help of new trucks.

Now, it is difficult to measure police productivity in the same way you do sanitation productivity, particularly because there are some situations that the best cops are going to resolve without issuing summonses or making arrests.

But at no point did the Giuliani administration dig in its heels and say it wasn't going to honor the prior sanitation bonus program on the basis that Sanitation Workers were more productive than two or three decades ago merely because they were being required to work full shifts while taking advantage of better technology.

On the Other Hand . . .

But that was the unstated assumption behind the city's case in the PBA arbitration: that more aggressive policing tactics combined with computerized tracking that made crime patterns more evident were what brought crime down so sharply. (A 15-percent increase in the number of cops since Mr. Giuliani took office in 1994 might also have been cited, but for some reason the mayor tends to downplay that factor in the crime drop.)

Mr. Giuliani has not fully grasped the lesson inherent in the reign of one sports figure he admired: the late football coach Vince Lombardi.

Mr. Lombardi's authoritarian nature was summed up by one of his defensive tackles with the Green Bay Packers, Henry Jordan, who said the coach treated all his players the same: "like dogs."

The players put up with Mr. Lombardi's verbal abuse and his exhausting practices because he was able to convince them early on that, if they submitted to his discipline, he had the intelligence to lead them to victory, with the attendant glory and financial rewards.

Mr. Lombardi became a legend, but so did his teams.

In Mr. Giuliani's case, he has been decidedly reluctant to share the glory or to compensate the officers of all ranks who have been pushed hard to burnish the crime statistics. Inevitably, starting a couple of years ago with the acrimonious contract negotiations, rank-and-file cops began asking themselves what exactly they were getting out of their additional efforts.

And when the shooting of Amadou Diallo unleashed a simmering public resentment of the high-handed conduct of some cops carrying out the NYPD's aggressive enforcement policies, Mr. Savage began wondering aloud about whether such policies were counterproductive. If those policies were antagonizing the public, leaving many cops further alienated from both the communities they served and a city administration that was giving them no tangible reward for doing this unpopular work, who exactly was benefiting?

Mr. Giuliani, it is clear, has focused much of his attention on his political future and horizons that stretch beyond New York City.

It is fine for his advisers to privately remark on the political reality that even as the Diallo shooting and the rallies it sparked have hurt his standing in the city, it has helped him upstate, where the Reverend Al Sharpton is still reviled for his outrageous conduct in the Tawana Brawley case 11 years ago. But how does that help the cops who will still be working the streets of the city long after Mr. Giuliani has left City Hall?

No Mayor Culpa

Mr. Savage and, presumably, many of his members, understand that Mr. Giuliani's ambitions have sometimes affected his better judgment. Both the mayor and Mr. Safir disregarded warnings from the Street Crime Unit's former commander against rapidly expanding the unit without proper training and supervision for its new recruits. Yet neither man has issued anything approaching an apology, to either the city or the troops, for the miscalculation that is a contributing factor to four officers facing murder charges, their careers in the NYPD almost surely over even if they are acquitted.

It goes back to the lesson of Mr. Lombardi and others who tried unsuccessfully to follow in his mold: If your players believe in you, they will give you more than might reasonably be expected. Once they begin to doubt you, they are likely to either quit on you or rise up against you.

Mr. Savage cast the loudest, most-emphatic doubt so far within the NYPD with his actions and, especially, his words last week. Two months from now, when his members' ballots are counted, we'll have a better idea as to whether he established himself as a worthy leader in their eyes with that bold, refreshingly unorthodox stand.

Savage lost the union election, a victim of membership anger over the two-year wage freeze that Giuliani succeeded in having imposed on the union through a 1997 contract arbitration. The winning candidate, Pat Lynch, was the only one in the four-man race who had not been a member of the PBA board when that ruling went against the union. Jim Higgins, the candidate favored by Police Commissioner Howard Safir, finished last in the member balloting.

Giuliani's Toxic Cynicism

(March 31, 2000)

"The general atmosphere toward police is toxic, especially within the minority communities," Detectives' Endowment Association President Tom Scotto advised his members in the March 20 recording on the union's hotline.

The following day, the man who has emerged as the city's leading toxic agent offered up some evidence as to why that atmosphere exists in the wake of the killing of Patrick Dorismond during a confrontation with undercover cops March 16.

Explaining why he decided to release details of Mr. Dorismond's past brushes with the law, including a juvenile conviction that was legally sealed under Family Court regulations, Mayor Giuliani said, "There's a principle of logic that says people act in conformity with their prior behavior. And even in a courtroom, you're allowed to introduce prior acts of a person accused of a crime if those acts occur frequently enough that they create a pattern of behavior."

Accused Only by Mayor

The courtroom analogy falls apart, however, once you remember that Mr. Dorismond had committed no criminal act, nor was he suspected of one, when an undercover cop initiated what turned into a fatal encounter.

This may have been a Freudian slip by Mr. Giuliani, who seems desperate to find some evidence that would suggest that, if Mr.

Dorismond did not necessarily deserve to die, it was his fault that the fatal shooting occurred.

But, seasoned courtroom lawyer that he is, I wonder if there is anything accidental about any of the mayor's utterances over the past two weeks. It seems more likely that, like a three-card monte dealer, he is trying to distract the crowd so it will lose focus on the shady business being transacted.

An anti-drug operation, authorized by City Hall and using tens of millions of dollars in overtime money, degenerated into a fishing expedition in which an innocent man was approached on the street by an undercover cop looking to buy marijuana.

From that legally dubious starting point, matters got worse, ending with Mr. Dorismond's death. The Manhattan district attorney's office is investigating whether the officer whose gun killed Mr. Dorismond, Detective Anthony Vasquez, acted criminally, or whether the shooting was just a horrendous accident.

But determining the Detective's culpability is almost a secondary issue here. More to the point, why is the NYPD having officers initiate encounters with people who are not suspected of doing anything wrong?

The cheap and easy answer—and frankly, the only one that really makes sense—is that it is hoped they will turn up a few guilty fish and pad arrest statistics. This kind of operation is not the way to make an effective dent in street-level drug sales. The best way to do that is to put some time into surveying an area, getting undercover officers to blend in while observing just who is making the sales and how, and then moving in with certainty that you are busting the bad guys.

But that takes time, as opposed to the quick hits that may produce arrests of low-level sellers but are unlikely to cripple an entire drug operation. The arrests generated don't have real significance other than to produce numbers that can be used by the mayor to tell voters who buy this kind of cynical game that, as much as he reduced crime in the past, he's still improving upon his own achievements.

Making Cops' Jobs Harder
So what if, as Mr. Scotto puts it, these kind of operations add to the "toxic atmosphere" that exists between cops and the minority community? The mayor doesn't seem terribly concerned about whether he is making the working lives of cops more difficult, and he isn't expecting many votes from blacks and Latinos anyway.

And as this story has played out, it has allowed Mr. Giuliani to further exploit a strategy he already had in place for the Senate race: to put Al Sharpton on the opposing ticket alongside Hillary Clinton.

On March 20, while taking the mayor to task for his efforts to publicize and exaggerate Mr. Dorismond's past criminal record, Ms. Clinton told her audience at the Bethel AME Church in Harlem, "At just the moment when a real leader would try to reach out and heal the wounds, he has chosen divisiveness. He has led the rush to judgment."

Mr. Giuliani's campaign manager, Bruce Teitelbaum, immediately fired back that "Mrs. Clinton is shamelessly doing her best to exploit this for political purposes just like she did when she rushed to judgment and called the police officers involved in the Diallo case murderers during her visit with her pal Al Sharpton."

The following morning, the mayor was even more explicit. "Mrs. Clinton and the Reverend Al Sharpton are reading from the same script," he said.

An 'Insulting' Question

At the end of his press conference, a reporter asked whether reasonable people might disagree about whether it was Mr. Giuliani or Mr. Sharpton who was the polarizing force in this incident. The mayor replied that, having spent more than six years in office, "I think it's insulting for you to compare me to Al Sharpton."

This is a valid response if the issue pertains to making major accomplishments while handling huge responsibilities. Mr. Giuliani, like him or not, produced some important prosecutions as U.S. Attorney, and the crime reductions during his tenure, coupled with the Wall Street boom and a strong national economy, have had a large hand in revitalizing the city after a decade of high crime and economic problems led to a decaying quality of life in many areas within the five boroughs.

Mr. Sharpton deserves much credit for spotlighting the case that exposed systematic racial profiling by New Jersey State Troopers. But arguably his most-significant achievement during the last 20 years has been transforming himself from a rabble-rousing street hustler into a legitimate spokesman for black residents' concerns. While a considerable feat, that required no great administrative talents or gift for inspiring others to work hard on behalf of a government.

Higher Standard Needed

But conversely, the greater responsibilities shouldered by Mr. Giuliani demand more responsible behavior on his part. And in that context, it is not clear that Mr. Giuliani occupies the moral high ground in a comparison with Mr. Sharpton over the years.

Mr. Sharpton earned his greatest and most lasting notoriety for his role in the Tawana Brawley case. It is hard to overstate just how irresponsibly he behaved during that sorry episode, smearing Steven Pagones and making increasingly outlandish demands upon state officials while perpetuating an awful hoax.

But Mr. Giuliani, who often excoriates the media for being too forgiving or too lenient regarding Mr. Sharpton, has also benefited from reporters' short memories.

The mayor of this most multi-ethnic of American cities has rarely faced criticism for his own disgraceful role in the early 1980s, while a member of President Reagan's Justice Department, in placing Haitian refugees in detention camps. Mr. Giuliani's justification for not granting them political exile from the repressive Duvalier regime was to claim that they had left Haiti not to escape political persecution but to seek greater economic opportunity here. You could have made the same morally dubious argument, with as much validity, about Russian Jews who emigrated here during that era.

Put Mr. Sharpton's slandering of Mr. Pagones on a scale with what Mr. Giuliani was willing to do to boost his standing in the Reagan administration—he soon after was appointed U.S. Attorney in Manhattan—and you could make a good case that Mr. Giuliani's actions did a larger harm.

Mr. Sharpton after the Brawley fiasco had two moments of conspicuously incendiary behavior: his remarks about Jewish "diamond-dealers" at the funeral of Gavin Cato, the seven-year-old boy whose death touched off the Crown Heights riots in 1991; and his "white interloper" comment during a boycott of a department store in Harlem two weeks before a crazed man killed several people inside the store and set it on fire.

Fanning PBA Flames

And alongside those incidents, we have Mr. Giuliani, at a 1992 Patrolmen's Benevolent Association rally that had already degenerated into a mini-riot, repeatedly using an expletive as part of a scathing denunciation of Mayor Dinkins.

Mr. Giuliani's defense of his speech on that occasion was that he was unaware that two blocks east of where he was speaking, unruly cops were blocking traffic and harassing motorists and pedestrians on the Brooklyn Bridge. He also contended that he earlier had played a role in quieting much of that overstimulated crowd after hundreds of officers tried to storm City Hall.

But knowing of some of the violence that had already occurred, and aware that emotions were running high, rather than appealing to cops to take care that the rest of their rally was peaceful and unmarred by vitriol, Mr. Giuliani made statements that could only fuel the anger that was in the air.

Which is just what he is doing now by continuing to flay Mr. Dorismond, the dead victim of an incident that wouldn't have occurred except for a highly questionable policing strategy.

The mayor's stated reason for not attending the Dorismond funeral March 25—that "the person involved may have been involved in a crime"—sounded particularly soulless alongside Detective Vasquez's statement that day extending "heartfelt condolences" to Mr. Dorismond's family.

The justification the mayor gave for his illegal release of information about Mr. Dorismond's conviction for punching a friend at age 13 was that dead people have no legal guarantee of privacy. In making that argument, he adopted the sleazy tactics associated with lawyers who try to defend their criminal clients by claiming that their victims' prior behavior suggests that maybe they asked for what they got.

The person for whom the mayor is going to these extremes in trying to make his case is not Detective Vasquez. Rather, this is all about trying to escape the consequences of his own actions in continuing dubious crackdowns at a time when the city's crime problem pales as a potential danger alongside the growing suspicion and distrust separating the police from minority communities.

This latest incident, regardless of whether criminal charges are brought against the officers involved, may be the deciding factor in whether U.S. Attorney for the Eastern District Loretta Lynch imposes an outside monitor on the NYPD.

Styling Himself As Victim

This would be more than a huge political blow to Mr. Giuliani. Given how closely tied the successes and failures of the Police Department are to both his emotional being and his place in the city's history, Ms.

Lynch's ordering such a step would for Mr. Giuliani be the equivalent of a cop being asked for his gun while he's placed on modified assignment.

If he had heeded his own initial advice to avoid making judgments until the incident was thoroughly investigated, it would have been akin to passively awaiting a decision from the U.S. Attorney. By stridently attacking Mr. Dorismond and all those sympathetic to him, from Democratic elected officials to Ms. Clinton and Mr. Sharpton, the mayor is doing advance work for a later claim, should Ms. Lynch order a monitor, that he is the victim of a political hatchet job.

Such a claim may be hard to sustain this time, however, judging by two surprising editorials in the *New York Post*—normally the mayor's most-ardent media booster—that took him to task for "insensitivity" both in his reaction to the Amadou Diallo shooting and his attacks on Mr. Dorismond.

Mr. Giuliani disregarded the *Post*'s advice against "stonewalling" this time, indicating that even his friends were incapable of gaining his ear. He may still believe that acting like a relentless executive with little concern about the senseless shooting of a decent man will play well among his core voting constituents, particularly those who like politicians who talk tough to black leaders.

But if that is his political calculation, it is fair to ask whether Mr. Giuliani is acting in a fashion that is contrary to the best interests of the city, not to mention his police force. If he's determined to pursue this strategy to a Senate seat, perhaps he should give up his day job.

The Demise of a
Once-Great Union

Charles Hughes (*left*) and James Butler over 30-year reigns became two of
the most powerful District Council 37 local presidents, but were tarnished
by the scandal that rocked the union in the late 1990s, with Hughes going
to prison for embezzling more than $2 million and Butler losing a reelection
bid in 2002 amid questions about his high salary and questionable financial
practices. Photo reprinted courtesy of the *Chief-Leader*.

Beginning in the mid-1960s, District Council 37 of the American Federation of State, County and Municipal Employees (AFSCME), established itself as the largest and most-influential public employee union in New York City and, arguably, the nation. It began its ascent in the late 1950s when it was taken over by Jerry Wurf, a firebrand with roots in the working-class Brooklyn neighborhood of Brighton Beach and the Young People's Socialist League.

When he moved on to head the national union in 1964 after a bitter internal struggle that led to him narrowly defeating AFSCME President Arnold Zander, Wurf brought in as his successor Victor Gotbaum, another Jewish kid from Brooklyn who had grown up amid labor ferment and, after being tapped by Zander in the late 1950s to run AFSCME's Chicago district council, had sided with Wurf.

Gotbaum was thrust almost immediately into a city welfare strike, and after that ended with some significant gains for both union members and the clients they served, he won huge battles to represent the bulk of New York City's hospital workers and its clerical employees. He was aided mightily in those efforts by an old friend from the Chicago district council, Lillian Roberts, who had a particular appeal to the largely minority, female workers they were courting.

Gotbaum built on the structure put in place by Wurf, using the formal collective bargaining rights that had not come to city unions until the mid-1960s to not only improve salaries and working conditions but to win other benefits for members through union-run dental clinics and legal-services programs that few unions had at the time. When a fiscal crisis threatened the city's solvency in 1975, Gotbaum became a key figure in the series of deals that brought it through the storm, agreeing to defer wage increases his members were due and committing billions of dollars in pension funds to the purchase of municipal bonds that were considered toxic in the normal markets because of the city's teetering credit rating.

Even as the city was climbing back from the brink of a bankruptcy that could have jeopardized his members' pensions, Gotbaum sought out a new challenge. It was inevitable, given his strong personality and that of Mr. Wurf, who was naturally cantankerous, that tensions arose in their relationship, and Gotbaum decided to oppose his reelection as AFSCME president. His bid quickly foundered, but not before dividing the local presidents within his union and forcing Gotbaum to align himself with some bad characters during a tense period in which he sometimes traveled with armed local presidents acting as bodyguards.

Both he and Wurf were committed battlers for the working people they represented. This didn't mean that they were wholehearted believers in the democratic process. Some of the most-activist locals in DC 37 were known for frequent turnover of their leaderships; Wurf and Gotbaum took steps to minimize the risk that a bad contract or a wave of anger bubbling up from the rank and file might cost them an election.

There were stories of local votes in which members mailed their ballots to a post office box and Wurf's allies opened the box and the ballots prematurely to ensure that the right candidate won. During Gotbaum's era as executive director, one local election was supposedly tipped when a box of ballots got tossed into a stairwell. These colorful tales of chicanery were actually just peripheral to their subversion of true union democracy through the very structure of DC 37's election process, in which members did not actually vote for the union's leaders.

That was instead done by delegates from within the locals, the largest of which, School Employees Local 372 and Clerical-Administrative Workers Local 1549, between them represented 50,000 of DC 37's 125,000 members. Since the delegates could often be enticed—using sweeteners that ranged from stipends of close to $10,000 to trips to exotic locations as part of their regular duties—to vote in blocs for the candidates favored by their local presidents, the two giant locals when banded together could virtually guarantee the executive director's job security—or end it.

Wurf and Gotbaum were both strong-enough leaders that while they made accommodations for the presidents of those two locals, they established limits, both to keep them under control and to prevent an uprising from the 55 other local presidents. But by the early 1980s, Gotbaum had come to the conclusion that Roberts, for all her talents as an inspirational organizer, lacked the skills and judgment necessary to succeed him when he would turn 65 in 1987. He eased her out by getting her a job as the state's Industrial Commissioner, calling in a favor from Governor Hugh Carey for past political support and his cooperation during the city fiscal crisis.

Determined that his successor be black, as were a majority of the union's members, Gotbaum turned to Stanley Hill, a former president of DC 37's social-services employees local who was part of his executive staff. Their personalities were vastly different, and so were their management styles.

Gotbaum was brassy and strong-willed, but he had a knack for choosing people to head union lobbying and negotiating units who could be just as outspoken and did not punish them if they said or did something that upset government officials or those from other unions. Hill was a more-amiable man, a former star athlete who wanted to rule by consensus but also had a reputation for deflecting blame onto others when problems arose. He was less inclined to be confrontational in dealing with local presidents, particularly those who had leverage over him through the number of delegate votes they controlled. And so by the 1990s, word was drifting out of the union's Barclay Street headquarters in lower Manhattan of serious excesses and questionable spending.

Smaller locals representing not more than a couple thousand members were running up tabs for holiday parties of $80,000 or more. In one case, the bill for the party was not paid to the large Long Island wedding and bar-mitzvah emporium that catered it but to a small travel agency in East Northport. Millions were spent on DC 37 cruises in the Bahamas at a time when the workers it represented were facing layoffs; millions more were spent on education conferences in which the union was being charged a rate for close to 1,000 guests that exceeded the rate the hosting inn quoted to couples looking for a weekend getaway.

There was also a peculiar contract vote. A deal that would freeze wages for two years—which had previously been rejected by the United Federation of Teachers—snaked its way through DC 37 in a most-unusual fashion, with the votes by locals spread out over several months.

The union had suffered through an 18-month wage freeze a few years earlier, after then-Mayor David Dinkins laid off a couple thousand of its members and said more jobs would have to be cut unless the membership bit the bullet. Dinkins was succeeded in 1994 by Rudy Giuliani, a Republican who had made his reputation as a tough prosecutor of corrupt politicians and mobsters and was neither terribly sympathetic to the workers DC 37 represented nor owed the union's leaders anything, since they had endorsed Dinkins in both of their battles for the mayoralty.

Giuliani in 1995 had told the union that without a two-year wage freeze to get the city budget into balance, he would have to resort to massive layoffs; there were some within DC 37 who believed the body count could be as great as 30,000. Hill had felt the pain when just a couple thousand of his members were cut loose by Dinkins, and he had no doubt Giuliani, unconcerned that the loss of even 10,000 union members could badly hinder the effective delivery of city services, would fire a lot more if need be,.

His members, because they held jobs that—while as varied as accountants, construction laborers, civil engineers, and boiler operators—did not have much public cachet, were more vulnerable to layoffs than the teachers who voted down the wage freezes. Nonetheless, they were by a narrow *but decisive margin rejecting the contract's terms. Just one local had not counted its ballots—Local 1549—and then, astonishingly, it reported that more than 10,000 members voted in favor of the terms with about 2,000 against, a large-enough margin to ratify the pact unionwide.*

The presidents of the third- and fourth-largest locals, representing hospital workers and social-service employees, both charged that the Local 1549 voting had been rigged, based on nothing stronger than a gut belief that its members—who were among DC 37's lowest paid—could not possibly have supported a two-year wage freeze that strongly, layoff worries or not. One of them wrote to the president of AFSCME, Gerald McEntee, requesting an investigation. McEntee, whose own electoral fortunes depended on the support of both Hill and Local 1549's president, Al Diop, ignored the request.

Eyebrows were further raised when a newspaper profile of Hill noted that he had been permitting Diop to live in DC 37's penthouse suite, with Local 1549 paying the tab. This, too, brought no stirring in the AFSCME bullpen. But in early 1998, word began seeping out that the president of Local 372, Charles Hughes, whose membership had recently surpassed Local 1549's to become DC 37's largest employee group, had plunged the local $10 million into debt, some of it through lavish personal spending, some through questionable payments made to him for overtime he claimed he was owed, and some of it through a series of loans from DC 37 to cover the local's operational expenses.

Suddenly AFSCME was involved and vigilant. By that time, however, so was the Manhattan district attorney's office, which was also focusing on some strange practices in smaller locals, including the purchase of holiday turkeys for members at prices that were roughly double what would have been paid buying them retail in a supermarket.

The local president who served as DC 37's turkey vendor was Joe DeCanio, whose members were laborers deployed primarily in maintaining the city's streets and highways. He had inherited the business from the man he succeeded, Vincent Parisi, whose family owned a Manhattan bakery sufficiently renowned that Frank Sinatra used to purchase bread from it.

Parisi was reputed to have organized-crime connections and styled himself as a tough guy. DeCanio was soft in comparison, and as prosecutors leaned on him in the fall of 1998, he began providing them a road map to all the corruption in DC 37. That included not only the systemic looting of members' dues money but the fixing of the contract vote a couple of years earlier.

Before it was over, more than two dozen DC 37 officials pleaded guilty to criminal charges or were convicted in court. Hill, who was apparently not involved in the criminality, was forced to step down as executive director, and AFSCME, which had already seized control of Local 372 when it ousted Hughes in February 1998, took over the district council as well late that November.

With McEntee's top assistant, Lee Saunders, serving as DC 37's administrator, financial controls were put in place after it was discovered that Local 1549—where Diop had stolen more than a million dollars while also playing a key role in fixing the contract vote—had not been audited for the previous four years. But Saunders, given extraordinary powers in the effort to clean up the union, left untouched the system for electing DC 37 officers, despite the protests of union reformers who had been calling for giving members the right to vote months before the scandal burst into public light.

Saunders and McEntee were cool to the reformers, seeming more comfortable dealing with those members of the union's Old Guard who had not been taken down by the scandal. They left the decision on direct election of officers to union delegates, who not surprisingly were unwilling to relinquish their greatest source of power. A feud over who would run DC 37 led to a bargain between the Old Guard and the reformers under which Lillian Roberts, who had not been involved with the union for nearly two decades, was to serve as a transitional leader, the fond memories of her work during the union's glory days making her an appealing candidate as it sought to put its sordid decline in the rearview mirror.

She was in her late 70s at the time, but she quickly decided she was unwilling to serve as just a caretaker leader for two years, and in 2004, in the first election since the scandal broke six years earlier, she narrowly gained a full term over Charles Ensley, the social-service employees local president who had asked AFSCME to investigate for election improprieties back in 1996. The fact that she had not distinguished herself during two years in office was irrelevant to the delegates; it did not matter three years later, either, when she defeated Ensley by an even wider margin. When local presidents and their delegates were the tools of the election process, accountability to the members was purely optional. The mechanism that Wurf and Gotbaum had used to ensure their longevity in office by safeguarding against dissidents seizing power remained alive and well, even as the once-vibrant union seemed to be on a respirator.

Targets: Friends of Rudy

(October 30, 1998)

In March 1997, Joseph DeCanio, the president of Laborers Local 376 of District Council 37, became the first official of that union to endorse Mayor Giuliani's reelection.

In doing so, he was not unlike the canary sent into the coal mine to make sure that it does not have too much methane gas to make it hazardous to humans. If the canary makes it back still breathing, it is safe to send larger creatures into the shaft.

Mr. DeCanio's endorsement of the mayor did not, as it turned out, set off any explosions, and six months later, on September 11, 1997, DC 37 Executive Director Stanley Hill gave the mayor the endorsement of the 120,000-member union.

200 Got $11,000 Raise

Less than three weeks later, the Giuliani administration announced a new career ladder for the Assistant Highway Repairers represented by Local 376 that for 200 of them meant an immediate $11,000 pay raise.

The deal was remarkable in several respects, not the least of them the fact that this huge boost came at a time when most of DC 37's rank and file was receiving 3-percent pay hikes that averaged less than $1,000 a year.

It also was negotiated outside the regular bargaining protocol. A story in DC 37's *Public Employee Press* (*PEP*) about the raise at the time identified the union's "key negotiator" on the deal as Associate Director Marty Lubin, Mr. Hill's top lieutenant.

Making it all the more unusual was the appearance of First Deputy Mayor Randy Mastro at the announcement ceremony. The *PEP* article quoted him calling Mr. DeCanio "a dear friend and a great union leader." He went on to add, "When Rudy Giuliani makes a commitment, he keeps it."

It's not unusual for officeholders to reward their union supporters at the bargaining table. It's also common for mayors to have someone in city government handling what might be lumped under the heading of union patronage and endorsement coordination.

The choice of Mr. Mastro for that role raised some eyebrows last year, partly because he was negotiating endorsements with union leaders in his City Hall office. There was also a certain incongruity in choosing as the primary patronage dispenser the official who was also the mayor's main agent against corruption, as Mr. Mastro—a former top prosecutor under Mr. Giuliani in the U.S. Attorney's Office—was in the drive to purge the Fulton Fish Market and the private carting industry of mob influence.

All this became an afterthought once the mayoral election was over, and early this summer Mr. Mastro left the administration to resume his law partnership at Gibson, Dunn & Crutcher.

DeCanio under Scrutiny

But it is suddenly a ripe subject again, with Mr. DeCanio having emerged as a man at the center of the Manhattan district attorney's investigation into possible corruption at DC 37. Subpoenas issued earlier this month asked the presidents of 44 DC 37 locals to turn over any business records they had involving transactions with Mr. DeCanio personally or with his family's bakery in Queens, which union officials say catered numerous DC 37 events.

Back in July, Mr. DeCanio acknowledged to this newspaper that he had served as a conduit between a supplier of holiday turkeys and two DC 37 locals and had received "commissions" for his efforts. Other officials of the union say the number of locals involved was much greater.

Mr. Mastro, asked October 24 about the clouds gathering over Mr. DeCanio, said, "I'm not familiar with any of the circumstances. I haven't seen any of those materials that you're talking about."

Asked about his impression of Mr. DeCanio during his dealings with him, he said nothing particularly stuck in his mind, remarking, "The mayor was endorsed by over 50 union leaders."

It was pointed out to him that Mr. DeCanio's endorsement, as the first one from a DC 37 local president, carried greater significance and therefore might be expected to have been more memorable. Mr. Mastro, after a long pause, replied, "I don't have any comment on the situation."

But a half-hour later he called back to say, "In my experience, I found Joe DeCanio to be an honorable person. And in terms of any investigation that may or may not be pending, I have no comment other than to say one should not prejudge."

Christopher R. Lynn, the commissioner of the city Tax Appeals Tribunal, was the Department of Transportation (DOT) commissioner at the time the Highway Repairer career ladder was created. He contended Mr. Mastro's significant involvement in reaching the agreement on the career ladder stemmed not from political considerations but because he was asked to intervene in a disagreement between Mr. Lynn and the Office of Management and Budget (OMB).

Issues in Dispute

"Ordinarily, it would go to [Labor Relations Commissioner] Jim Hanley," Mr. Lynn said regarding responsibility for negotiating the deal. In this case, however, he remarked, his desire to set up the career ladder ran into the opposition of John Murray, a veteran OMB official who was the agency examiner responsible for DOT.

Mr. Murray, according to Mr. Lynn, was not primarily troubled by the $2.2-million cost involved in granting the large raises to 200 employees promoted into Highway Repairer titles.

Rather, he said, Mr. Murray was "concerned that [a career ladder] increases permanent headcount," undercutting the Giuliani administration's efforts to trim the number of full-time employees on the payroll even while it pays thousands of per-diem workers in their place.

Mr. Murray was also, according to Mr. Lynn, "adamant" that ending the seasonal status of Assistant Highway Repairers could jeopardize the city's entitlement to Federal funding to cover the cost of 80 percent of any new road surfacing project.

"When the head of an agency disagrees with OMB, you go to your deputy mayor," Mr. Lynn said.

Calls to Mr. Murray seeking his version of the dispute were not returned.

Asked whether politics played a role in the timing of the mass promotions, coming shortly after the DC 37 endorsement and five weeks prior to the election, Mr. Lynn responded, "Absolutely none. This was my initiative. I started it the week after I came to DOT" in mid-1996.

Dead-End Jobs

Mr. Lynn said Mr. DeCanio had immediately impressed upon him the low morale that had been created by substandard working conditions and little chance for advancement among those in the Highway Repairer title series.

"Folks had been there for 11 or 12 years and were still provisional," Mr. Lynn said. "We had a mess. We had a system that no one could make sense of," in contrast to the Department of Environmental Protection, where employees doing comparable work had a career path.

Mr. Lynn said he found Mr. DeCanio to be "smart, dedicated, a total advocate, honest."

The last adjective raised a question as to whether he knew Mr. DeCanio was a prime target of the DA's probe.

"Nope," he said. When told why Mr. DeCanio's dealings may have prompted scrutiny, Mr. Lynn retorted, "We're talking bread and turkeys. This is a major corruption issue?"

It is if there were kickbacks involved, and the suspicion is what seems to be the engine powering DA Robert Morgenthau's year-long investigation of DC 37. The probe appears to be approaching climax and last week prompted a remarkable editorial in the *New York Times* under the title "Plundering a Municipal Union."

The editorial began, "A wave of indictments is expected . . ." Given the *Times'* caution about dabbling in bold speculation, the inference to be drawn is that if "wave of indictments" were a stock, the prudent investor would be placing a high-volume buy order.

Spotlight on Hughes

The editorial went on to single out Charlie Hughes, the already-banished former president of Board of Education Local 372, for his excesses, which plunged the local $10 million into debt and led to his being dunned by DC 37's international union for nearly $2 million in payments he received that it deemed improper.

Mr. Hughes, like Mr. DeCanio, is another DC 37 leader who had strong ties to Mr. Giuliani and whose local and individual members seem to have benefited.

He was the focal point of a television commercial that was prominently featured in Mr. Giuliani's reelection campaign. It began with a videotape of Mr. Hughes extolling the mayor's virtues and ended with the two—a black man who as a youth worked in the Georgia cotton fields and a white man raised in the comfort of Long Island—embracing.

By then, Mr. Hughes had already reaped the rewards of his support. In late 1996, at a time when other DC 37 members were receiving no additional money as a two-year wage freeze ran its course, the hourly workers at the Board of Education represented by Local 372 got a $250 bonus, and those who were annualized received $350.

Action Boosted Members

Mr. Hughes was also able to increase his membership by a couple of thousand—while other DC 37 locals were simply trying to prevent reductions—as the indirect result of a provision in the United Federation of Teachers contract negotiated by then-Labor Relations Commissioner Randy L. Levine that exempted teachers from hallway and cafeteria monitoring duties. That required the massive hiring of additional school aides to assume those chores.

It is the likely imminent indictments of officials like Mr. Hughes and Mr. DeCanio that had the *Times* editorial calling for DC 37 to be placed into trusteeship, in essence stripping Mr. Hill of his powers.

But their predicaments also raise questions about whether the mayor—who as U.S. Attorney for the Southern District was regarded as the sharpest, most-aggressive prosecutor seen here in decades—turned off his smell detector as he lined up labor support for his political advancement.

Gotbaum's Revised History

(December 4, 1998)

For much of last week, Victor Gotbaum attempted to rewrite history so that the continued implosion of District Council 37 would not weigh too heavily on his own legacy.

He did this under the guise of flawed nobility, by claiming that he had made a mistake in choosing Stanley Hill to succeed him as the union's executive director 12 years ago but that he had no alternative.

As Victor spun it to countless reporters, he would have preferred giving the job to Lillian Roberts, but she left to become State Industrial Commissioner, leaving him with no choice but to knight Mr. Hill as his replacement.

From 'No Leader' to Adequate

"When she left, I felt Stanley was adequate," Mr. Gotbaum said in an interview November 25, a considerable boost in his evaluation considering that he had told *Newsday* columnist Dennis Duggan two days earlier that Mr. Hill "never projected the personality or the force of a leader."

It's an interesting fairytale, based on a true story. The facts are a bit more complicated.

For one thing, by the time Victor was ready to retire in 1987, Lillian Roberts was long gone from the job to which Governor Carey had appointed her at Mr. Gotbaum's request. She had been dumped unceremoniously by Governor Cuomo, who arguably owed his election to DC 37's support in 1982.

"He forced Lillian Roberts out," Social Service Employees Local 371 President Charles Ensley said of Mr. Gotbaum, a perception shared by another half-dozen union veterans who did not want to be identified. Indeed, Mr. Hill told a DC 37 delegate assembly November 24 that Ms. Roberts, who could not be reached for comment, had accused Mr. Gotbaum of lying about her departure.

And between the time that Ms. Roberts left as DC 37's associate director and Mr. Hill's appointment as executive director, Mr. Gotbaum had five years to reconsider his options and go in another direction if he chose.

The unspoken issue in nearly all Mr. Gotbaum's interviews on the subject was race. When I asked him how heavily that entered into his choice, he responded, "Race always figures in the equation for me. I make no bones about it: the labor movement needs more black leadership. I felt a real responsibility to bring in a black leader."

But he had just gotten through a half-dozen interviews in which he suggested that Mr. Hill met only half that criteria, and he acknowledged again, "I didn't view Stanley as a No. 1 person."

Were there any white officials at the time in the union who he thought were up to the job?

"There's a lot of people," Mr. Gotbaum replied.

Not Exactly Affirmative Action

The idea of affirmative action, when carried out properly, is that if you have candidates for a position who are more or less equal in ability, then race can be a consideration in whom you choose for the job. Yet here was Mr. Gotbaum arguing that he believed that a number of white candidates were qualified to fill his shoes, but he instead chose a black candidate about whom he had serious doubts.

There is nothing affirmative about such a choice.

When that notion was broached to Mr. Gotbaum, he replied, "It's still a democratic union. There was a strong feeling on the part of a lot of the black leadership that they wanted Stanley."

To which Mr. Ensley, who was part of DC 37's black leadership then and now, responded: not necessarily, and certainly not to the exclusion of other candidates if they were better choices.

"Victor controlled that union with an iron hand," Mr. Ensley remarked. "He could have picked anybody and they would have received" approval as his replacement.

"I think Victor is an old-line liberal and he wanted to do something because of race," he continued. "But often the old-line liberals didn't understand race and how to play that card. If he had thought Stan inadequate, he had time to seek someone else out. If he thought Stan was inadequate and he put him in anyway, then he did a disservice to all of us. Maybe he set him up to fail."

That last thought assumes an unseemly cynicism on the part of Mr. Gotbaum, who for all his personal flaws was in many ways one of the most important and powerful labor leaders of this half-century.

Pivotal in Union's Rise

He could be cruel and crass and self-indulgent, but he had an unusual grasp of the big picture, which made him the pivotal figure in turning DC 37 into the largest municipal union and one of the best in the country. He helped to pull the city back from bankruptcy, and made decisions in governmental elections that were as right for his members as they were sometimes risky. Unlike Mr. Hill, who tended to prize loyalty over talent in choosing much of his staff, Mr. Gotbaum hired people who could be as independent and abrasive as he was, and he generally got more than his money's worth in return.

But several DC 37 veterans theorized last week that Mr. Gotbaum did not want his successor to be so good that his own accomplishments would fade from memory, and that his taste for the good life could be more easily indulged if the executive director who followed him needed to retain him for advice.

Mr. Gotbaum said that his role as a consultant to Mr. Hill lasted "about a year" and that he couldn't remember how much he was paid. A spokeswoman for Mr. Hill said the consultancy ran for "several years." Mr. Ensley said it was his understanding that Mr. Gotbaum was paid about $100,000 annually, and that DC 37 paid for his secretary and supplied him with a car and driver as well.

Hard Feelings on Layoffs

Just when tensions began between Mr. Hill and Mr. Gotbaum is not altogether clear, but there is no question that there were hard feelings over the layoffs made by Mr. Gotbaum's wife, Betsy, during her tenure as Parks Commissioner in 1991. DC 37 officials said at the time that they were convinced that Mr. Gotbaum was advising his wife on where to make the layoffs, in the process persuading her to get rid of senior workers because they were making higher salaries.

The one layoff that stood out was that of Joseph Zurlo, who had spent more than 40 years in the Parks Department and became president of DC 37 under Mr. Gotbaum. He fell out of favor because he sided with Jerry Wurf, the caustic president of the American Federation of State, County and Municipal Employees, when Mr. Gotbaum tried to wrest control of the national union from the man who had brought him in to run DC 37.

The blood feud that resulted left scars that still have not healed: when Charlie Hughes, his life and his power within DC 37 crashing down on him, lashed out at Mr. Hill during a union trial in March, he accused him of opportunism dating back to the days when they were on opposite sides of the Wurf/Gotbaum war.

In pressing on with that war, Mr. Gotbaum forced local leaders to take sides, and sometimes he gave power to allies who with half a chance were sure to abuse it. Among them was one local president who had the habit of mispronouncing the word "Negro" and another who sometimes referred to Mr. Gotbaum in front of other union officials as "that effin' Jew." Both those men were also suspected of being a few degrees south of honest.

Both were still around—they have since died—when Mr. Hill stepped into the job. It is likely that before the investigation by the Manhattan district attorney's office is through, they will have been posthumously implicated in the corruption that has turned DC 37 into a reeling, wobbly giant.

'I Put Clamp On'

"The illegal difficulties occurred after I was gone," Mr. Gotbaum said. "I think I put the clamp on it," he remarked when asked about the plundering tendencies of one of those men.

"The big difference," Mr. Gotbaum said, "was they were afraid of me."

There is consensus among veteran union officials that on this matter he is right: that Mr. Gotbaum was enough of a lion-tamer to keep the wild beasts under control and that any scams they ran on his watch remained small-time.

But again, this raises the question as to why he would for a moment believe that Mr. Hill, a man who would rather be liked than feared, would be able to keep petty grifting from turning into a land rush of larceny.

Some locals became racketeering enterprises and had elections no more honest than the rest of their business. The Thanksgiving turkey giveaway during Mr. Hill's tenure turned into an operation in which union members' dues lined the pockets of the people who were supposed to represent them.

'Lucky to Have Jobs'

One leading player in the turkey trimmings was Robert Taylor, who until recently was the president of Motor Vehicle Operators Local 983. When union members came to him with complaints about their treatment in one city agency, he allegedly replied, "You're lucky you have jobs." When those members went to Mr. Hill and produced evidence that Mr. Taylor was bankrupting the local, Mr. Hill ignored it. After all, Mr. Taylor's vote was one he could always count on at the DC 37 executive board.

And if there's one lesson Mr. Hill seems to have picked up from his predecessor, it's that sometimes you hold your nose rather than sniffing your supporters too closely.

Mr. Gotbaum has reason to feel regret about what has happened to DC 37 since he left it. But as Mr. Ensley noted, his waxing sanctimonious while taking shots at Mr. Hill is "really unattractive."

Mr. Gotbaum knew Mr. Hill's limitations when he chose him. It is unfair to raise someone up and then knock him down for failing to be any better than you believed he could be. No matter how much his failing may now be harming your own reputation.

Stern Reaction from DC 37

(March 5, 1999)

Back in 1966, Henry Stern was a precocious 30-year-old Executive Director of the Parks Department whose high-handed style quickly earned him the resentment of employees represented by District Council 37.

Shortly before the Memorial Day weekend that was to launch the opening of the city's beaches, a few employees were transferred for what union officials thought were arbitrary reasons. And so when the weekend began, from the sands of Orchard Beach to the shores of Coney Island, not a lifeguard could be found until a call was made to Parks Commissioner Tom Hoving at his summer home, who, after the cause of the sick-out was explained, countermanded Mr. Stern's transfers so that the beaches could open with proper supervision.

The Christmas Tree Caper
This was not enough to deter the intrepid Mr. Stern. And so the union guerillas struck again that December when Mayor Lindsay, upon pulling the switch that was supposed to light the Christmas tree in City Hall Park, discovered by the continuing darkness that someone had unscrewed all the bulbs.

A month later, Mr. Stern paid the price for that embarrassment. "I was transferred to another assignment at the same salary," he later recalled with an impish grin. "I couldn't really be fired: I was a member of the Liberal Party."

He was speaking on a warm June day in 1997, noting how the pendulum had swung more than 30 years after his first go-round in the Parks Department. Mr. Stern no longer found DC 37 troublesome.

Its executive director, Stanley Hill, had made mild but futile protests as DC 37's membership in the Parks Department steadily declined, even as the ranks of Work Experience Program participants grew. The WEPs by then outnumbered unionized employees by about three to one, and Mr. Stern's ability to muster them into an unpaid army, according to private advocacy groups, had allowed city parks to improve even as his budget was cut 20 percent by Mayor Giuliani.

No More 'Reign of Terror'

"Our employees are now working with us," Mr. Stern said that morning as he conducted a quick tour of Bronx parks. "You don't have any sense that the unions are fighting with us, trying to establish their primacy or sabotage us. It's very different from the reign of terror in the '60s."

Until now.

The passage two years ago of the state Social Services Law as part of a welfare reform effort has provided DC 37 with the legal ammunition to challenge the Parks Department's use of WEPs. The law prohibits participants in the program from performing work that either should be done by unionized employees or has been done in the past by them.

And new, more aggressive leadership at DC 37 in the person of Administrator Lee Saunders is firing away, having brought two lawsuits in the past month on behalf of locals that have lost hundreds of members while the WEPs are increasingly used to clean the parks and do some skilled labor.

During a press conference last week announcing the second lawsuit, which was brought on behalf of Motor Vehicle Operators Local 983, there seemed to be remnants of the tensions that have permeated DC 37 since the battle between reformers and regulars there began in earnest last year. There was a certain uneasiness in the interactions between DC 37's chief negotiator, Dennis Sullivan, and Local 983's president and counsel, Mark Rosenthal and Arthur Schwartz, that reflected differences in their approaches to both negotiations and confrontations with the Giuliani administration.

But the nervous energy in the air represented a step forward from Mr. Hill's ambivalence about doing anything to antagonize the mayor unless it was absolutely necessary.

Mr. Stern has been circumspect since the first lawsuit was filed early in February on behalf of City Park Workers, and through a spokesman he turned down a request for an extended interview on the changing relationship he has with DC 37, citing the pending litigation. But clearly the rediscovered militancy within the union does not gladden his heart.

Differing Traditions

Back in 1997, when he was asked how Parks had become the city agency that made greatest use of the WEPs, he said, "Our idea from the start was, 'Give us as many of the WEPs as you can and we will put them to work.' It ties in with the Civilian Conservation Corps. Park work was traditionally work for people who were unskilled."

Mr. Sullivan last week described the unskilled labor inherent in many parks jobs as a ticket for generations of city workers toward the middle class and away from dependency.

Mr. Stern, who dryly refers to the Dinkins administration era that interrupted his two tenures as Parks Commissioner, spanning 12-plus years, as "when I was away," has a different view. He spent part of his time out of government as head of the Citizens' Union, and made clear during that period that he believed the city's workforce had grown too large and that the wages and benefits it was paid could not be supported.

The equation changed, however, once he returned to power upon Mr. Giuliani's election and, thanks to the WEPs, was able to more than double the number of workers at his command even as those who received wages and fringe benefits were cut nearly in half.

Mr. Stern's eccentricities—his penchant for referring to his staff by "park names," the use of employees to walk his dog Boomer and chauffeur the golden retriever to agency events, his accusing a contractor who cut down eight trees of "premeditated arborcide"—sometimes overshadow his talents as an administrator with a particular skill for securing money for Parks' capital budget from both public and private sources.

But keeping the city's parks in reasonably good shape despite the loss of mayoral aid to an agency already decimated by cutbacks under

Mr. Dinkins is less about genius than about having a captive, unpaid workforce at his disposal. Mr. Stern is not unlike a manufacturer who becomes prosperous by farming out his work to Third World countries where employees can be paid a pittance and wouldn't dream of filing a grievance.

Enthusiastic Executor

As was noted by Michael Power—a carpenters union official who, back before DC 37 got back to that old-time religion, sued the Giuliani administration, charging that WEPs illegally displaced his members—Mr. Stern is merely acting as a particularly enthusiastic executor of Mr. Giuliani's labor policy.

When Mr. Sullivan last week remarked, "The real reform of welfare is a job," it seemed intended as an ironic commentary on the gap between Mr. Giuliani's frequent comment that "work is ennobling" and policies that suggest that it is particularly ennobling if it costs the employer nothing.

Mr. Sullivan said the lawsuits were part of a DC 37 effort to redirect the city's workfare program, so that it produced long-term jobs for participants and provided them with meaningful benefits during their city service.

Mr. Stern's spokesman noted that through the more intensive Parks Career Training Program, 1,227 WEP workers have been groomed and then placed in full-time jobs in the private sector. Mr. Stern, asked several weeks ago how many WEPs he had hired, responded that "dozens" had become regular employees. DC 37 officials expressed skepticism about that claim, but even if it is accurate, it's a pretty modest achievement given the thousands of WEPs who have been deployed by Parks over the past five years.

Union officials believe that the primary purpose of WEP has not been to promote self-sufficiency but to afford the mayor the opportunity to proclaim that he has transformed the city's public assistance culture, while drastically slashing the welfare rolls.

They may argue that they are more genuinely interested in a successful workfare program than Mr. Giuliani, but their primary motivation is also self-interest. Mr. Rosenthal last week spoke of the plummeting morale among his 550 members in the Parks Department, who see their opportunities for advancement thwarted by a lack of civil service exams while at the same time they find their work increasingly being performed by superficially trained welfare recipients.

Devaluing Workers

There is an implicit message in that transition about just how expendable those unionized workers are, and how little the skills they have acquired are valued by the administration.

Mr. Saunders last month spoke about a line being drawn in the sand. The battle will be fought, however, in the courts and figures to be a long time in its resolution. In throwing down the gauntlet this way, though, he has delivered a double-barreled message.

The union's members understand that rather than simply taking cover as in the recent past, DC 37 is ready to hit back on their behalf. For the mayor and Mr. Stern, the message is as clear and as pointed as Mr. Giuliani's proclamation to those on welfare: the free ride is over, and we're going to make you work for everything you want.

Delusions of Entitlement

(May 14, 1999)

Six months ago, in arguing that Charlie Hughes had no criminal intent when he appropriated nearly $2 million in union funds for his own purposes, his lawyer, Gerry Shargel, said that while undergoing a mental breakdown, Mr. Hughes came to believe that his spending was appropriate.

"He was clinically depressed. There came a time when he thought he was entitled to more money from the union," Mr. Shargel said.

It is no secret that Mr. Hughes, in addition to the troubles that led to his ouster as president of Board of Education Local 372 of District Council 37, has had serious family problems to deal with in recent years.

Touchdowns and Table Dances

But to fully buy Mr. Shargel's argument on behalf of his client, it would be necessary to assume that four other Local 372 officials who were indicted along with Charlie Hughes last week, including his son and son-in-law, were similarly delusional as they ran up $670,000 in credit-card charges for personal entertainment ranging from Super Bowl tickets to visits to topless clubs.

The key words in Mr. Shargel's explanation of this behavior may not be "clinically depressed"; more likely, the magic phrase is, ". . . he thought he was entitled to more money from the union."

That's because the sums of money involved and the manner in which much of it was spent suggest nothing so strongly as a sense of entitlement on the part of those who found themselves in Manhattan Supreme Court May 5 on the wrong end of indictments for plunging Local 372 deep into debt with their self-indulgence.

Charlie Hughes faces as much as 25 years in prison if convicted of the charges against him, among them numerous counts of grand larceny. Mildred Stephens, the 76-year-old former Treasurer of Local 372 who faces a similarly lengthy prison stretch if convicted, seems to have taken part in schemes that garnered Mr. Hughes half of the $2 million he is accused of taking more from a sense of loyalty than from baser motives.

But in some ways, the alleged crimes of their four co-defendants, none of whom face more than 15 years in prison, are more telling about what happened to this local, which was collecting $15.5 million in membership dues annually at the time that it fell $10 million into debt, according to its Administrator, Zack Ramsey.

Those four men are Martin Hughes, Local 372's ex-third vice president and Charlie's son; James Rose, Charlie's son-in-law and former associate editor of the local's newsletter; and Richard Louis and Joseph Alfano, both of whom were special assistants to the senior Hughes.

Their personal spending at union expense, as detailed in the indictment, started with relatively small numbers. The overt acts listed in the indictment for 1994 were Martin Hughes's spending of $1,100 to rent hotel rooms and cars in connection with the Super Bowl that year, and his paying $1,600 to buy tickets for a Knicks playoff game during the NBA finals that June.

But the spending began to accelerate the following year. The indictment indicated that Martin Hughes and Joseph Alfano began planning their itineraries early for the 1996 Super Bowl, making the first of what would amount to $26,000 in related charges on their Local 372-issued American Express cards in February 1995.

After the '96 Super Bowl, Martin Hughes filled out his sports calendar for the year by spending $5,250 on tickets for college basketball's Final Four championship games and another $9,522 that August to book airline tickets for the 1997 Super Bowl. Along with Mr. Alfano, he then spent a total of $22,732 on tickets for that Super Bowl.

Membership's Privileges

By April 1997, Martin Hughes and Mr. Alfano had put down hotel room deposits totaling $7,340 for the following year's Super Bowl, and in August the two men combined to put $29,400 worth of Super Bowl tickets on their union charge cards.

To keep themselves amused between football games, the Local 372 Boys Club members turned their attention to indoor activities: on May 8, 1997 Martin Hughes and his brother-in-law, James Rose, spent $2,200 of Local 372 dues money during a visit to a strip club. On October 9, the younger Hughes and Richard Louis ran up a bill for $1,840 in another visit to a topless club; on October 10, perhaps tuckered out from their endeavors the evening before, they made a return visit but charged only $803 worth of entertainment.

Martin Hughes and Mr. Louis did another back-to-back session in the land of 1,000 table dances the following month, running up a two-night tab of $2,202.75 at the expense of Local 372 members.

Three days later, perhaps having made some new friends, Mr. Hughes charged another $2,200 worth of Super Bowl tickets. During the next two months, he made three separate purchases of plane tickets to the Super Bowl at a cost of over $2,500.

Mr. Louis, having gotten a taste of the good life on dues-payers' nickels, now charged more than $6,000 in Super Bowl tickets and plane tickets on his own local-issued credit card.

At this point, Martin Hughes, Joseph Alfano, and Richard Louis had run up more than $48,000 in Super Bowl charges, and none of them had so much as set out for Pasadena, California, where the game was being played.

Going in Style

When they did, Mr. Alfano set the tone early, charging $141 for a ride to the airport via car service. Martin Hughes then stepped up to the counter and upgraded his airline tickets for the flight to California at a cost of $2,693.50, or more than the typical Local 372 member earns monthly before taxes. He, Mr. Alfano, Mr. Rose, and Mr. Louis spent another $2,700 renting four separate cars once in California. Their transportation costs covered, the four men then spent another $1,600 in union funds on meals, $1,700 on merchandise and footwear, and $3,600 on hotel rooms. And Martin Hughes and Mr. Louis, as a diversion from the spectacle of the Green Bay Packers vs. the Denver

Broncos, spent another $2,450 at a topless club. Throw in the $945 Mr. Alfano spent on ground transportation to get him to the airport in California and then back to his New Jersey home, and the 1998 Super Bowl cost Local 372's 26,000 members more than $63,000. For about 25,994 of them, the bill probably seemed a bit high.

Of course, that's only if they weren't comparing it to the $590,000 in unauthorized retroactive payments Charlie Hughes received, or the $700,000 in overtime pay that he collected during 1997. And alongside the $100,000 he spent taking 14 friends and relatives on a July 1997 trip that covered Egypt, Israel and the Czech Republic, Paris and London, the Super Bowl junket taken by his son and three associates looks like one of those boys-will-be-boys things that you do when the folks are away.

In some ways, though, it is easier to feel sorry for Charlie Hughes than for the four young men implicated in the whole mess that began to crash down on Local 372 just days after that 1998 Super Bowl, when the American Federation of State, County and Municipal Employees suspended Mr. Hughes and his board and placed the local under administratorship.

From the time that he was younger than his 30-year-old son, Charlie Hughes was president of Local 372, making it into a politically potent union that improved the lives of its members, most of whom were part-timers with no pension rights three decades ago. He was always extravagant, on behalf of the local as well as in his personal life, and his annual Christmas parties at the New York Sheraton attracted many of the biggest political figures in the city, because those same politicians counted on him for generous contributions.

Child of Segregation

Charlie Hughes grew up in Millen, Georgia, during a period when segregation was for the first time being seriously challenged in the Deep South. His adolescence was marked by the remaining vestiges of a life in which color overshadowed ability in determining how high you could rise. He attended an all-black high school, spent summers picking cotton in the fields of Millen, and was the first black person permitted to work behind a cash register in that town during his teens.

He came to New York at age 20 and took a job as a school lunch helper, and at 27 he was running Local 372.

When he was 40, Charlie Hughes recounted in a 1983 interview, he took his family to a hotel in Switzerland where Queen Elizabeth had stayed and asked his teenage daughter, Charisse, what she thought. Charisse, who is now married to James Rose, with the worldliness affected by adolescents, responded, "Eh."

To which Mr. Hughes retorted, "If you only knew."

And that exchange helps explain how people like Martin Hughes and Joseph Alfano could have helped bring Local 372 to the brink of ruin while Charlie Hughes's life teetered out of control. They did it casually, with the unearned sense of entitlement that comes from growing up privileged without knowing hardship. Like Martin Hughes, Mr. Alfano comes from a family with strong roots in DC 37: he is the grandson of the late Vincent Parisi, the former president of Laborers Local 376.

Mr. Parisi has always been regarded as a somewhat shadowy figure in DC 37's history. During then-Executive Director Victor Gotbaum's feuds with AFSCME President Jerry Wurf in the late 1970s and his battles with some DC 37 local presidents in the early 1980s, Mr. Parisi became known as "Gotbaum's muscle," someone who often traveled with him as a means of discouraging those inclined toward physical harm or intimidation of the DC 37 leader.

He also was the turkey broker for numerous DC 37 locals during the 1980s, although those who were aware of the practice say he did not extract the kind of profits from that role that have recently led to the indictments of several current union officials.

Children of Privilege

Martin Hughes and Joseph Alfano came to Local 372 as young men who had been raised in comfort. They were less likely to see its members as Charlie Hughes once described them—"the core of America." If they focused on anything, it would not be the battles fought on behalf of members who even now do not live especially well but rather on the treasury built through those battles into a pot ripe for the plundering.

Union veterans said it was the sight of Martin Hughes driving into work at the wheel of a BMW, rather than his father driving a similar car with Georgia plates, that stuck in their memories. It was an image of someone living well without having done anything to earn it, breeding a mind-set that would be oblivious to the seeds of self-destruction being sown.

The contrast in the appearance of father and son last week in Manhattan Supreme Court before Justice Brenda Soloff was striking: Martin Hughes at age 30 looking coolly elegant in a dark suit; Charlie at age 58 and looking at least a decade older was dressed like a pensioner in a khaki-colored jacket and red plaid shirt.

The father had grown up in the shadow of racism, had struggled his way to success, and then—calculatedly or out of control mentally—perverted his dream by taking advantage of those he spent more than half his life helping. The son grew up without struggle and seemingly aspired to nothing more than living luxuriously off other people's dues money.

Last June, after Lee Saunders and Mr. Ramsey stabilized Local 372's finances, they were able to rescind part of a dues hike that had been imposed a year earlier to try to cover some of Charlie Hughes's excesses. Local 372, which was founded in the Abyssinian Baptist Church in Harlem in 1941, the same year that Mr. Hughes was born, began its rebirth.

And last week, Charlie Hughes stood in an ancient courtroom, not having endured nearly as well as his local, his booming preacher's cadences reduced to a soft "not guilty."

His son awaited his turn in the dock, perhaps seeing for the first time in his life a glimpse of the experience behind his father's long-ago musing, "If you only knew."

An Absence of Leadership

(October 8, 1999)

Early in the press briefing called by District Council 37 Administrator Lee Saunders September 30 to discuss a report fleshing out how the union's 1995 wage contract vote was fixed, a reporter asked a question of Larry Weinberg, the general counsel for the American Federation of State, County and Municipal Employees.

The questioner sought to ascertain why AFSCME President Gerry McEntee had waited until last November to investigate that contract vote when Charles Ensley, president of DC 37's Social Service Employees Local 371, had made a written request for such a probe in March 1996.

Mr. Weinberg replied, "That letter did not contain a single factual allegation regarding the ratification vote."

And so, presumably, Mr. McEntee disregarded it as merely the complaint of one unhappy local president who had opposed the contract, without bothering to look into the matter.

Not the Only Doubter

What was arresting about last week's report from Kroll Associates was that it made clear that Mr. Ensley was not the only local president who had doubts about the voting. But aside from James Butler, the president of Hospital Workers Local 420, he was the only one who was willing to voice his suspicions publicly.

In some quarters, that would be considered leadership. In DC 37, it is considered making a nuisance of yourself—Mr. Ensley is widely disliked among that portion of the union's high command that has so far escaped indictment.

That is why there was more than a bit of chortling coming from DC 37's headquarters in mid-August after Mr. Ensley's sure-thing bid for an AFSCME vice presidency ran aground. The two officials who were elected in his place wound up occupying prominent places in the Kroll report—if anything, too prominent.

One of them, Mr. Butler, was put in the position of explaining why the officials who ran his local's contract vote had no records they could supply to investigators about the overwhelming vote against the deal.

The other, Helen Greene, was cast in the role of unwitting dupe as her vote was tampered with by Mark Shaplo, who was the prime villain in the report if for no other reason than the guilty plea he's already entered in the criminal case brought by the Manhattan district attorney's office.

Mr. Shaplo, according to the report, indicated that he fixed the vote in Health Service Employees Local 768, which Ms. Greene heads, because her position as secretary of DC 37 would have made it embarrassing if her local had voted against the wage contract. The report does not specify who Mr. Shaplo feared would be embarrassed.

But when DC 37 released a partial local-by-local breakdown of the contract vote to this newspaper in early 1996, Local 768's count was among those excluded. During an executive board meeting last week just prior to the press briefing, Mr. Ensley and Ms. Greene wound up in a shouting match over what had prompted her to keep her local's vote under wraps until now.

'Just Makes You Wonder'

"It just makes you wonder about that stuff," Mr. Ensley said.

Ms. Greene could not be reached for comment. It was far from clear, however, that she was involved in the chicanery. One union official surmised it was more likely that she withheld her vote totals either as a favor to other supporters of ex-DC 37 Executive Director Stanley Hill, who needed some political cover at the time, or because she knew revealing the count in the local would have raised questions that supported Mr. Ensley's suspicions.

The Kroll report was by necessity an incomplete document. Several former DC 37 officials who are under indictment or who have already pled guilty to charges refused to speak to Kroll's investigators. The report seemed designed not to reveal any information that would hamper the ongoing investigation by Manhattan DA Robert Morgenthau that has produced the indictment of two dozen former DC 37 officials and, late last month, a fresh batch of subpoenas, according to comments Mr. Weinberg made to the executive board.

But the net result of that discretion, Mr. Ensley complained, is that "they would have you think the whole thing was orchestrated by Shaplo, Lubin, and John McCabe."

Mr. McCabe is the former head of DC 37's White-Collar Division who has pled guilty to rigging the balloting at Clerical-Administrative Employees Local 1549 along with Mr. Shaplo. Marty Lubin, DC 37's former associate director, has been indicted on similar charges, along with Local 1549's ex-president, Al Diop.

Mr. Ensley is among the host of DC 37 officials who find it hard to believe that these men acted without the knowledge of Mr. Hill, notwithstanding the former executive director's recounting to the Kroll report of how he learned the vote was fixed and his "Say it ain't so, Marty" reaction.

"Stanley was not stupid in that way," said one veteran union official when asked whether it was possible that his closest aides kept Mr. Hill in the dark. "And he was with Shaplo 24 hours a day."

Mark Rosenthal, the president of Motor Vehicle Operators Local 983 and the man who persuaded Joseph DeCanio to go to the DA's Office a year ago with what he knew about the rigged vote, was also skeptical.

Unlikely Masterminds
"To think that Shaplo was the mastermind, and Joe DeCanio, is a sad state of affairs," he said.

Mr. Saunders seemed to be of a similar opinion. At one point during the press briefing, he stated that he was not absolutely convinced that an honest vote would have led to the wage contract's defeat.

This prompted a question about why DC 37 officials would have taken the risk of fixing the vote if they weren't sure they would lose otherwise.

Mr. Saunders responded, "I find this situation so deplorable that I will not even try" to figure out what the co-conspirators were thinking.

One way to interpret the comment is, Why are you assuming there's any logic to the actions of nitwits?

Hatchet Man with Clout

Mr. Shaplo, to be sure, cut a wide swath at DC 37's Barclay Street headquarters. He was Mr. Lubin's top assistant and a longtime friend of Mr. Hill's, and so he was perceived as a hatchet man with clout. He was also widely regarded as a hustler who never stopped chiseling—a perception that was borne out when he pleaded guilty in March to receiving more than $50,000 in kickbacks as part of a turkey-brokering scheme with Mr. DeCanio.

Joseph Vicinanza, the president of Accountants Local 1407, said there had been times when "I've seen Mark take hamburgers home. I've seen him walk out of executive board meetings and take a 'care package' home—and he was making more than 100 grand a year."

Mr. Vicinanza was speaking from anger. The Kroll report quoted anonymous sources saying that Mr. Shaplo rigged the voting in Local 1407 because he disliked Mr. Vicinanza. (This suggested an interesting paradox: on the one hand, Mr. Shaplo picked a local where he didn't like the president; in the other cases, he seems to have picked them because they were headed by people he deemed important. Of course, that's assuming that the other three local presidents, Mr. Diop, Ms. Greene, and Victor Guadalupe, were unaware of his machinations.

Dom Fallucci, Local 1407's vice president, put an ironic perspective on the vote fraud when he remarked, "It's a slap in the face to Joe and the members. It's like they were saying you guys can't be trusted with the vote."

Mr. Vicinanza said he had numerous brushes with Mr. Shaplo in the past. "Mark thought he was the commander-in-chief, and he screwed over my local a couple of times," he said. "And I told Stanley. And I told Mark, 'My members pay your salary.'"

Believes Hill's Honest

Yet Mr. Vicinanza, who right to the time when Mr. Hill was ousted defended the former executive director as a decent man who was betrayed by his underlings, still clings to the belief that Mr. Shaplo could have operated as he did without Mr. Hill's knowledge and consent.

"Stanley may have said to them, 'We need this contract at all costs,' and Mark in his infinite wisdom may have done it that way," Mr. Vicinanza said. "Personally, I don't think it was Stanley."

But that opinion comes in defiance of the indisputable history of Mr. Hill's final years in office: complaints by rank-and-file members to Mr. Hill about irregularities and misspending by the leaders of their locals going unheeded.

And his inaction, whether out of weakness or because he was a willing orchestrator of the transformation of the union into a corrupt enterprise, created a climate in which ordinary members, staff, and some local presidents became convinced that reporting wrongdoing was a risk they could not take.

Mr. Vicinanza said his own willingness to speak up was sometimes overcome by his desire to move into an executive board position and the knowledge that making waves would not help that ambition.

The Kroll report noted, "Many of those interviewed stated that they believed members were powerless to complain about abuses in the electoral process. They believed that the leadership of DC 37 would take no action, or no meaningful action, against persons engaged in electoral or financial fraud. In some cases they believed persons in the leadership to be complicit in the abuses."

The report continued, "Some of those interviewed stated that there was a climate of fear at DC 37. They reported that they were fearful not only of inaction on the part of the council, but of physical harm and other retribution from those who had committed misconduct, or their agents."

Some local presidents who were Hill loyalists told investigators from Kroll that they were surprised at the relatively strong votes in favor of the contract by their members.

Others, including officials from Emergency Medical Service Local 2507 and Electronic Data Processing Local 2627, were frankly skeptical about the vote tallies when they learned of them.

And the presidents of Recreation Workers Local 299, Highway and Sewer Foremen Local 1157, and Uniformed Park Officers Local 1508 were more than skeptical—each knew that the tallies listed for their locals were far beyond what the actual number of votes had been.

A $10-Million Mistake

But for all the misgivings and all the suspicions, Mr. Ensley was the one local president who put it in writing and sought an investigation. He was rebuffed. In the two and a half years that passed before AFSCME began to look at DC 37's operations in earnest, the union's assets shrank by about $10 million despite an increase in locals' per-capita payments that turned into a dues increase for most members.

Some DC 37 officials scoff at the notion that Mr. Ensley is a reformer, arguing that he often played politics to get Mr. Hill to provide service to his members at Local 371. But the issue should not be whether Mr. Ensley qualifies for secular sainthood.

What should matter is that it was he alone among the executive board members—as well as the presidents of the smaller locals—who was willing to say publicly more than three years ago that DC 37's emperor had no clothes and was taking the union to the cleaners anyway.

Even allowing for the fact that he can sometimes be abrasive in reminding fellow officials that he led the charge while others opposed him or sat on the sidelines, it's a bit mind-boggling that Mr. Ensley's willingness to put himself on the line has made him a reviled figure among many at DC 37.

"After receiving a report saying 22 of the 56 locals were involved in some irregularities, the leadership is offended at me," he said with some amusement.

Mr. Ensley believes that Mr. Saunders—notwithstanding his emphatic denials—took part in the effort to derail his bid for an AFSCME vice presidency. He is also convinced that the DC 37 administrator, deliberately or not, made a major error in allowing Veronica Montgomery-Costa, who at the time had just taken over as president of Board of Education Local 372, to run the local's delegate election, a process he charges was co-opted to ensure that she cast all the local's votes for Ms. Greene and Mr. Butler.

He has written Mr. Saunders, with a carbon copy to Mr. McEntee, asking him to look into the persistent rumors that something was amiss in the Local 372 vote. A spokesman for Ms. Montgomery-Costa called this newspaper a couple of weeks ago to say she bore no responsibility for how the delegate process was carried out, since it was handled by an election committee appointed by Mr. Saunders.

When I asked the spokesman, Bill Green, for the names and phone numbers of the Local 372 election committee members, however, he suggested I could get that information from Mr. Saunders. The DC 37 administrator's chief spokesman, in turn, expressed incredulity that Ms. Montgomery-Costa's spokesman would suggest she could not provide those names and numbers.

Serious about Change?

It is just this sort of dance around the maypole that leaves Mr. Ensley wondering whether true and lasting reform will matter to Mr. Saunders and his superiors in Washington once DC 37 patches up its disfigured image and DA Robert Morgenthau signals that he is through indicting union officials.

"Everybody's interested in turning the page," Mr. Ensley said October 1. "I want to move on, too, but not without confronting the people who were involved in the scandal. I'm not convinced that people are really committed to getting to the bottom of this thing."

As was the case concerning the contract vote, Mr. Ensley isn't bringing a single factual allegation to bear in his latest letter demanding an investigation. But he has a credibility born from being right about the rigged vote. Mr. Saunders, as Mr. McEntee's right-hand man and his agent for cleaning up DC 37, shoulders the weight of AFSCME's indifference when Mr. Ensley sounded the alarm last time.

Coca-Cola can sometimes be used to remove stains. Some blemishes, however, are so ingrained that, rather than using sweet stuff, a more caustic agent is needed for cleansing.

Mr. Saunders has to get past the personality conflicts and deal with Mr. Ensley's concerns in a more visible and concrete fashion. Until he does, many union members and officials may still believe that if they try to do the right thing, they'll pay a price for it, while those who go along with a corrupt program continue to sop up the gravy.

Sad Tale of Two Charlies

(June 9, 2000)

The parallel worlds of Charlie Hughes converged and collided in a 15th-floor criminal courtroom June 5 as he was sentenced to three to nine years in prison for stealing $2 million of his members' dues.

The sentencing memorandum prepared by Mr. Hughes's lawyer, Sarita Kedia, for consideration by Manhattan Supreme Court Justice William Leibovitz cited the honors he had received during 30 years as president of Board of Education Local 372 of District Council 37 and letters by prominent politicians singing his praises and regretting his fall that were written after he pleaded guilty in April to looting his local's treasury.

"A decent man" who inspired others with his idealism was a recurring theme sounded by people like City Council Speaker Peter Vallone, Council Majority Whip Victor Robles, Queens Borough President Claire Shulman, and U.S. Representative Gary Ackerman.

Anatomy of a Fall

But Ms. Kedia's brief also contained measured, clinical assessments that cut through Mr. Hughes's veneer to explain how he had arrived before Justice Leibovitz in disgrace, an ailing man whose life was spinning from sad toward tragic.

A letter written early this year to Ms. Kedia by three officials of Forensic Sciences Medical Group stated that the results of their most recent neuropsychological testing of the longtime union leader

161

"strongly reinforce our earlier impressions that Mr. Hughes is suffering from a dementing process that specifically undermines his judgment, insight and social inhibition. This information, coupled with his history of significant substance abuse, makes it virtually certain that he was not able to adequately appreciate either the nature of his acts or their consequences."

That assessment was delivered more than three months prior to Mr. Hughes's decision to plead guilty to grand larceny with an assurance of a sentence of no more than three to nine years. The neuropsychological experts who delivered this pronouncement concluded their letter to Ms. Kedia by stating, "We would note, most sadly, that although this information may be useful legally, it portends a grim prognosis for him clinically."

The details of the two examinations of Mr. Hughes by Drs. Mark J. Mills, Clifford A. Smith, and Wilfred G. van Gorp provided in Ms. Kedia's brief laid bare the demons with which Mr. Hughes struggled even before the criminal conduct that led to his downfall. As described by longtime acquaintances who were interviewed by the psychologists, they provided a startling contrast with the public image of Mr. Hughes that so many prominent political and union officials presented.

In essence, Mr. Hughes lived a double life for at least a decade: the charismatic, philanthropic labor leader whose political support was avidly sought overshadowing the troubled, at-times delusional man unable to cope with a mentally ill wife and his own raging emotions.

In November 1998, after examining him for the first time and interviewing family members and longtime acquaintances, Dr. Mills wrote to Gerald Shargel, the principal of Ms. Kedia's law firm, and said Mr. Hughes's daughter, Charisse, was among those who remembered his erratic behavior as beginning at about the time in 1993 that his wife, Shirley, was diagnosed as schizophrenic.

'Craziness' and Cocaine

But another longtime acquaintance who was not identified by Dr. Mills called the mood swings a manifestation of Mr. Hughes's "craziness," something he said he had begun to observe years earlier. Another unidentified acquaintance said Mr. Hughes's problems were exacerbated by his wife's mental condition and his increased use of cocaine.

This acquaintance recalled that during a trip to Israel a decade ago, Mr. Hughes told him that "God had spoken to him telling him he was great and would have an important role in the unification" of Judaism, Christianity, and Islam. This man also told Dr. Mills that he was so concerned about Mr. Hughes's abuse of alcohol and cocaine that "he consulted a drug counselor and another local member about the possibility of an 'intervention.'"

At the time of Mr. Hughes's substance abuse and grandiose visions, however, politicians were paying tribute to his good works, with many, not coincidentally, also lining up to accept his union's campaign contributions.

Charlie Hughes, who is 59 years old, grew up poor in Millen, Georgia, in an era when it was as segregated as the rest of the Deep South. Starting at age 10, he spent summers picking cotton and plowed land with a mule. He went to all-black schools and was the first person of color allowed to work at a cash register in one of the town's stores.

He came to New York at the age of 20 and got a job as a school lunch worker, became a shop steward two years later, and in 1968, at the age of 27, was elected president of Local 372. His early and intense interest in civil rights was later accompanied by a passion for improving not only the wages and working conditions of his members but also the nutritional quality of the food served in the city's public school cafeterias.

Aided Ethiopian Jews

He also developed twin concerns for Israel and the Ethiopian Jews who had migrated there. He established the Charles Hughes Center for Ethiopian Academic Advancement at Bar-Ilan University, the third-largest institution of higher learning in Israel.

On May 18, 1995, at a dinner in his honor at the New York Hilton, Mr. Hughes was given an honorary doctorate from Bar-Ilan in recognition that he exemplified "the highest moral values as well as a responsibility to reach out and help society."

Letters of tribute poured in from powerful politicians: New York's two previous mayors, a recently ousted three-term governor, and a sitting vice president.

"He is a man of great vision, and also deep faith," David Dinkins's letter stated.

"You have played, and will continue to play, a singular role binding the African-American and Jewish-American communities," Ed Koch proclaimed.

Mario Cuomo chimed in, "Of course, to those of us who know you, this act of kindness is but the latest demonstration of your leadership in the labor movement, your devotion to religious values, your work in behalf of freedom and human rights . . ."

Vice President Gore noted in his letter about Mr. Hughes, "Certainly, he is most deserving of this special honor, and I commend him for the work he has done in the past and the commitment he has made for the future."

Then-United Federation of Teachers President Sandy Feldman called Mr. Hughes "someone who really works hard to make a positive difference in people's lives."

'A Great Union Leader'

And Stanley Hill, who at the time was DC 37's executive director in no small part due to Mr. Hughes's political support, offered, "You are a shining example of what a great union leader and a true humanitarian should be."

But Mr. Hill, more than any of the political luminaries, had reason to know all was not right with Mr. Hughes. DC 37 had been forced to guarantee a multi-million-dollar loan to Local 372 from Amalgamated Bank ("Your Vision and Dedication Have Brought Great Meaning to the Lives of Others," the bank stated in its full-page ad in the commemorative journal for the Bar-Ilan doctorate festivities), and while Mr. Hughes was making the loan payments, he was also borrowing increasing amounts from DC 37 to cover his extravagant spending of his local's funds.

Mr. Hill had also been present the previous year for one of Mr. Hughes's most-famous and indiscreet comments at a retirement party for Arthur Tibaldi, the longtime treasurer of DC 37 who had somewhat reluctantly agreed to guarantee the loan.

Addressing the crowd at Pierino's, a restaurant near DC 37's lower Manhattan headquarters that was also favored by the corrupt officials of the now-defunct Transit Police Benevolent Association, Mr. Hughes, according to one veteran official who was there, said that when he arrived in New York, "I was a poor boy from Georgia with $60 in my pocket. Today I have $2 million, and I owe it all to the union."

That last remark was more literally true than he undoubtedly intended, but it would become clear that Mr. Hughes was not going to be terribly diligent about repaying what he would acknowledge as his debts to DC 37. By March 1996, Mr. Hill and Mr. Tibaldi's successor as DC 37 treasurer, Bob Myers, forced him to sign a document intended to establish a firm repayment schedule while limiting the advances he could take from DC 37 against his members' future dues.

Wasn't Reined In

He routinely violated that agreement, and DC 37 officials did little to rein in his spending, even allowing him to spend $1.4 million on Local 372's annual education conference at the Friar Tuck Inn in the spring of 1997. (One of the Friar Tuck Inn's principals, Steven Caridi, later pleaded guilty to paying kickbacks to an official of Clerical-Administrative Employees Local 1549 in return for that local's business.)

Finally, Mr. Myers in July 1997 fired off a memo to Mr. Hughes urging him to honor his obligations. But that same month, Mr. Myers signed off on Mr. Hughes's request for a payment of more than $600,000 he claimed he was entitled to for overtime accrued over his years as president.

That same summer, Mr. Hughes hosted a reelection fundraiser for Mayor Giuliani at his Queens Village home. He also appeared in a campaign commercial that was perhaps the most memorable of that race, which began with Mr. Hughes extolling the mayor's virtues in a speech to union members and concluded with him embracing Mr. Giuliani.

His political support of the mayor was rewarded with a significant growth in membership after a 1996 UFT contract ended teachers' obligations to serve as hallway and cafeteria monitors. Someone had to do the work, and by a happy coincidence the several thousand additional employees who were hired to do it went into Local 372's bargaining unit.

And so by the end of 1997, Local 372 had surpassed Local 1549 as DC 37's largest local, and Mr. Hughes spoke openly of "changes" that he expected in recognition of his new stature. He was said to have an eye on a post as one of two DC 37 vice presidents on the board of its national union, the American Federation of State, County and Municipal Employees.

Hill Finally Acted

Those posts happened to be occupied by Mr. Hill and his closest political ally, Local 1549 President Al Diop. It is not certain whether it was the new political challenge by Mr. Hughes or, as Mr. Hill has said, his conclusion that Mr. Hughes was incapable of bringing his local's spiraling debt under control, but he finally took the matter to his superiors at AFSCME.

They arranged their own form of the "intervention" that the long-time Hughes acquaintance had considered a few years earlier by placing Local 372 under administratorship and stripping Mr. Hughes and his fellow board members of their positions on February 4, 1998. A thorough review of the local's books—which had not been conducted prior to that time—showed it was $10 million in debt.

There was a cadre of Hughes loyalists within DC 37 who made clear that they believed AFSCME had acted too hastily in removing him when he wasn't even under indictment—something the Manhattan district attorney would finally arrange 15 months later. For many of them, Mr. Hughes was a source of pride: a leader who overcame prejudice and improved the lives of the people he represented while transforming himself into someone of power and influence.

But they never perceived the stranger within Mr. Hughes, that other part of him that seemed bent on self-destruction and would drag his local with him into the abyss.

Ms. Kedia's brief included the reprint of a photo from the Bar-Ilan program of Mr. Hughes in 1961, shortly after he arrived in New York at age 20, sitting on the stoop outside what was then the Central Kitchen facility of the Board of Education in Long Island City. He was wearing the same type of newsboy's cap that he would wear to his criminal arraignment 38 years later, as well as a jaunty, slightly crooked smile.

Made Smile Work

It is the smile of a charmer who understands that you can get away with a lot more in life if people like you. It also suggests the insouciance that in 1963, when a DC 37 activist named Adele Nobles came around asking who might be interested in working as a shop steward, led Mr. Hughes to loudly question why anyone would want to work on behalf of a union that wasn't producing benefits for its members.

Ms. Nobles responded that if he thought workers like himself weren't being served, a wiser solution than complaining would be to get involved in making DC 37 better. Mr. Hughes took her up on the challenge and launched his career.

There was no way for him to foresee that career culminating the way it did before Justice Leibovitz, laying bare all his problems in an abject plea for mercy.

But exposing that side of Mr. Hughes bought him no special considerations from Justice Leibovitz. The compassion the judge expressed was for the union members "whose relatively high dues came out of their food and rent money . . . Defendant systematically and incrementally stole their money and betrayed their trust."

Mr. Hughes noticeably twitched when a court officer approached to handcuff him, as if startled at how swiftly his new world had beckoned.

"His clinical prognosis," Ms. Kedia stated in her court brief, "suggests that Mr. Hughes's condition will continue to worsen over the next few years, eventually leading to his premature death."

Five years ago, the Bar-Ilan dinner and the tributes it produced offered Mr. Hughes an advance copy of a eulogy for the good works of his public life.

His sentencing provided a glimpse of the other side of dying, when kind words won't obscure the reality of what has occurred.

She Didn't Stick to Story

(July 28, 2000)

Marie Alston Diggins seemed composed and unemotional on the witness stand July 19, her voice soft enough that she had to be frequently reminded to speak up as she testified about how Al Diop had been unusually involved in the 1995 wage contract vote of Clerical-Administrative Employees Local 1549 of District Council 37.

The story she told, however, virtually shouted Mr. Diop's guilt to the jurors in Manhattan Supreme Court Justice Bonnie Wittner's courtroom.

Ms. Diggins, who at the time chaired Local 1549's election committee, described Mr. Diop ordering an unusually large number of extra ballots, cautioning her to be "discreet" about discussing the ballot count, and, finally, crossing out the tally she brought him and changing 800 votes against the contract to "yes" votes.

Layoff Fear Invoked
"He said he wanted to make sure the contract is passed and that the members would never get a contract like this again. And they would lose their jobs," she recalled.

Manhattan Assistant District Attorney Jane Tully asked Ms. Diggins her reaction when Mr. Diop, who headed Local 1549 for 29 years, made the change. "I was just in total shock," she responded.

Later, she testified, after it was revealed that the vote on DC 37's 1995 wage contract had been fixed and that much of the fraud involved the Local 1549 count, an investigator from Manhattan DA

Robert Morgenthau's office left a note on the door of her home saying he wanted to talk to her about that election.

Alarmed, Ms. Diggins called Mr. Diop. "He told me not to worry about it," she said. "Just stick to the story and don't tell 'em nothing."

Mr. Diop's attorney, Ramon Pagan, never challenged much of Ms. Diggins's story during his cross-examination. Rather, he focused his questioning in two areas. He got her to admit that witnessing this alleged fraud did not move her to give up her position as Local 1549's election committee chair, and that two and a half years later, she went to Hawaii as Mr. Diop's guest for the convention of DC 37's national union.

And after ascertaining from her that the meeting at which Mr. Diop allegedly altered the ballot count occurred in his office at about 5 p.m. on January 18, 1996, Mr. Pagan called Anna Massy, a veteran Local 1549 official, to the witness stand. She testified that it was at right about that time that she was posing alongside Mr. Diop for a group photo at a hotel in Atlantic City where the local was holding a staff conference.

That latter claim, which was based on Ms. Massy's recollection that the photo was taken on the first day of the weekend conference, seemed a slender reed on which to hang Mr. Diop's defense, particularly since January 18 happened to be a Thursday.

Less Tainted than Others

But it may have been all Mr. Pagan had. Ms. Diggins was something of an unusual witness among those who provided damaging testimony against Mr. Diop and his co-defendant, former DC 37 Associate Director Marty Lubin, over the past two weeks. Unlike most of those who put the two defendants neck deep in the conspiracy to fix the contract vote, she, along with two witnesses against Mr. Lubin—John McCabe, DC 37's former white-collar division director, and Alice Tennis—had committed no other illegal actions besides her complicity in the alleged vote fraud.

And in Ms. Diggins's case, there was no plausible explanation for why she would have had any involvement in the scheme except that she had been thrust into it by Mr. Diop's hasty work with a pen.

If jurors—who got the case July 24, as this newspaper went to press—convicted Mr. Diop of fixing the vote in Local 1549, it figured to be largely on her testimony. And perhaps the greatest irony of that is that Ms. Diggins was not a member of Local 1549 at the time of the vote fraud and Mr. Diop shouldn't have been.

She belonged to Local 1549 for 19 years, before being promoted out of the bargaining unit in 1993 to a computer technician job in what is now the Department of Citywide Administrative Services. A year earlier, she had become the local's election chair, and she was not asked to step down from that post even though she was now a member of the union representing the higher title, Communications Workers of America Local 1180.

Mr. Diop, according to veteran DC 37 officials, received a promotion to a city job title more than two decades ago that should have moved him out of Local 1549's bargaining unit and into Local 1180. But he was given a "union leave," under a deal between DC 37 and city officials, that allowed him to stay in the bargaining unit and continue running the local while accumulating pension credit based upon service in the higher city title.

He was ousted in February 1999 by DC 37's national union for the same financial irregularities that he is scheduled to stand trial for in less than two weeks.

Witnesses' Shared Past

Two of the other primary witnesses against Mr. Diop last week—his former first vice president, James Edey, and Bob Myers, the ex-treasurer of both Local 1549 and DC 37—were involved in the same financial scams concerning Local 1549 funds that led to his second indictment.

Mr. Pagan did what he could to dirty up their characters over their abuses, knowing that prosecutors could not point out that his client engaged in the same alleged transgressions unless Mr. Diop testified in his own defense.

Mr. Pagan and Pam Hayes, Mr. Lubin's lawyer, elicited testimony from Mr. Edey and Mr. Myers on cross-examination about kickbacks they had received from various vendors, from restaurant owners to travel agents and the proprietors of the Friar Tuck Inn.

Like Mark Shaplo, the former top assistant to Mr. Lubin who was able to directly implicate both defendants in the vote fraud, Mr. Myers and Mr. Edey seemed to have spent much of their working lives skimming funds from a multitude of sources. And like Mr. Shaplo, they were surprisingly reluctant, given the plea bargains they had already worked out with the DA's Office, to own up to just how much they had actually pocketed.

Half a Loaf Denied

Mr. Edey, who under his deal is supposed to repay $50,000 to the local but will receive no jail time, was unwilling to admit to having misappropriated that much, even though the credit card and hospitality abuses coupled with the other scams amounted to more than $100,000.

Mr. Myers initially told Mr. Pagan that he stole between $15,000 and $20,000 by abusing his credit card over a five-year period. As Ms. Hayes walked him through cross-examination, Mr. Myers admitted, among other scams, to having received at least $15,000 a year in kickbacks from a travel agent for most of the 1990s, and roughly $5,000 annually from a restaurant near DC 37 with which the union did a steady catering business.

"When you agreed to pay back $50,000," Ms. Hayes said, referring to the restitution Mr. Myers will make (he, too, will avoid a prison sentence in return for his cooperation with the DA), "that was a fraction of the amount you took."

"Um hmm," Mr. Myers replied.

A Crime 'Family'

But try as the defense lawyers did to put distance between their clients and the thievery of most of the witnesses testifying against them, there were moments when there seemed no escaping the fact that, when Ms. Massy said the union's leadership acted as "a family," the term also applied to criminal activity.

Asked during his direct testimony whether he had been responsible for choosing the vendors who paid him the kickbacks, Mr. Myers responded, "There was a consortium of people." He then named Local 1549's six top officers—himself and Mr. Diop among them—as the members of that consortium.

Mr. Edey was the first official to testify that it was on Mr. Diop's order that Ms. Diggins requested 5,000 "overrun" ballots—10 times more than the local traditionally had printed to supply second ballots to members who did not receive or lost their first ones.

"Marie basically disapproved about the amount. We both thought it was too high," Mr. Edey said.

Ms. Diggins testified that after Mr. Diop told her to order more than the customary number of overruns, Mr. Edey had suggested 1,000. Mr. Diop, she remarked, "said no, he wanted to order 5,000.

"Mr. Edey," she continued, "said, 'What the hell do you want that many ballots?'" And Mr. Diop, in turn, "said he wanted it, so order it."

'Told Me Be Discreet'

Sometime after that conversation in late 1995, Ms. Diggins testified, "Mr. Diop called me to his office and told me to be very discreet about this election. He said he didn't want no one to know the outcome of this election before he turn in the result."

And Mr. Diop, she continued, went with her when she picked up the ballots from the DC 37 mailroom and checked in periodically as the ballots were being counted.

And then, she testified, on that Thursday night in mid-January that she took him the vote totals—totals she did not know had previously been doctored in a ballot-stuffing operation in which several witnesses directly placed Mr. Lubin—Mr. Diop made the alteration in the count that left her in "total shock."

But not quite that shocked, judging by what she did when he asked her for any additional copies she had of the memo containing her tally. "I gave him one more copy," she testified, but held on to a third copy, which was entered into evidence against Mr. Diop by Ms. Tully.

'He'd Take Care of It'

The first two copies of the tally, she said, she shredded at Mr. Diop's command.

"Afterwards," she said, "I told Mr. Diop I was going to return the next day with members of the election committee to destroy the overrun ballots that were left over. He told me not to worry about it; he would have it taken care of."

Nearly three years passed before the rigging of the contract vote came to light and an investigator showed up at Ms. Diggins's door. After finding his note, she said that during the course of that evening, she spoke to Mr. Diop at least five times by phone.

In their last conversation, she testified, "He said if the union don't pay for a lawyer, he would pay for a lawyer—not to worry about it."

She went to see prosecutors from the Manhattan DA's Office and "stuck to the story," making no mention of the altered tally.

But later she had second thoughts and retained an attorney. When Mr. Diop learned of her action, she testified, he called her and said, "Why did you get a lawyer? Because I was gonna have Mr. Pagan be your lawyer . . . You did not need a lawyer. I was gonna take care of that."

Mr. Pagan barely touched on those conversations during cross-examination. He devoted far more of his energy to trying to discredit a different story of Mr. Diop's alleged attempts to cover up the fraud—one actually less potentially damaging to his client—told by Mr. Myers.

A day after the *New York Times* in November 1998 published a front-page story that the contract vote was rigged, Mr. Myers said he attended a meeting that included many of DC 37's top officials at the home of its outside counsel, Buddy Perkel.

The meeting had barely begun, Mr. Myers testified, when Mr. Diop asked, "What about a cover-up—can we do it?"

Mr. Myers said others in the room quickly responded in the negative.

Mr. Pagan brought in Mr. Perkel to testify July 24 that Mr. Diop never broached the subject of a cover-up, saying, "It was never discussed." A short time later, he emphasized the contradiction in his summation to the jury.

Tougher to Discount
But when jurors begin their deliberations in the case, even if they are inclined to distrust Mr. Myers's testimony, there is still the matter of what Ms. Diggins had to say about Mr. Diop's alleged machinations, before and after the vote fraud. That testimony figures to be considerably harder for the jurors to discount.

Mr. Lubin faces a similar predicament when jurors weigh the testimony of Mr. McCabe and Ms. Tennis, both on its own merits and in regard to how it corroborates the testimony of the less-reputable witnesses against him.

Conspiracy cases are often hard to prosecute because the persons running such schemes try to enlist as their helpers others who use wide strike zones when it comes to ethics. If caught, this generally gives their lawyers plenty of red meat in attacking the character of any "turned" witnesses.

The problem for the defense in this case is that while for some of the prosecution witnesses, the fixing of the wage contract vote was just business as usual in a work existence dominated by scams, the participation of Mr. McCabe and Ms. Diggins seems to have been a far more complex decision.

Conflicting Pressures
Part of them understood how wrong it was to fix the vote. Part of them probably rationalized it with the thought that there could be severe consequences for some union members if the contract was voted down. And refusing to go along with the fixing when their help was allegedly sought by people with whom they had long working relationships would have placed them under suspicion and jeopardized their futures within the union.

Since neither defendant took the witness stand, the jurors will form their opinion about the likelihood that Mr. Diop and Mr. Lubin engaged in the crimes of which they are accused based largely on how they regard the witnesses against them. And neither Mr. McCabe nor Ms. Diggins seemed capable of engaging in dishonesty without some encouragement from the defendants.

Al Diop and Marty Lubin were convicted of rigging the DC 37 contract vote. Lubin served time in prison; Diop was found psychologically unfit to assist in his own appeal of the conviction.

DC 37, after the Gold Rush

(May 18, 2001)

Arthur Tibaldi sounded frail and uncertain even before he was asked whether he improperly double-dipped by collecting $169,300 in severance pay at the same time that he was receiving $223,000 in deferred compensation benefits when he retired from District Council 37.

"The attorneys were involved in it," the 76-year-old Mr. Tibaldi said May 10 of the payments he got upon leaving the union six years ago after 28 years as treasurer. "I wouldn't take anything without them saying it was all right."

He became more defensive when he was informed that the accounting firm KPMG had questioned whether he actually did anything in return for the $100,000 consulting fee that DC 37 paid him in his first year after retirement.

'Did Everything I Could'

"I was available to them at all times," Mr. Tibaldi said from his home in Whitestone, Queens. "I built up the health and security fund. I did everything I could."

Finally, a question prompted by KPMG's finding that he had charged the union for roughly $20,000 in meals near his home brought a wounded cry of defiance: "If you're looking for dirt, go ahead!"

He said he had never been interviewed by the auditing firm retained by DC 37's parent union, the American Federation of State, County and Municipal Employees, to find out how DC 37 had squandered more than $18 million in assets over a four-year period, with its largest local going $10 million into debt.

"I don't even know what they look like," Mr. Tibaldi, who by trade was an accountant, said of his brethren who stepped all over the reputation he spent years building.

During his last full year as treasurer, 1994, DC 37's assets fell by $1.5 million. In retrospect, that looks like a gold rush for the union's finances, given that assets dropped by $9 million in 1995 and another $4 million in 1996.

The figures for those last two years are explained partly by the rampant stealing some key DC 37 officials engaged in. But a more-compelling testament than even the thievery is contained in that part of the KPMG audit that gives an itemized accounting of the spending at a "Gala New York Reception" at the AFSCME convention in Chicago on June 19, 1996.

That event, whose cost was shared equally by DC 37 and its two largest locals, featured the serving of 9,000 chilled jumbo gulf shrimp, 2,500 smoked salmon canapés, nine roast steamships of beef, nine honey-glazed country hams, and appetizers too numerous to mention. The food bill, once tax and tip were included, came to $271,000. Add in a $74,590 drink tab—which included 6,351 name-brand mixed drinks and 1,938 "top-shelf liquors"—and you were looking at $345,000 for a single reception.

If the balance sheet for DC 37 that year isn't enough of a reference point, try this one for perspective: at that time, the union's rank-and-file members were 14 months into a wage freeze.

Yet neither Executive Director Stanley Hill, who presided over this orgy of conspicuous consumption, nor Bob Myers, who had succeeded Mr. Tibaldi as treasurer, was terribly concerned about how this might look.

Myers Came in, Deluge Followed

There are veteran union officials who will argue that the demise of DC 37 only got started when Victor Gotbaum decided the union could survive with Mr. Hill as his successor in 1987; that the bigger step toward the dive off a cliff came when Mr. Tibaldi packed it in and Mr. Myers was tapped to succeed him.

One former colleague of Mr. Tibaldi's last year called him "an old-fashioned man with an old-fashioned moral code."

Mr. Gotbaum had been forced to retire when he was 65. Mr. Tibaldi stayed on until he was 70 and had lost an election for the presidency of the accountants local he ran for 38 years. One of his defenders within the union said Mr. Tibaldi stayed on past retirement age "because he knew what was going on and tried to forestall it." But another union veteran said the only reason the corrupt officials who surrounded Mr. Hill did not force Mr. Tibaldi out earlier was that "he was the fountain of knowledge. He knew where all the bodies were buried."

This official, who asked that he not be identified, said that there had been suspicions that he was treated generously to buy his silence from the time it became known in 1996 that Mr. Tibaldi had received a retirement package in excess of $400,000.

"Everybody thought Tibaldi ripped off the union," this official said. "It was considered a payoff by Stanley to clear the decks for Bob Myers."

Mr. Myers had been the longtime treasurer of Local 1549, and signing the checks for a local run by Al Diop—coupled with serious health problems that included two strokes—apparently eroded whatever scruples he might have possessed. He would eventually plead guilty to grand-larceny charges and be spared jail time in return for testifying against Mr. Diop and other officials implicated in fixing DC 37's 1995–1996 contract vote.

Indulged Hughes

In addition to the money he pocketed, Mr. Myers was the individual who continued signing off on questionable requests for payment of hundreds of thousands of dollars to Charles Hughes, the longtime president of Board of Education Local 372. He had done so even though Mr. Hughes's spending and borrowing to meet local expenses had gotten so out of control that Mr. Myers and Mr. Hill forced him to sign an agreement that essentially placed him under a budget.

This briefly cut his spending down to normal levels, but as soon as he began pressing beyond the limits, Mr. Myers merely shrugged his shoulders, mentioned it to Mr. Hill, and kept right on approving payments to the Local 372 leader.

Mr. Hughes, his criminal defense lawyer would later argue in seeking to limit his prison sentence for stealing more than $2 million, was in the throes of a mental deterioration that had been accelerated by his abuse of cocaine.

But he wielded enough power, including the clout to guarantee Mr. Hill's continued reign as executive director no matter how badly he mismanaged DC 37, to make Mr. Hughes untouchable for a while. And according to Mr. Tibaldi's old supporter within DC 37, he, too, had been cajoled and pressured into making questionable loans to prop up Local 372.

"He realized he'd gone too far in guaranteeing the loans to Charlie's local," this official said.

It was at Mr. Tibaldi's retirement party, at a now-defunct restaurant called Pierino's that probably deserved landmark status for its role in two major union scandals (the other one involving the Transit Police Benevolent Association), that Mr. Hughes made the comment that would later haunt him. When he came to DC 37, he said in toasting Mr. Tibaldi, "I was a poor boy from Georgia with $60 in my pocket. Today I have $2 million, and I owe it all to the union."

Legitimate Double-Dip?

Mr. Tibaldi had no similar sense of grandeur. KPMG scalded him for allegedly double-dipping on the severance and deferred compensation payments, but Al Viani, the former chief negotiator for DC 37, said that more than a decade earlier the union had set up an annuity plan that was supposed to cover its top officials. There were no questions raised about the propriety of getting both payments, he said, when Victor Gotbaum retired.

"He was the straightest guy," Mr. Gotbaum said of Mr. Tibaldi May 11. "When I took my wife on a trip, he made me pay full cost for her. If he was corrupt, he could have become rich."

There are questions about why Mr. Tibaldi got a $100,000 consulting fee and then did no consulting. But you might as well ask why Mr. Gotbaum collected $200,000 for consulting services after leaving DC 37. If Mr. Hill was truly qualified to run the union, should he have needed to pay his predecessor to advise him?

The consulting fees to Mr. Gotbaum ended in 1990, supposedly because some people inside the union convinced Mr. Hill he no longer needed his counsel. The union's operation began heading steadily downhill soon after.

Today, Charlie Hughes sits in prison, suffering from a debilitating mental disease. Al Diop is in a state psychiatric facility, too depressed to stand trial for ripping off his local or to be sentenced for rigging the 1995–1996 contract vote.

Shamed but Unindicted

Mr. Hill, who was yanked out of office in November 1998 when AFSCME finally sensed just how bad things had been, sits at home in Queens, one of the few prominent DC 37 officials so far unscathed by the Manhattan DA's Office. And Gerry McEntee, the president of AFSCME who was slow in acting in no small measure because the unwavering support of Mr. Hill and Mr. Diop helped keep him in power, was reelected by acclamation a year ago, as if the political hurricane from this fiasco took a left turn around his doorstep.

Ultimately, the trouble that enveloped DC 37 was less a consequence of an "old-fashioned moral code" guy like Mr. Tibaldi being overpaid to leave than it was due to higher-ranking officials with no moral code at all deciding to stay at any price.

Butler's Banana Republic

(April 19, 2002)

The law firm of Bill Sipser, whose family has represented District Council 37's Hospital Workers Local 420 President James Butler for the past three decades, is currently advertising itself on subway trains as "Progressive pioneering law firm dedicated to empowerment of women in the workforce."

And so when Mr. Sipser April 9 resigned as Mr. Butler's counsel, citing "irreconcilable differences," it allowed him to escape the embarrassment of counting as his principal client a man who is resorting to any means necessary to prevent a woman who defeated him in a union election from stepping into his job.

Jim Butler, who came to New York from his native Savannah, Georgia during the early days of the civil rights movement, at the age of 68 has turned into Lester Maddox; instead of standing in the schoolhouse door vowing "Segregation forever," the only wrongheaded cause he is perpetuating is his own political survival. And just as the rabid Southern white supporters of Mr. Maddox stood by him because, in Randy Newman's words, "He may be a fool but he's our fool," Mr. Butler can still rely on a solid if diminishing band of loyalists.

AFSCME Inertia Props Him Up

Just as importantly, he can count on the governance system of his international union, the American Federation of State, County and Municipal Employees, which renders DC 37 powerless to curb him, and an AFSCME leadership that personifies the law of inertia. Until

180

either a judge puts an end to the nonsense or enough heat comes down on AFSCME President Gerry McEntee to force him to act, Mr. Butler will continue to stumble through his bad vaudeville routine, dragging his members across the stage with him.

When Mr. McEntee's top aide, Lee Saunders, was serving as DC 37's administrator, he adopted the phrase "We're back" to symbolize the union's emergence from the corruption scandal that erupted in 1998. But Mr. Saunders never took the necessary steps to guard against a recurrence of the flouting of union democracy for which DC 37 became infamous. Now Mr. Butler has added a postscript to Mr. Saunders's slogan: ". . . and we're not leaving."

Local 420 in late February held an election that was conducted by Mr. Butler's handpicked committee, with voting confined to a single polling site in Harlem, his political stronghold. It wasn't enough. Softened up by revelations that he was paying himself more than $250,000 a year while members' dues soared, questions about several million in dues money that was collected beginning in 1995 to provide a new local headquarters that still hasn't materialized, and Carmen Charles's claim that he called her a "stupid immigrant," Mr. Butler got outplayed on his home court.

So he began squawking about irregularities he claimed were committed by Ms. Charles, her supporters, and officials at the Health and Hospitals Corporation who were supposed to be sympathetic to his challenger. Those charges were treated almost as a sideshow to the circus that unfolded during the Local 420 meeting April 8 at DC 37 to address Mr. Butler's complaints.

Let's Call the Whole Thing Off

Instead, his election committee chairman, Reverend Alvin Meads, called for a division of the house, with those in favor of a new election stepping to one side of the room and those who were opposed moving to the other. Unexpectedly, more people lined up on the side for letting the result stand, and the flummoxed Mr. Meads declared he couldn't do a count and ordered a new election.

Such shenanigans aren't without precedent in DC 37's recent inglorious past. Lou Albano, who after 17 years as a capable, decent president of the Civil Service Technical Guild was defeated by 80 votes in late 1997, tarnished his reputation by allowing his own handpicked election committee to rerun the presidential vote. The pretext for that new election had a bit more substance than at Local 420 but not much: after the initial count was completed in the contest between Mr. Albano and Roy Commer, tallies for other offices were suspended because of the late hour. When the count was resumed nearly two weeks later, it was discovered that the ballots had disappeared from a locked room.

Suspicion immediately fell on the leadership of DC 37, which had both means and motive for the theft—a concern that Mr. Commer would be a lot more difficult to deal with—but Mr. Albano got the benefit of an undeserved break anyhow. The backlash this created within his local, however, turned what had been a narrow victory for Mr. Commer into a landslide during their second election.

That experience was far from the strongest argument to come out of DC 37 against having internal committees handpicked by a local-president-run officer elections. The accidental tour guide for prosecutors through the sewer the union became was Joe DeCanio, the then-president of Highway Repairers Local 376 who made a handsome living brokering overpriced turkeys and fixed elections to equally corrupt colleagues.

Turkeys Took Priority

Mr. Saunders, in his peculiarly roundabout effort at bringing reform to DC 37, imposed controls so that members would no longer be spending $50 for a holiday turkey, but he did not attach similar concerns to cleaning up local elections. When he was asked about Mr. Butler's machinations early in the Local 420 campaign, he responded that it was a local matter, the standard excuse given by past and present DC 37 executive directors for not curbing an abuse because doing so might create political problems for them.

In Mr. Saunders's case, however, the claim didn't even have the veneer of plausibility. From the time in February 1998 when he came in and placed DC 37's Board of Education Local 372 under administratorship because millions of dollars was missing from its treasury, it was clear that he had the authority to do whatever he thought was needed to clean up the mess.

It could be argued that Local 372 President Charlie Hughes's misuse of money was serious enough to eventually send him to prison, while the Manhattan district attorney's office looked at Local 420's records and found no cause for seeking an indictment. But Mr. Butler has never offered a believable explanation for why, seven years after the dues hike to renovate a building to house the union was imposed, that building is still uninhabitable.

Fast Shuffle on Audit

Mr. Saunders, who needed far less grounds than a district attorney does to act against Mr. Butler, gave him a pass on the building fund. He also looked the other way when Mr. Butler limited Local 420 board members' examination of an outside audit of the local's funds to a one-hour perusal in the union's offices; all other locals gave their boards copies of the audits to take home and study at length.

Mr. Saunders's failure to act in Mr. Butler's case is most likely the result of the political currents within the national union. He is known to have designs on succeeding Mr. McEntee someday. Mr. Butler has cultivated close ties with the national leadership dating back to Mr. McEntee's predecessor, the late Jerry Wurf, enabling him to ward off efforts by then-DC 37 Executive Director Victor Gotbaum and his top aide—current Executive Director Lillian Roberts—to hold him accountable for his spending 25 years ago.

Back in those days, Mr. Butler and his followers weren't above resorting to thuggery to get their way or to ingratiate himself with Mr. Wurf during the latter gentleman's acrimonious battle to maintain control of AFSCME when Mr. Gotbaum sought to take over the national union.

Mr. Butler became the muscle behind Mr. Wurf while Mr. Gotbaum enlisted the physical presence of Vinnie Parisi, Mr. DeCanio's predecessor at Local 376 and a reputed mob associate. Members of Mr. Butler's entourage traveled with guns, as did Mr. Parisi; one DC 37 official said the Butler group brandished the weapons primarily "just to scare the s--- out of everybody."

Opponent Was Stabbed

But there was one occasion, slightly over two decades ago, when the violence became more than a threat. James Carter, who had previously run against Mr. Butler, stood up at a union meeting to protest his stewardship, and one of the Local 420 president's supporters stabbed him with a knife. Vocal opposition within the local was scarce after that.

The primary conduit between the Local 420 leader and AFSCME during the past two decades has been Bill Lucy, the international's secretary-treasurer who is regarded as the other potential successor to Mr. McEntee.

Mr. Butler's ties to Mr. Lucy, and his own status since 1999 as an AFSCME vice president, make it extremely tricky for Mr. Saunders to lean on him, and the former DC 37 administrator clearly decided to take the course of least resistance. Which is precisely the way his boss likes to play it.

"Gerry McEntee never steps in," Mr. Gotbaum, who lost the political struggle with Mr. McEntee to succeed Mr. Wurf more than 20 years ago, said during an April 11 interview. "I don't think that's healthy, though; this is his largest, most prestigious council. In a way it ties Lillian's hands; she has no power of discipline."

Another veteran DC 37 official was even harsher in assessing the situation. "I don't think Gerry McEntee is prepared as a so-called leader to do anything about Butler unless he's caught with his hand in the till.

"Butler's got his own cult and they don't let go of him," this official, who spoke conditioned on anonymity, continued. "He's got this magnetism when he speaks—he may not be making any sense, but he's got the cadence down perfectly, like an old-time preacher."

'Ask the Lawyers'

A call to Mr. Butler produced an exercise in the kind of illogic this referred to. Questioned about how he could justify a new election when he hadn't demonstrated any wrongdoing by his opponent, he responded, "You ask the lawyers."

"Your lawyers?"

"Her lawyers. The election committee made a recommendation for a new election. That was it." He then disconnected the call.

A visit to Coney Island Hospital last Wednesday offered some insight into how Mr. Butler has been able to keep control over the local even as his spending has grown more outrageous and his conduct more dictatorial.

"I don't know nothing about it," Johnny Martinez, a housekeeping aide with 30 years on the job, said when asked about Mr. Butler's electoral machinations. "I'm not really involved with them; you ask them for something and then you wait."

Another hospital employee who apparently holds some position in the local was not as sanguine.

"I'm not saying nothing," she said when I approached her about the Local 420 meeting two nights earlier.

"Can I ask you why not?"

"Don't harass me!" she screamed. "I'm gonna call hospital police right now!"

An anesthesia aide named Frankie who would not give his last name offered a less-agitated if more conflicted case for Mr. Butler a few minutes later while standing in the hospital cafeteria, whose franchise is divided between Burger King and Subway. Six years ago, when Mr. Butler was still an active force on behalf of his 7,500 members, he played a key role in preventing the Giuliani administration from privatizing Coney Island Hospital. He was less successful, however, in his subsequent attempt to keep fast-food chains from taking over the cafeteria.

Frankie said he believed Ms. Charles during the campaign raised legitimate issues regarding how Mr. Butler's salary of more than $258,000 and unusually high member dues were examples of poor fiscal policy.

He said he decided to support Mr. Butler, however, after an article appeared in this newspaper two months ago in which Ms. Charles accused Mr. Butler of calling her a "stupid immigrant" and threatening her with deportation during a dispute over election rules.

Ethnic Divisions

"I think she used that as a catalyst to divide the membership," Frankie said. "Most Americans voted for Butler and most immigrants voted for Charles."

Wasn't it a relevant campaign issue if the local's president had made anti-immigrant remarks?

"It could be," Frankie replied. "But why bring it up to split the membership?"

"A lot of people got turned off because of the opposition raising that about Butler," he continued. "It became more of an issue of, 'We want our people in charge.' A lot of people opposed her because she was a woman. Why? That's just how it is."

That sense of fatalism about how things work is also why some union members are not turned off by Mr. Butler's salary, Frankie said. "We'd rather have someone making $258,000 fight for us than get together collectively on the issues," he said. "And as far as him going out and fighting for the members, he's the best. My point is, is Charles going to be able to do all that?"

The fact that she had been able to outpoll Mr. Butler in an election in which everything was tilted in his favor suggested she could outfight him at this point in his career, I replied.

"The bottom line is, if she's a qualified director or president, she'll be able to get herself in office," Frankie said. "But I go by what I hear. I hear he's been here 30 years and he makes $258,000. And I think, maybe I ought to start politicking."

Roberts Is Queen of Denial

(May 2, 2003)

When she finally realized she had maneuvered herself too far into a corner to escape, District Council 37 Executive Director Lillian Roberts tried to make it seem as if canceling a benefits-fund contract that was rife with favoritism was the unfair price exacted from her by malignant forces.

In a statement following the decision by a law firm in which her nephew is a partner to withdraw as the $180,000-a-year counsel to the DC 37 Benefits Fund Trust, Ms. Roberts asserted that the family connection "only recently became an issue because a political calculation was made by those who would like to seize power at District Council 37 that they cannot achieve this goal by 'democratic means.'"

The use of the phrase "democratic means" was particularly interesting in this situation. It was a poison dart aimed at DC 37 Treasurer Mark Rosenthal, who initially signed off on the questionable contract award but later balked when Ms. Roberts demanded that he renounce the finding of the union's ethics officer that she had engaged in a conflict of interest in steering it to her nephew's firm.

Diversionary Tactic

By blaming the political calculators in her midst, Ms. Roberts was attempting to focus attention away from the fact that it was Barbara Deinhardt, a well-respected arbitrator with no political ax to twist, who had found her conduct wanting. Mr. Rosenthal, after being foolish enough to go along with a deal whose odor should have repelled him from the start, merely recovered his better judgment in time to stop Ms. Roberts from dragging DC 37 back into the sinkhole of sweetheart arrangements from which it had emerged less than five years ago.

The recent revelation that DC 37 Special Counsel Richard Ferreri was not present during the interviewing of candidates for the Benefits Fund Trust legal services contract—contrary to what Ms. Deinhardt was told during questioning of Ms. Roberts and two close associates—makes the process by which that contract was awarded look even more suspicious than the ethics officer deemed it when she ruled Ms. Roberts in violation of the union's ethics code.

And it cast further doubt about the statement of Ms. Roberts that she, her nephew, attorney Ivan Smith, and DC 37 Associate Director Oliver Gray had seriously considered one other attorney besides Larry Cary, the partner in Mr. Smith's firm who got the contract.

Even more curiously, the participants in that meeting, according to a memo from Ms. Deinhardt to the Ethical Practices Committee that was obtained by this newspaper, stated that a mystery guest was present at the dinner meeting where the interviews were supposed to have been conducted. This man was identified to Ms. Deinhardt as "a former district attorney who had been involved in some way in an earlier investigation or review of the Funds, whose name was not recalled." The fact that Ms. Roberts, Mr. Gray, and Mr. Smith were all unable to remember the name of this individual raises questions about whether he really exists.

Peculiar Exclusions

As to the "second" attorney interviewed for the benefits fund job in addition to Mr. Cary, even if he was part of the conversation, the fact that neither Mr. Ferreri nor Mr. Rosenthal—who is a fund trustee along with Ms. Roberts and Mr. Gray—was involved in that process also is peculiar, to put it kindly. As Ms. Deinhardt noted, and Ms. Roberts and Mr. Smith have acknowledged, their relationship became essentially that of a mother and son after Mr. Smith's own mother was murdered when he was a child.

Given that closeness, there's no way that Mr. Smith should have been involved in an interview process in which a partner in his firm was under consideration. Ms. Roberts's predisposition to helping her nephew is an argument against her having any role in the process.

And Mr. Gray serves at Ms. Roberts's pleasure, meaning he was guaranteed to support her choice on any key matter unless he wanted to risk losing his job.

This leaves Mr. Rosenthal as the only trustee who did not have a vested interest in awarding the contract to Mr. Smith's law firm, Vladeck, Elias, Waldman & Engelhard. He said last week that he voted to retain the firm despite his having been excluded from the interview process because he was assured by Mr. Ferreri that the contract was a reasonable one and that Vladeck had a proven track record in handling this kind of business.

But he also accused Ms. Roberts and Mr. Gray of misleading him about Mr. Smith's role with the firm. "I was told that Ivan worked at Vladeck, not that he was a partner receiving a bonus," Mr. Rosenthal said.

No Real Difference

For Mr. Rosenthal to believe that this would have made the conflict of interest less unsavory is at best naïve. Because an associate in a law firm does not share in its profits, gaining a promotion to partner for landing a significant account would represent a bigger financial jump than is derived by a partner whose year-end bonus gets padded by such additional business.

As an early crusader for reform at DC 37 who played a major role in uncovering corruption there five years ago, Mr. Rosenthal more than most union officials should have known enough about the potential for impropriety to look carefully at the contract and the process by which it was awarded.

He said last summer that he was less inclined to criticize Ms. Roberts than he was previous DC 37 leaders because she had given him input about the union's operations that he was previously denied. He fell into the trap that awaits any outsider who suddenly is given power—that they will let their guard down once they discover that being an insider affords them a comfortable existence if they just go along with the program.

That said, Mr. Rosenthal relocated his moral compass in time to head off Ms. Roberts's attempt to send DC 37 sailing back toward the corruption that ran it aground five years ago when she looked to have Ms. Deinhardt's findings overruled. At every turn in this drama, Ms. Roberts looked to obfuscate and bulldoze rather than acknowledge that she had gone too far with union resources to benefit her nephew. Paying his college tuition was a noble thing; steering a contract paid for with union funds to his law firm was quite the opposite.

Never Sought Clearance
In an interview last August about the contract award, Ms. Roberts said she was going to seek an advisory opinion to ensure that nothing improper had been done. It seemed a natural enough assumption that the person she would ask was DC 37's ethics officer, but that did not occur. Other than issuing a statement last week after Vladeck resigned as benefit-fund counsel, Ms. Roberts has not responded to inquiries from this newspaper for the past three weeks about the failure to consult Ms. Deinhardt and other aspects of her conduct.

A week after a column that included her comments about the fund, Ms. Roberts was summoned for an interview by Ms. Deinhardt, who had launched a probe of the matter. The DC 37 leader consented to answer questions from the ethics officer then; it was only after the decision did not go her way three months later that she began asserting that Ms. Deinhardt had lacked the authority to open an investigation based solely on an anonymous letter and the column in which she justified the contract.

Fair Not Her Concern
Ms. Roberts had the option of accepting the finding and submitting the contract for competitive bidding, a process under which Vladeck might still have been chosen as counsel to the Benefits Fund Trust. Rather than take her chances with a fair process, however, Ms. Roberts chose to fight the decision. According to one person who discussed the matter with Mr. Rosenthal, the DC 37 treasurer was asked by Mr. Cary shortly after the Deinhardt report was issued how he felt about cases being made based on anonymous sources. Mr. Rosenthal, according to the source, said he was dubious about such cases; not long after that, Ms. Roberts tapped him to chair the Ethical Practices Committee.

But whatever misgivings he had expressed then, he quickly decided that the evidence that led to Ms. Deinhardt's conclusion was compelling. Contrary to what Ms. Roberts had maintained, the ethics officer had the power to launch an investigation without a formal complaint by a union member in cases where she had "reasonable suspicion that an Ethical Code violation has occurred," according to the code.

After a copy of the Deinhardt report was obtained by this newspaper three weeks ago, Ms. Roberts accused Mr. Rosenthal of leaking it and tried to get him barred from the Ethical Practices Committee's deliberations, only to be overruled by her executive board.

Political Winds Turn

On April 21, the committee presented its recommendation to the executive board—that Vladeck be stripped of the contract and barred from being part of the competitive-bidding process by which it would subsequently be awarded. The board unanimously approved the recommendation, dealing a stinging defeat to the executive director who had been chosen by acclamation 14 months earlier in large part because she was a reminder of DC 37's pre-scandal glory years.

It was the third time in four months that Ms. Roberts had overplayed a losing hand. In December, she had rejected a city severance offer and let nearly a month go by before she vainly tried to revive talks on the issue: several hundred union members were laid off in January with no additional compensation.

In March, Ms. Roberts rejected a city proposal on a job-training program over a 25-cent-an-hour difference between what she was seeking to have the participants paid and what the Bloomberg administration was offering. The city went ahead with the program, but the participants are receiving less money than they would have and without either fringe benefits or union representation.

Faint Lobbying

She has also been criticized over the union's less-visible role in the battle to save jobs by lobbying both in Albany and at the City Council. Some union officials have charged that Ms. Roberts allowed the erosion of strong lobbying and public relations operations that had been developed by former DC 37 Administrator Lee Saunders because she needed the funding to cover the salaries of herself and several key aides. At $250,000, Ms. Roberts is earning about the same as former Executive Director Stanley Hill, who presided over the union during its decay, but $100,000 more than Mr. Saunders was being paid as administrator.

"You have this huge union being ignored by City Hall and by Albany because it's not really there," said one union official who's been involved in budget battles at both places. "You don't hear much from Lillian; she sends out white papers."

Recently, DC 37 started a $500,000 TV ad campaign to rally public support for increasing taxes on the wealthy to avoid layoffs and other service cuts that would hit its members hard. Ms. Roberts is also hoping that an April 29 rally outside City Hall—the day this newspaper hits the stands—will increase pressure on Mayor Bloomberg to back away from his more-draconian cuts.

Loss of Faith

But Mr. Rosenthal said that by prolonging the dispute over the ethics finding, Ms. Roberts had undercut her own efforts in that area—even as she was imploring the DC 37 ethics committee to renounce the Deinhardt report because it added fuel to the city's drive to take over administration of union benefit funds as a cost-saving measure.

"The members aren't going to support a union they don't have confidence in," Mr. Rosenthal said. "No one's above the process—not even Lillian Roberts."

Asked about Ms. Roberts's written statement attacking unidentified enemies as having undermined unity within DC 37 and her prediction that they would be "exposed as malicious self-seekers," Mr. Rosenthal responded, "She should give the Deinhardt report to the delegates or publish it in the union newspaper and let the members decide."

'Doesn't Listen Well'

But another veteran union official said that was unlikely to happen, noting how doggedly Ms. Roberts had fought the ethics finding until the point where she risked having this week's rally overshadowed by the controversy over her own lapse in judgment.

"Lillian doesn't respond well to outside advice," he said.

Given how poorly she's been served by her inside advisers, that character trait does not bode well for her stewardship of a union facing far bigger problems.

Roberts Wins, DC 37 Loses

(February 6, 2004)

District Council 37 Executive Director Lillian Roberts, like George W. Bush, is considerably better at political infighting than she is at governing for the benefit of her constituents.

That talent accounts for her reelection victory by 8,200 votes last week in a contest in which Charles Ensley believed he would outpoll her by about 4,000 among union delegates.

The certainty of the Ensley forces that victory was theirs was on display past 11 p.m. January 27, even as the ballots were being tallied, with two of his key operatives speaking confidently about the outcome in the fifth-floor pressroom created for the occasion at DC 37's Barclay Street headquarters.

A Dramatic Turnabout

An hour later, however, a call to the first-floor room where American Arbitration Association representatives were finishing the count brought this response from another Ensley aide: "They're about to announce the results. It doesn't look good."

Moments later, just outside the pressroom, an elderly woman proclaimed in an exultant voice, "All right, she got it!" She then added of the forces behind Mr. Ensley, the president of Social Services Employees Union Local 371, "They don't know how to campaign. Lillian Roberts has been campaigning for 30 years; they was in their mothers' wombs."

In fact, there is just a 15-year age difference between the 78-year-old Ms. Roberts and Mr. Ensley, but the DC 37 leader had given her challenger a lesson in not counting on allies of convenience to put you over the top. Mr. Ensley's status as the candidate carrying the reform banner in this campaign evoked the old political clubhouse joke that the difference between regulars and reformers is that once you've bought a regular, he stays bought.

The swing of over 12,000 votes between Mr. Ensley's preelection estimate and the actual tally appeared to be the result of as few as eight delegates not honoring verbal commitments they had made to support him. The mystery about the identities of the defectors was cleared up a bit when two delegates from Civil Service Technical Guild Local 375, Rajiv Gowda and Ahmed Shakir, showed up alongside Ms. Roberts for her post-election press conference. Ensley campaign officials said it appeared that one or two other Local 375 delegates had reneged on a promise to vote for him, and at least three delegates from Clerical-Administrative Employees Local 1549 had gone back on their pledges to Mr. Ensley and their president, Eddie Rodriguez. A couple of other delegate reversals swung enough votes to turn the tide resoundingly in Ms. Roberts's favor.

It brought to mind something one official who took no position in the contest had said the morning of the election. Even as some of Mr. Ensley's backers predicted he would win by 7,000 votes or more, this official forecast a narrow victory for Ms. Roberts. Delegates' memories of long-ago slights so inconsequential that Mr. Ensley was unlikely to remember them, as well as old tribal loyalties, were sure to produce a few surprises when they actually cast their secret ballots, this official said.

Locals Have a Feuding History
Tense relations with Local 1549 existed long before Mr. Ensley's 22-year tenure as president of Local 371, a reflection of the differing education levels, salaries, and responsibilities of the social work and income maintenance staffs that are dominant presences in the two locals.

There are some veteran Local 1549 delegates who may never forgive Mr. Ensley for asserting—prophetically, it turned out—that their 1996 wage-contract vote was rigged, and for castigating their then-president, Al Diop, who turned the local into a major terminal of both vote-fixing and corruption. When Mr. Diop was on his way out five years ago, before he was criminally convicted for misdeeds in both those areas, one delegate said she would never renounce him because he was the only reason she had been able to go to Hawaii, as one of his roughly 300 guests at the 1998 convention of DC 37's international union, the American Federation of State, County and Municipal Employees.

For others within that local, Ms. Roberts is a symbol of achievement based on her past role in building DC 37 that cannot be tarnished by her mediocre record as executive director. And so some of them openly, some covertly—in what may have been last-minute conversions or perhaps just an official disclosure of how they had always intended to vote—bucked Local 1549 President Rodriguez to support Ms. Roberts.

The Local 375 defections likely have nothing to do with either old grudges toward Mr. Ensley or emotional ties to Ms. Roberts. They are probably attributable to her camp's having made plain its willingness to offer DC 37 committee assignments or other perks in return for support.

Winning Ugly

Such questionable tactics, which were described by other Local 375 delegates who were made similar offers to switch sides and declined, were consistent with the overall tenor of Ms. Roberts's campaign.

Close political races are rarely models of decorum. While Mr. Ensley's campaign was notable for its avoidance of sleaze, it also pivoted on the harshest kind of negative attack: that Ms. Roberts was incompetent. Her performance during 23 months in office suggested there was a large grain of truth in that charge, but that claim established a sharp tone at the outset, and she soon demonstrated her willingness to counter with what Mr. Ensley characterized as "loathsome" distortions.

Much of her campaign literature focused not on her actual opponent but on his running mate, incumbent Treasurer Mark Rosenthal. Mr. Rosenthal and others in the Ensley camp suggested this was a kind of back-door racial appeal pitched at African American delegates. That's a possibility, but it sometimes seemed that the assault on Mr. Rosenthal and his character was less about playing the race card than it was a matter of Ms. Roberts indulging an obsessive hatred she developed for Mr. Rosenthal after he refused, as chair of DC 37's ethics committee, to quash a finding by the union's ethical practices officer that she had engaged in a conflict of interest by steering a $180,000-a-year legal services contract to her nephew's law firm.

A Peculiar Inversion

The attacks on Mr. Rosenthal's character in her mailings seemed to embody what psychologists call projection: unconsciously attributing to him the bad impulses to which she herself submitted.

He and Mr. Ensley criticized her for bungling two negotiations with the city, one regarding severance buyouts for union members facing layoffs, the other a jobs program for welfare recipients. They also suggested that she scuttled the deal regarding the welfare recipients not over a 25-cent-an-hour difference between her wage demand and the city's offer but because she didn't want Mr. Rosenthal, who would have represented the program participants, to add 3,000 members to his local and increase his power within DC 37.

Ms. Roberts countered by calling the two men "amateur negotiators" for praising a deal reached by Transport Workers Union Local 100 President Roger Toussaint 14 months ago, placing her alone among municipal officials on both sides of the bargaining table in believing it was not a good, solid contract. She issued a leaflet arguing that Mr. Rosenthal was willing to sell out the job-training workers just to increase his dues collections, proclaiming, "While Rosenthal goes to the bank, poor single mothers pay the price." The flyer didn't try to explain how the program participants, who are now receiving 25 cents less per hour than the offer she rejected and lack both union status and health benefits, are better off as a result of her decision.

Hypocrisy on Pay

Her repeated harping on Mr. Rosenthal's compensation, which totaled $236,000—less than she receives as executive director—sounded discordant given her decision to reinstate the old salary levels from the prior, discredited regime of Stanley Hill rather than maintaining the less-generous pay plan adopted by DC 37 Administrator Lee Saunders. There were past and present union officials who wondered whether the sharp downgrade in the union's political action and public relations operations after Ms. Roberts took office was a consequence of limited resources to attract top people in those areas because of what was being spent on executive salaries.

And if she was willing to distort in those areas—not to mention questioning the ethics of Mr. Rosenthal for challenging her own— she was also willing to outright lie in a final flyer distributed within DC 37's headquarters on the day of the election. Scoffing at Mr. Rosenthal's claims about his role in rooting out corruption within the union six years ago, the flyer stated that he merely "fell into his Local's election scandal. He did not uncover the scandals that were going on in the other locals. How could he unless he knew in advance and was a part of it?"

A Scurrilous Assertion

Even by her own standards, Ms. Roberts was plumbing new depths with those assertions. More fair-minded critics within DC 37 who disparage Mr. Rosenthal as a blustery self-promoter nonetheless find it impossible to deny him credit on that score. He used his unique working-class appeal to persuade Joe DeCanio, a primary figure in both the stealing of members' dues and the rigging of the contract vote, to confide in him about the corruption. He then convinced him that he would be best served by telling what he knew to the Manhattan district attorney's office rather than taking the fall for higher-ups later on. It was the information Mr. DeCanio subsequently provided that brought the old regime crashing down, leading to more than two dozen criminal convictions and the placing of DC 37 under administratorship.

In the end, however, the willful lying as part of what Mr. Ensley called a "completely negative, mean spirited" campaign by Ms. Roberts may not have mattered. It seemed clear that for most of the pro-Roberts delegates, the election was not decided on the merits. If it were, they could not have so easily disregarded her record over the past 23 months.

Mr. Ensley's defeat produced reactions ranging from disappointment to despair among union members who had no direct stake in the contest. The problems Ms. Roberts has encountered in past negotiations with the Bloomberg administration have created doubts that she will be successful in getting a potentially pattern-setting contract that other labor leaders would embrace.

In the severance discussions in late 2002, she clearly misread the mayor's willingness to make layoffs without compensation when she walked out of a bargaining session after Labor Relations Commissioner Jim Hanley failed to improve on an offer of up to $5,000 for some members and three months of continued health coverage. Five weeks passed before she tried to restart the talks, and by then Mr. Hanley wasn't interested.

Still Defending Stance

When she was asked last week following her victory whether she felt vindicated after Mr. Ensley's shots at her capability, Ms. Roberts defended her stance in that negotiation, insisting she hadn't blown the opportunity to get something for the laid-off employees.

"That was always a lie and nobody ever printed the truth on it," she said. "None of the seven presidents that were there wanted the package," including, she said, Mr. Rosenthal.

There's a problem with that argument, though, besides the fact that Mr. Rosenthal, none of whose members were facing layoff, said he took no position on the offer. City labor leaders in recent years have rarely had reason to cheer over contract offers, but those who have been successful at some point realized that they had moved the line as far as they could and that making a deal was the best possible result. Ms. Roberts doesn't seem to have grasped that the Republican in City Hall today is not cut from the same cloth as John Lindsay, who too often for his own good bent when pushed hard enough by aggressive union leaders.

Mr. Rosenthal was among the people in the Ensley camp who predicted following the election that because a majority of the board consists of Ensley supporters, Ms. Roberts will have to honor their concerns.

One of his close allies, New York Public Library Local 1930 President Ray Markey, said that will be a two-way street, remarking, "Simply because Lillian says yes, we don't say no. It's not just her [responsibility] on the contract; we have to bring a contract back to our members. We have more input than we used to; we've got to work together in the best possible way.

"There's gotta be a cooling-off period," he added, referring to the lingering acrimony. "But I don't perceive warfare."

Mr. Ensley pointed out, however, that the reform wing of the union had helped elect Ms. Roberts 23 months ago, only to find itself marginalized soon afterward. Others questioned whether DC 37 President Veronica Montgomery-Costa, widely viewed as the Roberts forces' warlord, wouldn't counsel against making peace with her foes. In their view, Ms. Roberts takes no prisoners when crossed, and if mercy and vengeance were traded on the commodities market, they'd be placing a heavy buy order on guillotines, not olive branches.

'Come to Me for Healing'

Ms. Roberts did nothing to discourage such speculation. Asked immediately after her victory whether she would be reaching out to her opponents, she said, "I will work for every single member that we have, regardless of whether they were with me or not." She then added, "If they don't want to be healed, they won't come to me."

And the notion that she will have difficulty doing what she wants without controlling the executive board overlooks her success in co-opting the support of delegates who were in the other camp. She now has the hard, immediate currency of perks to offer those who come to her side, rather than promises that could have turned to snowflakes by the time the vote count was over.

It remains to be seen whether she honors last year's directive by the executive board that she take the legal services contract away from her nephew's firm and put it up for competitive bidding. She said last week that she would leave it to Ms. Montgomery-Costa to start the process that would change DC 37 officer elections from a delegate vote to a vote that involves the entire membership; since the current process serves her style and her president's so well, there is reason to doubt that this campaign promise will ever come to fruition.

AFSCME Head Skates

The defeat of Mr. Ensley also minimizes the chance that there will be any reform at the international union. AFSCME President Gerry McEntee's indifference to corruption when it involves his political allies has been a contributing factor in scandals within district councils from New York to Hawaii. If Mr. Ensley had taken over DC 37, it would have posed a real threat to Mr. McEntee's reelection hopes in two years; now the chance of putting together a winning coalition against him is virtually gone.

And so DC 37 figures to continue the drift of the past 23 months, in which it has been largely ineffectual on both sides of City Hall. When Mr. Bloomberg, in releasing his preliminary budget January 15, offered a $400 rebate to homeowners but insisted there was no money available for employee pay raises, Ms. Roberts's only response was to issue a statement saying, "We urgently need a fair contract now."

Missed Opportunity

A more-dynamic labor leader in her position would have called a press conference or come to City Hall to make the case to reporters and the City Council that her members, who typically are renters making less than $30,000 a year, needed a pay raise far more than anyone with the means to own a home needed a rebate. But no one on her political-action or public relations staffs thought it was worth expending the energy. Nor did her associate director, Oliver Gray, one of the few staffers ex-City Council Speaker Peter Vallone ever got rid of for lackluster performance.

Exiting the building around 1:20 a.m. following her victory, one of Ms. Roberts's supporters, giddy with the triumph and eyeing the snow blanketing the street, sang, "It's beginning to look a lot like Christmas . . ."

For those at DC 37 for whom the union means something more than the perks and healthy paycheck that go with riding shotgun on the gravy train, it looks more like another three years of winter closing in.

Elegy for a Flawed Fighter

(December 2, 2005)

More than one speaker at Jim Butler's funeral November 22 wondered, and not kindly, why more elected officials and union leaders were not present to pay last respects to the man who for 30 years was president of Hospital Workers Local 420 of District Council 37.

That question, and its unstated answer, summed up the contradictions of Mr. Butler's life.

He was a deacon in the Ebenezer Baptist Church in Flushing—where the funeral service was held—who brought the fervor and imagery of his religion to his union work.

Left Office under Clouds

He was also ousted from office three years ago after questions were raised by his reelection opponent, Carmen Charles, about a salary that exceeded $258,000 and spending habits that at best were questionable.

After his handpicked election committee ordered a new election under dubious circumstances and she defeated him for a second time in 2002, a thorough investigation of union finances led Ms. Charles to bring a civil suit that led to a default judgment of $1.6 million against Mr. Butler when he failed to appear for a court hearing.

When a reporter from this newspaper called him about the verdict, he contended he had no money other than what he received from Social Security and his union pension. "If I were in his situation, I would say the same thing," Ms. Charles said the day after his funeral.

At the time of his death at age 73, she said, "The lawyers were trying to find his assets."

Mr. Butler attempted to ostracize her when she first challenged his spending, and on the day when she took office, he left the premises grudgingly, with police called at one point to help ensure a peaceful transition of power.

But unlike others who feuded bitterly with Mr. Butler over the years—retired DC 37 Executive Director Victor Gotbaum and the current occupant of that post, Lillian Roberts—Ms. Charles attended the funeral and seemed to do so for more than appearance's sake. She was among those who rose to their feet when a gospel choir consisting of past and present Local 420 members performed a stirring rendition of "Order My Steps in the World."

"I cannot bask in my glory without giving Jim Butler the credit," she said during a phone interview the following afternoon. "Jim Butler is responsible for my being a labor union leader. The first time I went to one of his union meetings, it lit a fire in me."

Bill Lucy, the secretary-treasurer of the American Federation of State, County and Municipal Employees who was the closest link between Mr. Butler and DC 37's international union, put it this way to the 400 mourners crowded into the church: "All of us knew Jim as a fighter for union members in general and for Local 420 members in particular. If he liked you, you knew it right away. If he didn't like you, you knew it a little bit sooner."

Giuliani Roused Battler in Him

One of those who fit the latter category was Rudy Giuliani, and several speakers referred to Mr. Butler's clashes with the former mayor over the threatened privatization of city hospitals and their services and the layoff of Local 420 members.

They were natural adversaries, both of them tough and stubborn and cantankerous and on a collision course from the time Mr. Giuliani took office in 1994. Mr. Butler mispronounced the mayor's name as "Juliana" in the same way that 30 years earlier Michael J. Quill had expressed his contempt for City Hall's chief occupant by referring to him as "Lindsley."

His blood boiled when Mr. Giuliani justified cuts at Health and Hospitals Corporation facilities by saying that the hospitals existed to treat people, not serve as "a jobs program." Others viewed the then-mayor's words as hypocritical and insensitive; Mr. Butler smelled something racial in such taunts from a man who was not averse to larding city agencies with patronage hires. That compounded the Local 420 leader's natural protectiveness toward a membership that was among the lowest-paid in city government.

Mr. Butler took it personally when DC 37 settled a wage contract in late 1995 that, in return for union members accepting a two-year wage freeze at its outset, protected all of them from layoffs except for the members of his local. It was a fundamental difference between him and the union's executive director at the time, Stanley Hill, who had witnessed the pain of tens of thousands of members being laid off during the mid-1970s fiscal crisis, and was in charge of DC 37 when a couple thousand members lost their jobs in 1991 at the hands of a mayor he helped elect, David Dinkins.

Mr. Giuliani raised the specter of as many as 30,000 layoffs unless the city got budget relief elsewhere, and Mr. Hill was sufficiently intimidated to settle for the two-year pay freeze in return for a no-layoff clause. He was weak enough not to insist that this clause had to apply to all DC 37 members, regardless of Mr. Giuliani's explanation that giving such protection to Local 420 members would compromise his hopes of finding buyers for up to three city hospitals.

Smelled Vote-Fix

Infuriated, Mr. Butler campaigned against the contract, producing an overwhelmingly negative vote by his rank and file. When an even larger vote in favor was produced by Clerical-Administrative Employees Local 1549, whose members were only slightly better able to deal with a two-year pay freeze, Mr. Butler's reaction—accurately, it would turn out—was, "They stole the vote."

He rallied opposition to the mayor's attempt to sell Coney Island Hospital to a private company, leading to a lawsuit that produced a court ruling nullifying the sale because Mr. Giuliani had failed to consult the City Council.

The mayor's revenge was exacted in the spring of 1998, when he ordered the layoff of more than 900 Local 420 members while sparing the jobs of hospital clerical staffers represented by Local 1549. Lest anyone be misled into believing that this was merely the consequence of a need to keep clericals but not hospital aides, three dozen clerical supervisors represented by another union that had opposed the mayor politically were also targeted for layoffs.

Mr. Hill's agreement to the contract that turned the city's budget situation from large deficit to healthy surplus, and his strong support of Mr. Giuliani's 1997 reelection, were not enough to spare Mr. Butler's members. It was only after Mr. Hill went to then-Senator Al D'Amato, a power in national Republican circles who could influence Mr. Giuliani's future political ambitions, that a compromise was reached under which the threatened employees would either be offered a buyout or given help in finding other jobs within HHC or in other city agencies.

Mr. Butler initially agreed to the deal, although he was conspicuously absent from the City Hall press conference announcing it. Over the next week, more than 300 of his members were placed in other city agencies, but Mr. Butler complained that those who remained at HHC were being forced to work overtime and denied vacations. Even with them putting in extra hours, he said, services were being stretched too thin.

Butler Scuttled Deal

And so he balked at signing the memorandum of understanding, and 17 days after that deal was reached, 550 Local 420 members were laid off. Mr. Giuliani said hospital staffing was now at its proper level and there would be no adverse impact on services. Mr. Butler responded, "Juliana has got Stanley in his back pocket," adding, "Somebody got to carry the cross."

Brooklyn City Council Member Yvette Clarke, who won election with Local 420's support after her mother, Una, rode that support to become the first Caribbean American woman elected to the council 14 years ago, put it this way: "There are those who negotiate in a certain manner, and there are those who are no holds barred. Jim Butler was no holds barred."

It was in the midst of those battles with Mr. Giuliani that the out-of-control spending that led to the 2003 court judgment against Mr. Butler began: raises and overtime payments that were not approved by his executive board, large tabs for vacations and other luxuries.

Also Helped the Afflicted

Unlike some labor leaders whose out-of-town travel consisted primarily of junkets to fair-weather resorts, Mr. Butler also took delegations of union members to help those struck by natural disasters, as well as sending them money.

But the mourners last week were decidedly blasé about the money spent taking union officers and other supporters on trips to the Caribbean that, while billed as educational, were far more about fun in the sun.

"Jim Butler didn't just go down to Bermuda or the Bahamas and take a vacation," declared the Reverend Timothy I. Mitchell, whose father is the pastor of Ebenezer Baptist. "He took a whole lotta people with him." On the dues of a whole lotta other union members.

That unspoken reality helped explain why some prominent officials who were assisted by Mr. Butler over the years were absent from the nonetheless-packed church. It might also explain the need of so many of those who did show to scold them for their absence.

Invisible Attendants

"I'm sure those other labor leaders and other elected officials must be here somewhere. I just can't see them," said the Reverend Wendell Foster, who told the crowd that both he and his daughter Helen had been elected to the City Council over the objections of the Bronx Democratic organization largely because of Mr. Butler's help.

Queens Congressman Gregory Meeks recalled being elected to the State Assembly more than a decade ago when Mr. Butler sent the union's "Freedom Bus," best known for transporting Local 420 members to hospital rallies, into the housing projects in his district, where members went door to door rousing enough people to give him the 247-vote margin that launched his political career.

And the Reverend Al Sharpton, another fiery leader whose passion for the less fortunate has always uneasily coexisted with questions about his money, spoke of Mr. Butler's loyalty and his feeling for working people who struggled to make do.

He told a parable of a minister who was more intent on being respected for his righteousness and the fine-looking church in which he preached than on "feeding the sparrows."

'Butler Never Backed Up'

"I remember Jim Butler," Mr. Sharpton said, "because when other labor leaders would think about what election they could turn . . . he would get up early in the morning to take care of sparrows like me. He would feed the sparrows." He then added, "He never backed up."

Those were the memories that would warm Mr. Butler's wife, Eloise, his son, Robert, and the other family members and supporters inside the church. One sign of the impact Mr. Butler had came when a minister began his remembrance by invoking his trademark call on the picket line, "All fired up!" and the crowd responded, "Can't take no more!"

For them, he would live on as a larger-than-life presence at the barricades, whose mantra, one eulogist said, was an almost-exuberant declaration, "It's crisis time." Una Clarke recalled Mr. Butler's battle against the privatization of Brooklyn Central Laundry by Mr. Giuliani, the facility for HHC's citywide laundry services at Kings County Hospital. "He taught me well what courage is," she said of that struggle. "I know whatever the organizing is up there, he's organizing. Let's rejoice in a life that was well lived."

Became What He Hated

There would be no attempt that night to reconcile the contradictions in a man whose fierceness in seeking justice and a decent living for his members was later transferred to a fight to retain power that featured the kind of bullying he found so repugnant in others.

In 1998, when his longtime colleague, then–Local 372 President Charlie Hughes, was subjected to an internal trial after it was found that his local was $10 million in debt, Mr. Butler questioned why Mr. Hughes's superiors hadn't curbed his excesses before it reached that point. "Why didn't they pull Charlie close?" he asked an acquaintance. "You can't have that kind of stuff going on."

The truth was that attempts had been made, however ineffectual, by Mr. Hill to get Mr. Hughes's spending under control, and he simply wasn't going to bow to somebody else's judgment that what he was doing was intolerable. By the end of Mr. Butler's career, the same seemed true of a man who in years past had sometimes privately showed that a keen, subtle mind lay beneath the surface bluster and fiery rhetoric.

Ms. Charles, who saw both sides of Mr. Butler to a greater degree than most, was asked how a man who could inspire her and so many of those who turned out to say goodbye could have clouded his legacy as his power began to slip away.

"I will not try to surmise what happened," she said. "But he had a great vision, and sometimes people lose their vision."

Same Old Song for DC 37

(September 18, 2009)

It is said that on his way out of District Council 37 in early 2002, after providing some cosmetic surgery for the scandal-scarred union without ever getting to the cancer within, Lee Saunders expressed regret that he hadn't used his power as administrator to require direct election of union officers.

It is likely that sentiment didn't translate to action for the same reason that DC 37 once again finds itself under a cloud of financial irregularity: for those with power over its operations, political considerations always outweigh the best interests of the union's 125,000 members.

It's why the September 4 press release from the American Federation of State, County and Municipal Employees announcing it had placed DC 37 Local 2054 into administratorship should have been accompanied by a recording of Levi Stubbs leading the Four Tops in singing "It's the Same Old Song." All that has changed are the names of the local presidents charged with malfeasance and the executive director who tolerated them despite glaring evidence of wrongdoing. And as usual, AFSCME, where Mr. Saunders is the top aide to President Gerry McEntee, intervened too late and for reasons that seem less pure than advertised.

Delayed Despite Risky Business

The international union's press release noted that its action was coming six weeks after its own audit had found major problems with Local

2054's operation, including the loss of more than $1 million "due to risky investments" that violated its regulations and "no program or mechanism in place to protect against depletion of the local union's remaining assets."

Given that kind of loss and the lack of financial controls, it would have seemed urgent to act sooner than that, particularly since the head of the AFSCME judicial panel, John Seferian, on August 17 had found the Local 2054 president at the time, Colleen Carew-Rogers, guilty of two counts of unauthorized spending.

But fiscal mismanagement is so much a part of DC 37 tradition largely because by itself it has rarely been grounds for decisive action by AFSCME. Two other factors probably had a greater role in rousing Mr. McEntee and his minions from their usual torpor: a coup within the local September 1 that led to Ms. Carew-Rogers's ouster and the retainer of attorney Arthur Schwartz by the local's executive board, and inquiries by the *New York Times* about the developments.

Mr. Schwartz is a well-known advocate for union dissidents and earned the wrath of Mr. McEntee by bringing a lawsuit a decade ago accusing both DC 37 and the international of being part of a racketeering conspiracy. The fact that there was more than a grain of truth to the charge, given AFSCME's having turned a blind eye to massive corruption until the Manhattan district attorney's office set up a branch office inside DC 37 to deal with the malefactors, made the charge particularly tough to stomach even though the suit eventually vanished without a trace.

And when the *Times* in November 1998 reported that not only had a cavalcade of cronies of DC 37 Executive Director Stanley Hill looted their locals under his nose, they had also rigged a union wage contract vote, it took the scandal beyond the local embarrassment it had been when the transgressions were being reported primarily by this newspaper and the *Daily News* and made it a national story. That forced Mr. McEntee to fake meaningful action by deputizing Mr. Saunders to clean up the union and set a tone of "zero tolerance" for wrongdoing.

Most people think of "zero" as a fairly absolute concept, but the folks at AFSCME seem to apply it on a sliding scale, with loyalty or lack of it considered a mitigating factor.

A Clear Double Standard
Thus Roy Commer, a president of Local 375 who not only criticized Mr. McEntee but raised questions about the union's contract with

a prescription-drug supplier that employed the AFSCME leader's daughter in a ranking position, was yanked from office at the first possible opportunity based on unauthorized spending on membership mailings of less than $11,000 and his failure to speedily make reimbursement when he was ordered to do so. On the other hand, Helen Greene, a top DC 37 officer who was also president of Local 768, would have gotten off scot-free for making thousands of dollars of personal charges on her union credit card—and publicly lying about it—if she hadn't been criminally convicted in Manhattan Supreme Court.

Ms. Carew-Rogers spent more without the authorization of her board at Local 2054 than the amount for which Mr. Commer was stripped of not just his leadership post but his union membership. Yet Mr. Seferian, who constantly reminds us of why his nickname is Kangaroo John, cleared her of the biggest expenditure despite finding her justification for it "dubious" and did not require her to make restitution for the two charges on which he deemed her guilty, letting her off with a decidedly limp reprimand.

Given the fact that Mr. Commer's local was in no financial turmoil at the time of his ouster, while AFSCME had already flagged Local 2054 for being in dangerous waters, prudence—if not even-handedness—would have seemed to require Mr. Seferian to act strongly against her. It was his failure to do so that led her subordinates on the local's board, at Mr. Schwartz's direction, to remove her from office two weeks ago.

But a day after the change was made, the man who had been chosen by the board as her replacement, Carlton Berkley, came to the local's offices along with his vice president, Linda Bowman, to discover Ms. Carew-Rogers shredding documents, and their attempts to stop her were blocked by a DC 37 official. When Mr. Berkley appealed to DC 37 leader Lillian Roberts, according to Mr. Schwartz, she told him, "I'm waiting for a directive from the international."

A Weekend Surprise
By the following day, a Thursday, Steve Greenhouse, the *Times* labor reporter who broke the 1998 vote-fixing story, was making calls to DC 37 about the Local 2054 situation and getting the kind of non-response that the union's press office seems to strive for. At some point, someone there apparently concluded that they should at least

contact their international union's spokesman, Chris Policano, about the situation. Shortly before 6 p.m. on the Friday that began the Labor Day weekend (after this newspaper had already gone to press), Mr. Policano issued a statement saying that AFSCME had imposed a trusteeship.

The timing was interesting, to put it mildly. The press release cited just one new detail that prompted swift action: while it noted the Local 2054 board was within its rights to remove Ms. Carew-Rogers, it stated that choosing someone other than the local's vice president to replace her violated the local's constitution.

Was this supposed to be more alarming than AFSCME's own discovery, in an audit it issued on June 22, that Ms. Carew-Rogers had either failed to impose or disregarded appropriate financial procedures, in the process losing more than a million dollars in member assets through risky investments that violated AFSCME's own Financial Standards Code?

Mr. Policano, asked those questions last week, apparently decided not to try to explain the inexplicable and did not call back with a response.

Suit: 'A Bad-Faith Act'

Mr. Schwartz filed a lawsuit in U.S. District Court in Manhattan September 8 charging that imposing the administratorship was "a wholly bad-faith act [because] AFSCME has known of the financial deficiencies in Local 2054 for a long time and has taken no action," claiming the international union stepped in primarily because it was worried about the effect he might have on the future course of the local.

It seems at least as likely, however, that the *Times'* interest in the story was what moved AFSCME to once again fake meaningful action. National coverage of a new scandal in a union wracked a decade ago by similar shenanigans would have brought the same kind of outcry about negative publicity by the heads of other district councils that led Mr. McEntee to finally cashier Mr. Hill long after it became obvious he was either indifferent or powerless to stem the crime wave overwhelming the union and draining its assets. Until then, Mr. McEntee had ignored the warning signs—from a written demand by one prominent local president that he investigate whether the 1996 wage-contract vote had been fixed to the looting of DC

37's largest local by its president—that Mr. Hill was the wrong guy to lead his flagship district council.

Calls Roberts Soft on Allies

Mr. Schwartz contended last week that Ms. Roberts was also the wrong person to lead DC 37, and for many of the same reasons. He noted that she had not even acted to strip Ms. Carew-Rogers or Michael Hood—the deposed president of Local 1505 who has acknowledged some financial irregularities and withheld the local's books for more than three years from the woman who eventually unseated him—of their DC 37 vice presidencies, which pay each of them $18,000 a year. The reason, he said, was as simple as it is mortifying: they may be grossly incompetent at the very least, but they are reliable "yes" votes for Ms. Roberts at the DC 37 executive board.

"It's like Lillian World 2009 is similar to what existed in 1998: 'if you're my friend, I won't bother you,'" Mr. Schwartz said. "'And I'll give you release time,'" meaning the officials involved can get paid while not reporting to their city jobs because they are purportedly conducting union business.

Those who cross Ms. Roberts, however, find that retribution is swift. Local 375 President Claude Fort said last week of his onetime ally that "if she is challenged or you ask questions about expenditures," retaliation soon follows.

Five years ago, when Ms. Roberts asked Mr. Fort not to seek an AFSCME vice presidency in deference to the then-head of Local 2054, Joan Reed, he obliged, even though his local has nearly 2,000 more members. When she died, however, he sought the spot again and did not step aside when Ms. Roberts told him that Local 372 President Veronica Montgomery-Costa, her most-powerful supporter on the executive board, wanted it as well.

Questioned $300G Dinner

His decision to run unsuccessfully earned him bad will, Mr. Fort said, but it was not until he began asking questions last summer about a party at the AFSCME convention in San Francisco on which DC 37 reportedly spent $300,000 that Ms. Roberts wanted to "kill" him politically. He said trumped-up charges soon followed that a close aide of his had a no-show job and that Mr. Fort was enabling him.

Cuthbert Dickerson, the president of Local 374 and a Roberts supporter, challenged Mr. Fort's narrative and his chronology, claiming the charges were prepared against him before he pressed for how much had been spent on the dinner at the convention. But when asked whether the figure had been in the neighborhood of $300,000, Mr. Dickerson said, "That sounds about right."

The fact that DC 37 is still partying like it's 1998 should be troubling to anyone familiar with that dark decade in the union's history. Back then, the large expenditures on holiday parties and education conferences reflected not just extravagance with members' dues money but, as the later prosecutions made clear, kickbacks in which local presidents split the proceeds of the inflated bills with vendors and, in one case, a local may have laundered a payoff to the president of another in return for having his members rolled into the larger local.

No Confidence but No Challenge?
Although more than a few union officials shake their heads and roll their eyes when discussing Ms. Roberts's leadership and the decline of DC 37 during her seven-plus years in office, she may not face serious opposition when she seeks her third full term next year at age 84. This is largely due to an election system in which DC 37's officers are not really accountable to their members, since they are elected by union delegates rather than a rank-and-file vote. Aside from the fire officers' union, where nine board members directly elected by the rank and file choose among themselves for president, DC 37 is the only municipal union where the membership does not vote for its leader.

The problems inherent in this system became clear with the 1998 scandal. The two men who were eventually convicted of stealing the most from the union, Charlie Hughes of Local 372 and Al Diop of Local 1549, represented about 40 percent of DC 37's members and exercised tight control over their delegates. This meant that they could make or break an executive director, since they needed to enlist the presidents of no more than a handful of DC 37's 56 locals to provide a majority in the delegate voting. Mr. Hill was not possessed of the kind of political courage that would lead him to ask questions about the two men's activities that might trouble either one, unless, as in Mr. Hughes's case, a local president's ambition suddenly posed a threat to his own power.

Could Swing Board Majority

That dynamic may also have played a part in Ms. Roberts's lack of response in recent months when Local 2054 board members came to her with their growing concerns about Ms. Carew-Rogers's spending and her autocratic behavior. Local 2054 is one of the largest of the 51 locals that are not part of the "Big Five" that each represent at least five percent of the union's members. If it were led by someone not tied to Ms. Roberts, it could swing the balance of power on the DC 37 executive board, so that her next term would be beset by checks on her authority similar to what she endured when she first defeated challenger Charles Ensley but did not have a majority on the board.

The basic flaws of the governance system have left not only her and Mr. Hill but Victor Gotbaum, the last truly strong DC 37 executive director, forced to tolerate varying degrees of knavery by local presidents as the price for continued control over their boards.

Yet when Mr. Saunders became DC 37 administrator and was granted sweeping powers by Mr. McEntee, he opted not to change this election system. It was generally believed that he shied away for political reasons of his own: he hopes to succeed his boss someday, and diluting the power of the heads of the two largest DC 37 locals might have eventually cost him important support if he faced opposition.

Change of Heart on Democracy

He went away, but the potential for a recurrence of corruption because of the governance structure lingered. It was summed up concisely in an article in this newspaper in December 2003 written by a veteran union official who had seen DC 37 at its best and worst. "We still need to do more to make sure that corruption can never return to DC 37," that official wrote. "More democracy is the answer. We need to amend our constitution to provide for direct election of DC 37's officers by the members. We must truly make the leadership fully accountable to the membership."

The author of those noble words was Lillian Roberts. It's possible that she put her name behind them only because she was seeking a full term as executive director the following month and faced a tough challenge from Mr. Ensley, then the reform-minded Local 371 president whose warning about contract vote-fixing had been ignored nearly eight years earlier by Mr. McEntee. But if she believed them then, she changed her mind soon after her narrow victory. By the latter part of 2004, she had backed away from her position in support of direct election, saying she would leave it to union delegates to decide.

Delegates Reap Loyalty's Rewards

The delegates themselves are not exactly unbiased observers, however. Just as local presidents who side with Ms. Roberts have been rewarded financially, delegates who Mr. Ensley thought he had locked up in the 2004 election wound up voting for her instead and received committee assignments that were accompanied by stipends as rewards. There are other perks for those whose votes and loyalty can be counted on: in 1998, the last AFSCME convention for many DC 37 officials before their fancy hotel accommodations at union conferences gave way to prison cells, Mr. Diop took a delegation of more than 300 from Local 1549 to Hawaii with him.

That's an awful lot of member dues money being spent to keep union officials happy. It doesn't cost the local presidents or the DC 37 executive director anything, though, and helps guarantee that the delegates will vote the right way, which has nothing to do with whether members' interests are being served.

And as long as he can count on DC 37's votes when he runs for reelection, Mr. McEntee sees nothing wrong with this arrangement. Mr. Saunders may be less of a political hack, with more concern for the people AFSCME represents, but his decision to back off from taking action he knew was necessary to reform the union a decade ago does not foster much hope that he will play any role in meaningful reform whenever Mr. McEntee finally packs it in. Which means that there is no assurance that whoever succeeds Ms. Roberts when she bows to reality and retires will, even if more capable, govern any differently.

An Unearned Honor at Parade

Last Saturday, amid the turmoil at Local 2054 and questions about whether there are locals beyond Mr. Hood's where similar problems are just waiting to surface, Ms. Roberts served as grand marshal of the Labor Day Parade. The press release from the AFL-CIO New York City Central Labor Council, rather than citing any accomplishments she had to justify the honor, noted that the choice coincided with DC 37's 65th birthday.

It was an appropriate if unintended commentary on a ceremonial union leader playing yet another ceremonial role, just as she and her superiors in Washington dress up actions that are a pretext for the political machinations that are the only thing they do with much skill.

The Rise and Fall of a Militant Whose Vision Went Sour

Roger Toussaint vowed to restore Transport Workers Union Local 100 to "the great, fighting union" it had been in the 1960s, but his knack for alienating former allies and a dubious decision to lead a transit strike near Christmas in 2005 wound up splintering the union politically and prompted him to step down as president midway through his third term in office. Photo reprinted courtesy of the *Chief-Leader*.

For all those who followed him as president of Transport Workers Union (TWU) Local 100, the ghost of Michael J. Quill posed a dual challenge: be militant on behalf of your members, and when you take the ultimate risk of leading them out on strike, make sure you come back with a better contract than anyone would have thought attainable.

It was a heavy burden to bear, particularly considering that Quill, during 32 years as the leader of what was then a predominantly Irish-Catholic union of bus drivers and subway conductors and motormen and track workers, threatened numerous strikes but only pulled the trigger once.

He gained notoriety for repeatedly taking the talks to the contract deadline during the 12 years from 1954 through the end of 1965 that Robert F. Wagner served as mayor of New York City, and then, with the chaos of a massive job action hanging like a metaphorical ball due to drop at midnight on New Year's Eve, somehow a solution would materialize.

The drama was carefully choreographed: Quill and Wagner had a friendly relationship and invariably found a way to resolve their differences comfortably in advance of the witching hour. No one, least of all the city's newspapers, had moral qualms about dragging out the proceedings enough to give residents a good scare (and in the process, boost circulation at a notoriously quiet time of the year).

In November 1965, Manhattan Congressman John Lindsay was elected mayor, a tall, handsome, patrician-looking reformer whose victory running on the Republican and Liberal lines was trumpeted as a rebuke to the Democratic clubhouse politics that characterized the Wagner years (to such an extent that Wagner himself gained his third term in 1961 by campaigning against "the bosses," which some viewed as an homage to . Franz Kafka).

Lindsay had vowed to get tough with the increasingly militant city unions, and there was no one who better symbolized the hard-driving labor leader than Quill. Egged on by editorial writers, the soon-to-be new mayor vowed there would be no backroom last-minute sweetheart deal in which the city gave away too much to the union. He sounded contemptuous of the time-honored dance between the union and his predecessor, and seemed determined to start his administration with a bang by standing up to the man whose past dealings with the American Communist Party led some to sneeringly refer to him as Red Mike.

Quill, not amused by Lindsay's hard line, pulled the trigger on a strike that began on January 1, 1966. Legend has it that at one point during the negotiations, the two men came face to face, and the new mayor, citing a demand that the union had made for an additional paid holiday, asked what day he had in mind. Quill, in his sharp Irish brogue, was said to have replied, "Yer birthday."

When the city went to court and obtained an injunction threatening union leaders with jail unless they ended the walkout immediately, Quill told reporters, "The judge can drop dead in his black robes."

Off to jail he went along with several colleagues, but in a city so dependent upon mass transit to get not only residents but commuters from neighboring suburbs to their jobs, the strike took an increasing financial toll. And so Lindsay, who had ridden into battle to the whoops of the editorial pages, now found them besieging him to end the paralysis of his city. The price he paid was an overly generous contract. Quill, whose shaky health had not improved from his time behind bars, paid a steeper price—three days after the 12-day walkout ended, he suffered a fatal heart attack. This only served to burnish his standing in the eyes of his members and made him an impossible act to follow as head of the union.

Until then, city employees who went on strike faced the penalties of the Condon-Wadlin Act, which called for firing for walkouts and a three-year period before they could be reinstated. The very harshness of the law made it largely unenforceable. When President Reagan 15 years later fired more than 11,000 Air Traffic Controllers for an illegal strike, it took close to a decade to bring staffing back to where it had been, and that was with the entire country from which to recruit. Practically speaking, firing 30,000 transit workers and replacing them quickly enough to keep the subways and buses running safely would have been a far more difficult task.

And so New York State's Legislature at the direction of Governor Nelson Rockefeller scrapped Condon-Wadlin in favor of what became known as the Taylor Law. It guaranteed the right of public employee unions to collective bargaining and to have employee dues paid to the unions through payroll deduction but also substituted more-realistic, and thus far-more-effective, penalties for striking. Workers would lose two days' pay for each day of a walkout, and their unions would be subjected not only to huge fines but to the potentially more-damaging loss of dues-checkoff provisions.

The state also created a new entity, the Metropolitan Transportation Authority, to run both the city transit system and the commuter rail lines that extended into its suburbs on Long Island and in Westchester County. The chairman of the new agency was to be appointed by the governor, giving him power over future negotiations with the TWU that was arguably greater than the mayor's.

By 1980, the city had a mayor, Ed Koch, who had gained election three years earlier, in part by vowing to get tough with the unions in ways that Lindsay was unable to after being knocked back on his heels by the transit strike that launched his administration. The TWU president at the time, John Lawe, was a far more genial man than Quill, but he was facing turmoil within his ranks, as the makeup of the union had rapidly changed over the previous decade and a militant faction of black workers was looking for power within the union. This forced him to take a tough stance in contract negotiations. Koch was eager for a showdown, and the state's labor-friendly governor, Hugh Carey, did not intervene.

When Lawe somewhat reluctantly led his members out on strike, it became clear how much the game had changed since Quill's successful walk-out 14 years earlier. The most-significant shift initially had to do with a change agreed to previously in the expiration date of the TWU contract: from the final day in December to the last day in March. April began with unseasonably mild weather, the kind made for invigorating walks. For his war with the union, Koch suddenly had hundreds of thousands of foot soldiers—with a fashion trend launched of women wearing sneakers for the trek to their jobs and then changing to more-traditional kicks at their desks—as a rebuke to the notion that the TWU could still shut the city down.

The strike nonetheless lasted for 11 days before the union admitted defeat and accepted a contract offer only marginally better than the one it had deemed insulting enough to walk off the job. The pain had just begun: workers were zapped with the loss of 22 days' pay, leaving them financially pinched enough that they would have struggled to keep up with their dues payments if the money was still being withheld from their checks each pay period. But the right to dues checkoff had been stripped, and it proved to be a more-crushing financial blow to the union than the $900,000 fine imposed by a state judge. By 1982, the union had to plead with a judge to restore dues-deduction procedures so it could avert looming bankruptcy.

Lawe stepped down as president around that time, replaced by Albert "Sonny" Hall, a politically savvy union leader who was able to stabilize its operation. But increasingly he found himself under challenge by the largely minority militant wing of the union, and by the mid-1990s, when he took a step upstairs to run the TWU's international union, he appointed first a Latino successor and then a black one in an attempt to maintain control over the union.

But the militant faction, known as New Directions, was continuing to make inroads among the rank and file, and in 2000 it finally elected a president, Roger Toussaint.

Toussaint had come out of the political turbulence of his native Trinidad, and he brought the radical politics he was immersed in there to the union. At a time when unions including the TWU were being forced to accept concession-laden contracts by Republicans at both City Hall and in the Governor's Mansion in Albany, Toussaint argued that union members should be standing up rather than taking their lumps in hopes that better days would soon be upon them, and the promise of being more militant in dealing with transit-system management gained him a solid victory.

In his first contract negotiation in late 2002 (the union under Mr. Hall had succeeded in getting an expiration date of mid-December, offering the potential of weather once again becoming workers' ally if they did the unthinkable and walked off the job), he raised the threat of a strike in response to the MTA's refusal to offer pay raises. When Mayor Michael Bloomberg, who had taken office 11 months earlier, went into court to seek injunctions and penalties should a strike actually occur, Toussaint responded with truculence worthy of Mike Quill, whom he frequently cited early on as a bridge to the sizable contingent of white members who may have been too young to have known the fiery founding president but certainly knew of him. With a single impolite suggestion that the mayor hold his tongue, Toussaint propelled himself forward as the tough guy the labor movement in the city needed at a time when union leaders had become better known for a series of corruption scandals.

Toussaint wound up settling a contract that while offering relatively modest wage increases provided a much-needed infusion of cash for the union's health fund and addressed a disciplinary system that was widely viewed as overly harsh.

When the pact was ratified by 60 percent of his members in early 2003, it seemed to augur a bright future for Toussaint. Yet he seethed that the margin wasn't significantly higher, railing against his political enemies within the union for undermining support. It seemed odd for a new president to be taking a big win so hard, particularly since the first year of the deal, providing just a $1,000 bonus rather than a lasting pay raise, made it inevitable that some members wouldn't be thrilled by the financial terms.

It inadvertently was a reminder that the esteem in which Mike Quill was held might be accounted for by his death so soon after his great triumph in the 1966 strike, before his penchant for quarrels could create future *conflicts within the union or the measures taken by elected officials to pre-vent a repeat could be used against the union. For much as Toussaint stewed over that contract not being universally acclaimed by transit workers, it would turn out to be his finest hour during eight years as president, a tenure that was cut short by his decision to step down and take a job with the international TWU at a point when much of the rank and file was in mutiny against him and his hopes of winning a fourth term had been severely compromised.*

Toussaint's Quiet Revolution

(December 27, 2002)

Somewhere in the wee hours of the morning of December 16, the day that his contract expired, Roger Toussaint recalled, he cut off negotiations with the Metropolitan Transportation Authority, "overcome by frustration," and told officials that he wanted to take a nap.

He intended, however, once he awakened to call his executive board together and "strongly recommend" that it reject management's most-recent proposal, setting the stage for a possible transit strike.

He awoke at about 7 a.m. and began packing his bags in his room at the Grand Hyatt Hotel. "Then they called us back to the table," he said, and a new wage offer was made, reigniting a process that 12 hours later would produce an announcement of a wage deal and the unlikely sight of the Transport Workers Union Local 100 president hugging MTA Chairman Peter Kalikow.

'A Historic Victory'
Four days later, Mr. Toussaint sat in his union office on the Upper West Side and described the deal, rich in health-benefit contributions and featuring a sweeping reform of New York City Transit's disciplinary procedures, as "a clear, historic victory."

But even as that morning's *New York Times* was making clear how costly the estimated $386-million health-benefits package made the deal for the MTA, Mr. Toussaint realized that his need to accept a $1,000 bonus instead of a first-year wage increase had presented an inviting target for his political opponents within the union as he prepared to send contract ballots out to his rank and file this week.

"I feel like someone who has gotten a job well done," he said. "I need to rest my weary bones, but I can't rest until I get the contract ratified."

He said having to accept a lump-sum bonus payable next July rather than a wage increase "was a disappointment, as was the fact that we didn't eliminate workfare. But that balances against a host of positive stuff."

The improvements were so significant that negotiators from other unions were effusive in praising Mr. Toussaint, and one veteran government official who does not particularly like him said he had done a good job by any standard, but especially so in light of the fact that he had no negotiating experience prior to his election two years ago.

One veteran labor attorney who previously did business with New York City Transit singled out Mr. Toussaint's success in changing a disciplinary system that he likened to "Stalinist Russia."

Larry Hanley, an international representative for the Amalgamated Transit Union who headed the ATU local representing Staten Island bus personnel for more than a decade, said, "The things that they accomplished here are so massive. For 20 years, the MTA bargained strategically, changing a clause here and a clause there, and they've crippled the unions because so much of their time was spent dealing with discipline. The fact that Kalikow publicly acknowledged the need to change the relationship with the workforce is significant."

'Everybody Wanted Out'

The climate within NYC Transit was so uncomfortable for many workers, Mr. Hanley said, that in recent years the transit unions had made improved retirement eligibility their biggest priority "just because everybody has wanted to get the hell out of there."

Mr. Toussaint said he made the case for revamping disciplinary rules by asking MTA negotiators whether the current system was improving performance, as opposed to simply making employees feel oppressed and disrespected.

"It eliminates the prospect of virtual house arrest for members," he said, referring to the requirement that employees on sick leave had to notify management if they were leaving home to visit the doctor or go to the pharmacy. (Thirty percent of the workforce with the highest sick-leave rate will still be subject to those rules.) "It includes a fresh-start approach," he said, under which absences in past years will not be counted against employees who take sick leave.

Perhaps the most significant breakthrough in this area was his winning the right for employees summoned to Step 1 disciplinary hearings to be paid for their time there if the original charges were not sustained. Not paying them for that time, Mr. Toussaint said, made supervisors more likely to hit employees with arbitrary charges, since management suffered no financial cost from having to replace the worker while he was at a hearing. Now, he added, "If they have an interest in watching their costs, they will be judicious about how many hearings they hold."

Another reform that has the immediate supervisor deciding on whether to discipline an employee carries a mutual benefit, Mr. Toussaint said. "It allows the supervisor greater discretion. And if he cuts you some slack, you owe him and you can't get in his face every time he says something to you. It humanizes the relationship."

One of the more-startling facts about the 15,000 cases in which transit workers faced discipline over the past year, according to Mr. Toussaint, is that 60 percent of those cases involved alleged time and attendance abuses, and 90 percent of those stemmed from NYC Transit's sick-leave policy.

'Cost Transit, Too'

"We showed that they had not benefited [from that policy]; that employee availability had not improved with the increasing volume of discipline," Mr. Toussaint said. "And they were spending an increasing amount of money—and we were, too—on lawyers and arbitrators."

Among the reforms in that area are an extension of the period, from three days to 30, in which employees can provide a doctor's note or other documentation of an illness or injury, and the elimination of cases that were brought simply because an employee had spent extended time on NYC Transit's sick-control list.

Mr. Toussaint said he told MTA officials, "The rip didn't work—try incentives," in convincing them to implement a policy under which employees who take no sick days in a year can receive two days' payment, and those with just one sick day can receive an extra day's pay for that year.

Unfair Accident Policy

Another sore point in the disciplinary process was that Bus Operators faced charges for any accident, regardless of whether they were at fault. Citing as an example cases where bicyclists ran into buses, some of them sitting at stops, Mr. Toussaint said, "I have operators who have been fighting a warning on their records for three years because they felt insulted, and so they refused to accept even a slap on the wrist."

The new contract provides that Bus Operators involved in an accident deemed "preventable" will not face discipline if they had no other such accidents in the previous 12 months, instead either reviewing the incident with a supervisor or undergoing retraining as a preventive step. Persons in that situation will not have their promotional opportunities affected by a single incident in that period.

In cases of major accidents involving serious injury or property damage of more than $15,000 that are deemed preventable, Local 100 gained the right to appeal such determinations to an arbitrator agreed to by both sides, with hearings to begin within 90 days of the finding and a decision to be rendered within 15 days of the hearing's conclusion.

To address union concerns on safety that were highlighted by the deaths of two track workers within 48 hours last month, the MTA agreed to a contract provision permitting employees or work gangs to formally protest conditions they believe are unsafe. If their supervisors disagree with their judgment, a manager will be called in for a final ruling. Employees who don't comply with his ruling will face discipline, but so will any supervisor or manager, the contract states, who "fails to correct a valid safety condition."

'Bind Members to Jobs'

The changes in areas ranging from safety and discipline to the added health-benefit funding and new money to provide child care and upgraded skills training, Mr. Toussaint said, "will give our members a sense of more connectiveness to the job. We hope there's a new relationship with the MTA where people buy into their responsibility to deliver service because they've been shown they're appreciated."

And although opposition to the contract within the union is developing based primarily on the wage terms—most specifically, the lack of a raise in its first year—Mr. Toussaint predicted the deal would be approved by at the least "a healthy margin." He noted that members indicated in a survey last spring that they placed their highest priority on maintaining adequate health benefits and what he called "dignity and respect" issues.

He cited the plight of Traffic Checkers, a small segment within the 35,000-member union, but one that felt particularly exploited because of a previous contract provision that guaranteed them between zero and 25 hours per week.

"Whether you got zero or five or 25 was up to supervision," Mr. Toussaint said. "That system fed a real classic plantation," which he viewed in racial terms because 99 percent of those in the title are people of color and 75 percent of them are women. Work was doled out in a fashion similar to the old dock-worker shape-ups, and some employees would sleep at the work location the night before, hoping to ingratiate themselves by being available well before shifts began the next morning.

"The MTA heard the message," he said, speaking of the rank and file in general. "And we appreciated that."

Media's Icy Blast

Not so much, however, that he gave them any indication that addressing those issues would assure them of no strike. The union's December 7 strike-authorization vote unleashed a torrent of media criticism, some of it clearly over the top. The most-blatant offender in this regard was the *New York Post*, which accused Mr. Toussaint of conducting a "neo-socialistic jihad" against the city and proposed that he be put "on ice." Alarmed at how this latter editorializing might fire up some deranged soul, the union increased security around Mr. Toussaint and at its offices.

But the "outside interference" he found most objectionable, he said, came in the form of the city's announcement four days before the contract expired that it would be going into court seeking penalties that would start at $25,000 per day against employees and double with each day on strike.

"Brother Bloomberg was doing what he felt he had to do, but that was a bit on the heavy-handed side," Mr. Toussaint said. "Our stance [on a possible walkout] was not pegged to the fines and injunctions. I had to make the determination as to whether what was available to us on the table would have warranted a strike, and whether the public would have perceived it as reasonable."

He continued, "There was one moment when I lost my composure, and I told the mayor to shut up. I took a deep breath and I gulped and I swallowed, and it still came out."

The night before the contract was to expire, the MTA finally moved off its offer of no raises without accompanying productivity, proposing a pay freeze in the first year, a $1,000 bonus in the second year, and a 2-percent raise in the final year of an agreement.

This fell so far short of what Mr. Toussaint thought his members would accept, said his special labor counsel, Basil Paterson, that "we suggested that they not make that offer public because we thought it was incendiary."

'Kept Up Momentum'

Mr. Toussaint said he believed it was "a blunder" on the MTA's part not to improve on its wage offer prior to the Sunday midnight dead-line he had set.

"I could have stopped the discussion at 10 o'clock and said, 'Put wages on the table or you're going to have problems at 12 o'clock.' But I didn't want to stop the progress and the momentum after they had made really big moves on noneconomic issues.

"And," he added, "the issue of wages was really being decided away from the table." He was referring to decisions he believes were being made by people close to Governor Pataki, a feeling borne out by the fact that the next wage offer came not from the MTA's chief negotiator, Gary Dellaverson, but in a one-on-one meeting with Mr. Kalikow, who was appointed to that post by Mr. Pataki. Mr. Kalikow's unwillingness to move off the no-wage-hike proposal for the first year over several hours of conversation, Mr. Toussaint said, was what briefly led him to believe he might have to ask his board for a strike vote. But then some sleep and a timely phone call got the talks moving again.

Offered Other Options

Much of the next few hours was consumed by proposals by the union that provided sustained money to employees in the form of step-pay-ments or longevity differential increases rather than a pay raise in the first year. These gambits were rebuffed, and Mr. Toussaint subsequently kept his own counsel to such an extent that when one union official was told to check out of the Hyatt, he surmised it meant a strike was imminent. But the MTA had finally agreed to the $1,000 bonus, plus 3-percent raises in the second and third years of the proposed pact.

For the average Local 100 member, the bonus was equivalent to what would have been received from a raise of just over 2 percent. But the money would evaporate for salary and pension purposes after this year, making it particularly attractive to management, which using a standard 10-year costing model puts a value on the payment of just .2 percent.

Mr. Toussaint wasn't thrilled about this, just as he had some misgivings about the terms under which the MTA's bus division covering Manhattan and the Bronx would be merged with its operation for Brooklyn and Queens. He was convinced, however, that this was as far as the MTA would go, and he believed the advantages in other areas of the deal far outweighed the negatives of those provisions.

A Surprising Calm

If anything surprised him about the emotionally charged negotiations, Mr. Toussaint said, it was that, except for the moment when he rudely rebuked Mr. Bloomberg and the time after he left the talks early last Monday morning believing they had reached a dead end, "throughout I felt extremely calm." He yielded to neither the outside pressures to settle cheap nor the temptation to overreact to management's reluctance to put money on the table for raises.

"If they thought he was going to cave, they found he wasn't," said Mr. Paterson. "I think he is a very impressive man with a remarkable memory and has a power of persuasion among his members without raising his voice. When you see him, you're not pushing him around and you're not frightening him. There may be a churning going on at some point, but you don't see it."

Mr. Toussaint expressed annoyance about the criticism of the deal from some of his former comrades in the New Directions wing of the union. He was asked whether they hadn't yet grasped that it was more difficult to accomplish some bargaining goals than it was to pick at the shortcomings from outside, as he himself was doing just three years ago.

Mr. Toussaint demurred. "You can do anything if you have the political strength to make things happen," he said.

The World v. Mr. Toussaint

(February 3, 2006)

"Sobering" was the word Roger Toussaint used January 24 in discussing the vote four days earlier by Transport Workers Union Local 100 members rejecting the contract he brought back to them after a three-day strike. "Just thinking through the impact of the vote, the perceptions of the membership, where we are in the labor movement."

The weekend that followed must have been a brutal one, even if he hadn't read the *Post* editorial about him that began "What a jerk," or the pronouncement by Baruch College political analyst Doug Muzzio that Mr. Toussaint had "lost control of his union. This is not a slap on the wrist. It's a punch in the face." Mr. Toussaint is not given to public displays of anguish, however—certainly not in front of reporters. And the humiliation implicit in having members reject—even if by just seven votes—the contract he presented them as the just reward of standing up by walking out did not change him in that regard.

Surrounded by Alligators

"I think as time has elapsed, I'm in a more-comfortable place mentally," he said during a 90-minute interview in his office at Local 100. "My Monday was better than my Saturday and Sunday. My Tuesday was better than my Monday."

Even so, to paraphrase the last Local 100 president to lead a strike, the late John Lawe, Mr. Toussaint was still up to his ears in alligators with no clear path to safety. Since the pact's defeat he had sought to deflect responsibility for the rejection in the direction of Governor Pataki, Metropolitan Transportation Authority Labor Relations Director Gary Dellaverson, his media critics, and the dissidents within Local 100, all of whom he accused of either bad faith or collaborating in a disinformation campaign that minimized the gains that the terms provided.

He even argued that some of the 11,000 union members who didn't vote on the contract may have believed their nonparticipation would count in favor of the deal, citing a practice he said was employed by Local 100 until the ratification vote following the 1980 strike. (Arnold Cherry, a driving force behind the 1980 walkout, said Mr. Toussaint had bought into an urban legend that many transit workers of that era believed. "It was an impression of the membership, but it wasn't actual," he said, explaining that sizable votes in favor of the contracts of that era resulted from Local 100 presidents turning out big margins from their stronghold in the Manhattan and Bronx Surface Transit Operating Authority.)

The Local 100 leader's rationales obscured one potentially ominous sign for Mr. Toussaint's political future: his members did not have enough confidence in his judgment to ignore the chatter from all sides against the contract and take him on faith when he told them it was a good deal.

"The contract was a successful conclusion of the strike," Mr. Toussaint insisted. "Even with the concession [members having to pay 1.5 percent of their health premiums], there was enough to construct a contract settlement and get our troops out of harm's way."

Noel Acevedo, a former ally who unsuccessfully challenged Mr. Toussaint's reelection in 2003, disagreed, saying the health premium contribution would have established "a precedent that we don't want for the current workers. And the fact that we went on strike raised people's expectations" about how good the contract terms should be.

Delay Let Opposition Mobilize

By one account, during the last two weeks of the ratification process, Mr. Toussaint was putting in 16-hour days traveling to work sites to preach the deal's virtues. Even with that schedule, which he adhered to on weekends as well, he couldn't get to every site by himself or answer questions that cropped up after his visits when union dissidents picked at key provisions of the agreement.

"He had lots of bodies out there against him, and his own staff didn't have enough information to answer some of the questions about the contract," one union official said. That was where Mr. Toussaint's fractious relations with one-time allies wound up costing him: activists who three years earlier could have been counted on to help sell the deal, using both their knowledge of its details and their influence within their shops, too often this time were leading the opposition. And by stretching out the vote so that it was concluded more than three weeks after the deal was reached, he allowed his enemies ample time to mobilize against it.

One example cited by several past and present union officials of a former supporter haunting him was John Samuelsen, an activist in the Track Division who had been the Local 100 acting vice president of Maintenance of Way until a falling-out with Mr. Toussaint last month. Two days after Mr. Samuelsen joined a half dozen officials in the Track Division in signing a December 8 letter asking Mr. Toussaint to shelve negotiations on the sale of the union's headquarters until a contract was secured, the Local 100 leader fired him.

'Too Many Enemies'

"He made one too many enemies," said Alan Saly, the former managing editor of the union's newspaper, the *TWU Express*. "Samuelsen turned around and actively campaigned against the contract. In this case it was personal: I think a lot of people just decided that the glass was half empty rather than half full. They were probably foolish to turn [the contract] down, but that's how they felt."

Mr. Toussaint said there were signs that many union members had been struck by morning-after remorse. "We're getting some calls for revotes" on the pact, he said. "The elation [at the deal's rejection] has given way to being stunned and then into fear and, by Monday, anger." He brushed off the suggestion that firing Mr. Samuelsen for his dissent on the building sale was a tactical error in the context of getting the contract approved. He accused Mr. Samuelsen of raising the building sale as a red herring to officially launch a campaign for Local 100's presidency that he had begun contemplating 18 months ago.

Mr. Toussaint said Mr. Samuelsen's duplicity could be seen in the fact that he had sent copies of the letter regarding the building sale to this newspaper and other media outlets before giving him a copy.

Mr. Samuelsen responded that he has made no decision on running for president, although he acknowledged that he intended "to oppose Roger and his slate" in some capacity. He said the stimulus for running for higher office came 12 months ago, not 18, and the source of it was a request from the former vice president of Maintenance of Way, Julio Rivera, whom he called "Roger's right-hand man."

Claims Alliance Sought

According to Mr. Samuelsen, Mr. Rivera approached him, said Mr. Toussaint did not plan to seek a third term, and that if Mr. Samuelsen supported Local 100 Secretary-Treasurer Ed Watt to replace him, Mr. Toussaint would back one of his allies, Patrick Lynch, in an election for the Maintenance of Way vice presidency. Mr. Samuelsen said he made no commitment at the time because "there was a lot of opposition to the notion of an Ed Watt presidency."

Mr. Toussaint scoffed at this explanation, saying he had never told anyone within the union that he wouldn't seek reelection.

Mr. Toussaint cast his clash with Mr. Samuelsen as an act of principle over political expediency, accusing his former ally of "trying to blackmail me" by raising the building-sale issue just a week before the original deadline for getting a new contract.

The practical effect, however, according to an official generally aligned with Mr. Toussaint, was to leave the Local 100 president "really isolated in his own union. With John Samuelsen against him, he has opposition broader than anything Sonny Hall or John Lawe ever faced."

Mr. Samuelsen traced Mr. Toussaint's troubles, which he called operational as well as political, back to his 2003 reelection, when five union vice presidents on his slate were defeated. From the outset, he has clashed with their replacements and is a defendant in a lawsuit they filed, and Mr. Samuelsen maintained that Mr. Toussaint "never recovered from that" weakening of his control of the upper echelon of the union's board.

One official who's dealt with Mr. Toussaint during his five years in office calls him "the most-paranoid guy I know." To some degree, the Local 100 leader's suspicions are reasonable: remnants of the union's old guard, including Mr. Hall, the ex-Local 100 president and retired head of the International TWU, have actively opposed him and made his life particularly difficult when the last two contract deadlines loomed.

No Dale Carnegie

But Mr. Toussaint has compounded his internal problems by taking harsh action against numerous former allies, with Mr. Samuelsen's firing from the vice president's post merely the latest example. He has justified the personnel moves by accusing those he has forced out of disloyalty or laziness, but the net effect has been to wind up running the union largely on the strength of his own will.

That approach failed him in the contract vote. Mr. Toussaint said the combination of harsh media critiques of the deal and the vocal opposition of union dissidents had a corrosive effect on his rank and file "even though membership knows better. They got to know better."

But the newspaper editorial statements he cited, "Raid on the pension," "Made out like bandits," should have actually made it easier to get the deal approved, since they contended that in securing a refund of past pension payments by about 20,000 members, Mr. Toussaint had bested the MTA in the post-strike bargaining.

"I think Roger likes to think transit workers are easily swayed by people, and that's not the case," Mr. Samuelsen said. The drawbacks to the deal were significant enough, he claimed, that if it hadn't been for "the relentless effort [to sell the deal] on Roger's part, it would have been a landslide against the contract."

He cited the health premiums concession as a large factor, notwithstanding Mr. Toussaint's claim that it was offset by other benefits, including the guarantee of lifetime health coverage for retirees and the awarding of Martin Luther King Jr.'s birthday as a paid holiday.

A Source of Envy?

Even the pension refund of up to $14,000—the source of the howling begun by editorial writers and taken up by Governor Pataki—was a mixed blessing from a political standpoint, Mr. Samuelsen said. Referring to the issue that caused the strike, the MTA's insistence on an inferior pension plan for future employees, he said, "The notion that we would not accept a two-tier pension because it would create division was a good one."

But in obtaining the pension refund as the sweetener that was supposed to make it easier to digest the requirement that transit workers pay a piece of their health premiums, Mr. Samuelsen said, Mr. Toussaint did nothing to satisfy the 10,000-plus union members who were not eligible for the refunds because they had not made additional contributions to the retirement system prior to 2001. "He succeeded in negotiating language that did bring division to the union" between those who would have collected and those who would not, Mr. Samuelsen said.

Although numerous workers in interviews with reporters cited the health premiums as their prime objection to the deal, one person involved in the talks said he believed the real issue for many of them was that the deduction was to be based on total earnings, including overtime.

Revising that provision so that the premium was assessed only against base salary might be all that would be needed to get the deal ratified by a comfortable margin, but the MTA would surely insist on savings somewhere else to make up for the resulting reduction in worker health contributions.

Mr. Toussaint said that when bargaining resumes, he will insist on a substantive change of that sort. He noted that after a 1992 contract deal made by Mr. Hall was rejected by union members, the agreement was subsequently ratified with just a couple of small tweaks: a $1,000 bonus was replaced by a 2-percent raise, and a productivity program was revamped to distribute a portion of the money saved to all employees rather than just those responsible for the savings.

'Won't B.S. My Members'
The Local 100 leader argued that this merely amounted to reshaping the terms rather than improving them, although the revised contract was easily ratified. "I'm doing labor in a different way than it's been done," Mr. Toussaint said. "If you're asking me to b.s. my members by turning a package around but having the same value, that isn't happening."

There is little to suggest, however, that Mr. Toussaint has nearly the leverage he enjoyed prior to the strike. A second walkout would not have as great an impact with the Christmas shopping season passed. It also would be tough to present sympathetically to the public, since at this point Mr. Toussaint's problem stems not from alleged MTA intransigence but rather his own members questioning his judgment about what constituted a fair contract.

The Local 100 leader said the dissidents within the union kept expectations unreasonably high and "it had more impact than I hoped on members' confidence. These guys want to be in a fantasy world where you go into the ring and you come out of the fight looking like Pretty Boy Floyd. But you don't play with strikes. Don't go there unless you have to, because you can't afford to lose a strike. That was the lesson of PATCO," referring to the union that was decertified after President Reagan in 1981 fired the nation's striking Air Traffic Controllers.

'Not Catering to Tribes'

Mr. Toussaint continued, "The labor movement's inability to respond to PATCO led to two decades of concessionary contracts. We could have gotten our heads handed to us; instead we established [the rejected deal] as an issue of perfecting our benefits package."

Members who complained that the health-premium charge was financing gains that in the short term benefited only segments of the rank and file, whether it involved a maternity benefit for female workers or the retiree health coverage and pension refund that many younger workers believed had no relevance to them, were missing the bigger picture, Mr. Toussaint said.

"You can [negotiate] as a union or you can do it in tribes," he said. "You decide whether you are a union that takes care of your retirees, or you tie them to a tree in the forest and let the animals get them. You decide whether you're going to take care of your [future members], or you're going to say, 'Eff 'em, we don't represent them yet.'"

"The setback here has broader implications. We're going into a period when health benefits are going to be under attack—as well as pensions—and we're deciding the future of the labor movement in the city and the state."

He seemed unnaturally calm about his own future as president of Local 100, considering how important contracts tend to be in deciding union elections. Given the number of prominent union officials who sought to torpedo the contract, it would seem that his best hope would be that several of them challenge his reelection and split the anti-Toussaint vote. While he surmised, "They're going to all want to put their hats in the ring," he added that just as "all of the motley forces have coalesced against this contract," he anticipated that they would seek to unite behind a single opponent this fall.

Sees Hall Calling Shot

"Sonny Hall will put it all together," Mr. Toussaint said, convinced, as are more than a few other past and present TWU officials, that the retired International TWU president is still trying to mastermind a coup. "The ultra-leftists are in bed with the conservative old guard."

The most-serious potential challenger is likely to be Barry Roberts, the vice president of the MaBSTOA Division of Local 100, who is also an International TWU vice president and was among those who during the strike urged members to vote on the MTA's final offer.

Mr. Toussaint is convinced a new contract will be put in place by election time, but others aren't so sure. Under the best of circumstances, government agencies don't look to sweeten the pot in a way that will cost them anything when a contract is voted down, for the simple reason that it would invite unions to always reject the initial contract deal.

And Mr. Toussaint's relationship with top MTA officials is 180 degrees south of the best of circumstances. "They hate Roger," one of his allies said. "Gary Dellaverson would shoot him if it was legal. They won't do anything to help Roger if there's no threat of a strike."

That much became clear when the MTA filed an arbitration petition January 25 in which it indicated that numerous key demands that it took off the table after the strike—including an inferior pension tier for new members that actually can't be considered by arbitrators unless both sides consent—are back in play.

If the contract winds up in arbitration, it's possible the panel will not have rendered a decision by the time voting in the Local 100 officer elections begins in the latter part of November.

Urges Big-Picture View

That would make Mr. Toussaint even more vulnerable, but he insisted that members ought to focus on where the union is going, regardless of the status of the contract. "We have tried to be for true, genuine reform," he said. "And so a big question in the election is, should we give the union back to the old guard, not so much in terms of ethnicity but in terms of the decisions that got us into the position we're in?"

He supplied his own answer and a prediction about his future that defies the signal of the contract rejection. "If you think there's a 50-50 support for me because of the contract [veto], you're wrong," Mr. Toussaint said. "There are those who look at what the alternatives are."

Did he feel any uncertainty about his chances? "No."

Then again, Mr. Toussaint predicted his contract would be "strongly ratified."

Hard to Be Toussaint in City

(December 29, 2006)

We were walking out of a TV studio early this year, talking about how Roger Toussaint had managed to complicate his reelection chances at Transport Workers Union Local 100, when one of my colleagues said, "Yeah, Roger's a hair-shirt sometimes, but the labor movement needs guys like him."

He was right on both counts, but a diminishing percentage of Local 100 members deemed Mr. Toussaint indispensable in the recently concluded union election.

On the one hand, they gave him what he needed most: a third three-year term as president. On the other, he actually received less support than the contract he brought out of last year's three-day transit strike that was rejected by a seven-vote margin in January.

Going the Wrong Way

When Mr. Toussaint was first elected in December 2000, he got 61 percent of the vote and his running mates won five of the seven vice president seats. Three years later, he was reelected with 60 percent but his opponents captured five of the seven VP slots. This time, the Local 100 leader got just 45 percent of the vote, and although his slate won back at least one vice presidency (another will be decided in a runoff election), his One Union slate lost seven seats on the Local 100 executive board.

This downward trend, even as he has further taken on a Metropolitan Transportation Authority management that his rank and file clearly views as oppressive, is explained by two factors: reservations about the contract he brought back and Mr. Toussaint's truculence beginning to wear thin as the results at the bargaining table fall short of the fiery rhetoric.

The toll of the past year—from vilification by much of the media for the three-day strike, to his members' initial rejection of the contract because it required them to pay 1.5 percent of their earnings toward their health costs, to the severe financial penalties against Local 100 and his own brief jail sentence for violating the Taylor Law prohibiting public walkouts—may account for why Mr. Toussaint declined to appear before reporters after he learned that he had retained his office but with less than majority support.

Instead, his top two lieutenants, Secretary-Treasurer Ed Watt and Recording Secretary Darlyne Lawson, addressed the media, with Mr. Watt declaring, "We are going to pull this union together."

Just how is an unanswered question. My call to Mr. Toussaint last week was parried by a call from a public relations aide to this newspaper's transit reporter, Ginger Otis, to convey that the Local 100 leader believed I had strayed too far from the Church of Roger in some columns over the past year and given too much space to his opponents' beefs during the election campaign. Mr. Toussaint has made clear by now that he considers constructive criticism to be an oxymoron.

After his election three years ago, he was furious with the camp of opponent Noel Acevedo for allegedly feeding members a steady diet of disinformation and was unhappy that 40 percent of them had swallowed it. If he has been chastened by the fact that 55 percent of his rank and file voted for one of the other four candidates for president, it is not readily apparent.

Some of those who admire Mr. Toussaint despite his warts said that his flagging support does not necessarily mean that he could be deposed in the next election.

'Weathered the Storm'

"I think for the moment he sort of weathered the storm," said Josh Freeman, the City University of New York graduate school professor and labor historian who authored a well-received history of Local 100 up through the 1966 transit strike.

With nearly three years before his next election and the chance to negotiate another wage contract in the interim, Mr. Freeman said, "He's got some time to address the issues, including the high level of factionalism within the union and dissatisfaction among the rank and file. But he's got some big challenges ahead, including the financial ones, with the [$2.5 million] fines and the loss of dues checkoff" that were assessed against the union by a Brooklyn Supreme Court justice.

Bill Henning, the second vice president of Communications Workers of America Local 1180, said notwithstanding Mr. Toussaint's decline in member support, his reelection was "a very important statement that the workers of Local 100 have reaffirmed their struggle and their determination to stand up to the boss."

Expressing a view that's not uncommon among union officials throughout the city, Mr. Henning said, "There's a bureaucracy at the MTA that almost takes glee in screwing the workers," focusing more on catching them in minor infractions and denying Workers' Compensation claims than on addressing working conditions that include safety and health hazards.

"If they spent that much energy on safety," Mr. Henning said of MTA officials, "I think we'd all be better off."

Mr. Toussaint's militancy is not so much a contributing factor to the bitter relations between the union and management, Mr. Henning said, as it is a reflection of rank-and-file anger.

'Right Guy to Lead Them'

"Roger's a son of a bitch," he said, "and that job requires a son of a bitch leading them against management."

The downside of Mr. Toussaint's hard-line attitude is that it has led to clashes with numerous former supporters and their exile from his inner circle and sometimes from staff positions. His talent for alienating old allies contributed to his contract's rejection 11 months ago and might have led to his election defeat if two vice presidents with whom he repeatedly butted heads, Barry Roberts and Ainsley Stewart, had run as a team rather than fielding separate candidacies for president.

"I don't think it's simply a matter of Roger's personality," Mr. Freeman said. "There's been a long history of bus workers [Mr. Roberts's political base] having a different perspective than the workers in the subways. And there's a long history of activism and dissent in the union that predates him."

No Free-Speech Fanatic

But he acknowledged, "Toussaint does not tolerate well dissent on his executive board."

Mr. Henning, his tongue firmly in cheek, remarked, "Sometimes it's tough to take counsel from people who aren't as smart as we know we are."

Speaking more seriously, he said that often it was healthier not to have a union dominated by a single group, since that limited the extent to which voices and ideas other than the president's would be heard.

Mr. Acevedo, who was elected Local 100 recording secretary on Mr. Toussaint's ticket six years ago but then, after a falling-out, opposed him for president in 2003, said he doubted Mr. Toussaint would seek to mend the rifts with the opposition on the Local 100 board, notwithstanding Mr. Watt's statement about uniting the union.

"I don't think it's in his character to do that," he said of Mr. Toussaint. "He's not someone who believes in working by consensus. We look forward to another three years of division and persecution, because I don't have any hope that he is going to change."

Larry Hanley, a regional vice president of the Amalgamated Transit Union, argued that this is an unfair caricature. If Mr. Toussaint is sometimes abrasive, he said, it reflects the obstacles he has encountered in trying to make substance and long-term gains more palatable to members.

'He's No Dictator'

"It's easy to say that Roger's a petty dictator, but that's not true," said Mr. Hanley, who formerly headed the ATU local representing Staten Island bus drivers. "He looks at members who just don't get it, and obstructionists—from both the left and the right [wings] of the union—and the approach he's taken a lot of times is just to use the force of his will to move the union forward."

Local 100 leaders for at least two decades before Mr. Toussaint assumed office six years ago pegged contract terms to "how they looked in the next election, not how the contract looked 20 years out," Mr. Hanley said. Mr. Toussaint in negotiating his first contract had to make up a $46-million deficit in the union's health-benefits fund that was created by the previous president, Willie James, who sacrificed funding in that area to gain a 5-percent raise in the first year of a three-year pact.

'Ended Key Giveups'

Mr. Hanley said Mr. James and other past Local 100 leaders including Sonny Hall—who became Mr. Toussaint's prime nemesis until he retired as president of the International TWU—had allowed the MTA to make incursions on work rules and disciplinary procedures in return for additional raises from the belief that the union's rank and file focused primarily on salary issues rather than job conditions.

Mr. Toussaint's 2002 contract, besides making up the deficit in the health fund by agreeing to freeze wages in the first year of the three-year pact, "managed to unravel 20 years of concessionary changes," Mr. Hanley said. "But when you took that out into the field, people didn't get it. Getting the Checkers full-time [status under that deal] was a great thing, but if you're driving a bus on Flatbush Ave., you may not appreciate that."

The question remains whether Mr. Toussaint is introspective enough to have learned something from the humiliating contract defeat he suffered. The deal that emerged from the strike was uncharacteristic of a man who prides himself on trade-union principles because it included a giveback—the health-benefits contribution by members—to pay for some of the gains.

Words Haunted Him

In fact, his message to members last December 20 after the strike began included the statement, "This is a fight over whether hard work will be rewarded with a decent retirement and over the erosion or eventual elimination of health benefits for working people." While he succeeded in blunting the MTA's bid for a lesser pension tier for new employees, the health-benefits contribution he agreed to amounted to an erosion of Local 100 members' rights in that area.

Mr. Toussaint has pointed out that in return he got members continued health coverage between age 55—when they first become eligible for a full pension and are more likely to retire—and 65, when they begin receiving Medicare. He also secured a pension refund for about 22,000 members that will be worth up to $14,000 for some.

He had twice previously sought to get that refund—covering additional contributions members made between 1995 and the beginning of 2001 in return for the right to a full pension at 55 after 25 years' service—via legislation, only to have the bills vetoed by Governor Pataki, who said the refund should be negotiated with the MTA.

Considering that the MTA had agreed to support legislation to provide a refund as part of its 1999 contract deal with Mr. Toussaint's predecessor, Mr. Pataki's position seemed rooted in politics. Mr. Toussaint, after soliciting members for their contract priorities, decided to pursue the refund in last year's bargaining rather than waiting and hoping that a new governor would be more inclined to grant the refund.

Trouble down the Road?

Once his members discovered that the health-benefits contribution was the price for it, a slight majority torpedoed the deal. It was resurrected by the arbitration award issued on the same day of Mr. Toussaint's reelection, offering a short-term windfall and a long-term political headache: by the time Mr. Toussaint seeks a fourth term—if he does—the refund money will have been spent but the health-care premium payments almost surely will still be taking bites out of members' checks. (Mr. Toussaint a year ago talked about scaling back the contribution under the next contract, but given the rate at which health costs have been rising, it's hard to see the MTA being amenable.)

While the Local 100 leader has contended that the narrow contract rejection resulted from misrepresentation to union members by his political enemies, Mr. Henning said he believed that was one time when his in-house critics' charge that Mr. Toussaint is a one-man band resonated with the rank and file.

"A deal was reached by Roger and Roger alone in a 'trust-me' mode," Mr. Henning said, referring to the process by which Mr. Toussaint ended the strike and did not inform either his board or his members that paying for a portion of their health coverage was going to be the price extracted by the MTA for union gains in other areas.

'Need Faith in Members'

"The contract was seen as Roger's rather than the union's," Mr. Henning said. Asked whether Mr. Toussaint made his command decision because he believed that to consult his board would have risked prolonging the strike and producing disastrous consequences for the union, Mr. Henning replied, "I think you have to have faith in the members."

Instead, even though transit workers eventually voted strongly for the contract when Mr. Toussaint resubmitted it for consideration in April, Mr. Henning said, "The discontent was palpable in that union, some of it coming from a good place, some of it from a bad place."

The "bad place," he said, emanated from Mr. Roberts's camp, noting that as vice president of the union's division at the Manhattan and Bronx Surface Transit Operating Authority, he was the lead signer on a petition presented to Mr. Toussaint on the second day of the walkout asking that management's final pre-strike offer be submitted to the executive board for a vote. This amounted, Mr. Henning said, to "repudiating the strike" while it was still going on, making it that much harder for Mr. Toussaint to stand firm against the outside pressures from elected officials and "the louder media."

If Mr. Toussaint proved one thing during the walkout, Mr. Henning said, it was that the stringent penalties under the Taylor Law and the more-conservative political climate since the 1966 transit walkout have not made strikes by public workers an exercise in folly.

"Fifty-seven percent of the public supported these guys, so I think it would be a mistake to say that the strike is an ineffective weapon," Mr. Henning said.

Can't Strike Next Time

It's not one that Local 100 will be able to use in the next round of bargaining, since the return of its dues-checkoff rights will be conditioned on a no-strike pledge. And the moving of the current contract's expiration date forward by a month, from December 15 to January 15, means that in future bargaining the union won't have nearly the same leverage as when it could hold the Christmas shopping season hostage.

The new governor, Eliot Spitzer, is unlikely to open the MTA vault to the union, but neither is he likely to use tough-guy posturing against Local 100 to bolster his standing for national office the way Governor Pataki did both before and immediately after the strike.

Mr. Spitzer has spoken about the need to improve the relationship between the MTA and its unions, which Mr. Henning said was an encouraging and refreshing indication.

"They have to create a whole new mind-set," he said regarding the MTA. "Governor Spitzer at the head of this can send a signal, and I hope he does."

Mr. Acevedo shared that view, although he said Mr. Spitzer's call for increased productivity raised questions about whether his concern for employees extends further than getting more out of them.

Mr. Toussaint may benefit from the changes on the executive board even though he no longer can count on even two-thirds of its members for support. Whatever incursions on his power were made, the board no longer includes some of his most-prominent critics, from losing presidential candidates Barry Roberts and Ainsley Stewart to Marty Goodman and John Mooney, who were defeated as part of Mr. Stewart's slate.

Will He Reach Out?

"Will he change his style?" Mr. Hanley mused. "I think he really understands that he has to enter a different stage of leadership" to mend some of the internal rifts.

Mr. Freeman said, "It certainly would be in his interest to work with some people on the executive board who disagree with him on some issues but agree with him on others. Whether he takes that opportunity remains to be seen."

"I have confidence that the majority of people on that executive board will pull together for the benefit of the members," Mr. Henning said. "And Roger's a very strong personality, but I think he fails to adjust at his peril."

All three of them are sizing up the situation from the cool perspective that is afforded by not being part of the internal feuding that has been ingrained in Local 100's DNA for more than a decade. Within the union, even those who do not harbor Mr. Acevedo's sense of betrayal are less optimistic, saying that Mr. Toussaint's opposition will have to reach out to him if there is going to be a smoother working relationship.

One veteran of the backroom bloodletting said, "I don't think he'll function any differently."

For Toussaint, Power
Is All That's Left

(July 25, 2008)

Roger Toussaint seems determined to prove that Neil Young's line about rock stars—"It's better to burn out than to fade away"—doesn't apply to union leaders. He came to office as president of Transport Workers Union Local 100 in 2000 pledging to engage his members and once again make them a force to be reckoned with. At the midway point of his third term in office, however, his presidency is teetering between crashing disappointment and Chaplinesque farce.

Earlier this month, Local 100 members by a roughly two to one margin approved a series of changes in the union's bylaws that seem designed to strengthen Mr. Toussaint's control of its operation, which the union's Web site declared would make it "stronger, more effective, and more responsive to its members."

Sinking into Undistinguished Company

Yet the Web site doesn't explain the bylaw changes, or even list them other than by their numbers on the ballot. Fewer than 5,000 valid ballots were cast out of a membership that approaches 39,000. There is the suspicion that Veronica Montgomery-Costa, who as president of Local 372 of District Council 37 has consciously aimed to discourage member participation in union operations, could produce a larger return than that if she permitted mail ballots for her local's elections.

This is not distinguished company for Mr. Toussaint to be in. But it is a measure of how far he has fallen from the lofty plateaus he set for the union during his early days in charge. His hopes of making it a mighty force that could rekindle memories of the union under the late Michael J. Quill have disappeared in the cloud of dust from which he conducts business primarily with an eye to retaining power.

The most significant of the bylaw changes authorizes Local 100's executive board to move its election forward by six months, to next June, even though the actual counting of the ballots won't be done until December 2009.

There is a logical explanation for this change that doesn't involve voting fraud, and it was provided last week by Steve Downs, head of Local 100's Train Operator Division and a member of the union's largest fraternity: former allies of Mr. Toussaint who are now critics of his regime.

According to Mr. Downs, the move is designed to strengthen Mr. Toussaint's hand at the convention of his international union, the TWU of America, next October. The new election date will coincide with the voting for Local 100 delegates to that convention, but the delegate ballots will be counted shortly after they are cast.

Mr. Downs said that if delegate candidates loyal to Mr. Toussaint do well in that voting, it will be presumed that the Local 100 president and his running mates on the executive board have also done well. This would send a signal to top officials of the international union, he said, that Mr. Toussaint is likely to retain his presidency and so they should finally give him the ranking position in the TWU of America that he is entitled to unless they want to create a powerful enemy.

This sort of thinking, however, seems a classic example of putting the cart before the horse. If members are alienated by the screwball logic of having an early election but delaying the vote count by six months, it is less likely that the show of strength Mr. Toussaint is banking on among the delegates will actually materialize.

'What the Hell Is He Doing?'
Which was why one admirer of the Local 100 president who never drank his Kool-Aid said of the election changes, "I think the amendment itself is idiotic. My first reaction is, Jesus Christ, what the hell is he doing?"

He then added, "It's a pity. I think Roger's smart and totally hon-est, monetarily, and yet he could fight a cockroach on what territory they're going to walk on."

John Samuelsen, a fallen-away ally who is expected to run against Mr. Toussaint next year, agreed with Mr. Downs's theory about the Local 100 leader's hope of sending a message to the international, speculating that he rejected the more-palatable way of doing it—by also counting the ballots for president next June—because that would put too much on the line. Referring to International President James Little, Mr. Samuelsen said of Mr. Toussaint's objective, "He's got to show Little that he can win [in order] for Little to include him on the team. If the ballots were counted in June and he lost, he would be of no use to Little."

But one quirk of the TWU of America's governance system is that a local president who holds international office can keep it even if he loses a local election. Terms on the international executive board run for four years, where Local 100's last for three, and Mr. Downs noted that next year is one of the rare ones in which elections for both are being held.

On the one hand, he said, Mr. Toussaint wanted to send a signal based on the delegate vote; on the other, the Local 100 president did not want anyone getting wind of the executive board results early if they were unfavorable to him and his running mates.

There are two reasons for that, Mr. Downs said: "They believe that if people find out that they've lost their offices, either they won't do their jobs well for the last part of their terms or management won't respect them or take them seriously during that time."

Of course, he added, "You would avoid either of those problems if you waited until November [when nominations would normally be taken and ballots mailed out] to hold your election."

Ally: 'Roger's in Control'

But one of Mr. Toussaint's dwindling band of supporters in the labor movement dismissed suggestions that the meager ballot return showed how little sway he still holds over his members and that the six-month delay between election and vote count would further antagonize the rank and file.

"Roger's in control," he argued. "Among those who are eligible to vote, he is going to be very difficult to defeat unless he totally screws up the contract," referring to upcoming wage talks for a successor agreement to the Local 100 wage pact that expires in mid-January.

But the qualifier he attached to his claim, "among those who are eligible to vote," speaks volumes about the loss of faith in Mr. Toussaint within the larger rank and file.

Still Reeling from Strike Fallout

Both financially and spiritually, Local 100 has still not recovered from the aftershocks of its December 2005 transit strike. The loss of automatic dues deduction from members' paychecks beginning in June of last year, one of the primary penalties for violating the Taylor Law, has forced Local 100 to ask members to voluntarily remit the money. Hard feelings that lingered from the contract reached after that strike—most notably, the requirement for the first time that members pay a portion of the cost of their health benefits—produced a less-than-ringing response.

The last time Local 100 disclosed the number of members who were up to date on their dues payments last year, only 17,449 were considered to be in "good standing." Mr. Samuelsen said this year there has been a steady growth in the number of members who were fully paid up, which was why 26,000 ballots were mailed out for the bylaw vote.

Even based on that number rather than the total membership, the return for that vote was shockingly low. The most votes on any of the 16 bylaw changes was 4,625, but Mr. Downs said 4,651 valid ballots were actually cast—about 18 percent of those eligible by virtue of being in good standing. The 3,150 who approved Amendment 1 on the ballot—the largest margin for any of the bylaw changes, in this case requiring at least one membership meeting a year—amounts to just over 12 percent of the members in good standing and about 8 percent of the total membership. "The key thing here," Mr. Downs remarked, "is most of the members didn't really care, or think it mattered whether they voted or not."

'Convinced Them Not to Vote'

Mr. Samuelsen put it even more harshly. "It's a testament to the damage he's done to the union," he said of Mr. Toussaint. "He's convinced the members that it's not worth it for them to vote."

He cited Mr. Toussaint's previous attempt to hold a revote on the 2005 wage contract after it was rejected by just seven votes out of more than 22,000 cast and his nullifying several elections in Local 100 divisions based on the claim that candidates were ineligible to run because they were either delinquent on dues payments or had urged members not to pay their dues (something Mr. Toussaint accused Mr. Samuelsen of in a trumped-up move to deny him a shop steward position). "Guys say, 'Why should I vote—the guys I elected are still working here with their tools,'" Mr. Samuelsen said.

After he negotiated his first contract as union president in late 2002, Mr. Toussaint bristled when only 60 percent of those who cast ballots—11,757—voted in favor of its terms. He said following the ratification count in January 2003 that it showed how much work he had to do to overcome the interference from his political enemies both within the local and in the international.

But a determination at that time to convince members to embrace his trade-union ideals has been replaced by a cynical approach to the problems that have arisen since dues-checkoff rights were revoked. In some cases, critics of Mr. Toussaint have been declared to be in bad standing even when they produced documentary evidence that they were up to date on dues payments.

Smaller Electorate, Bigger Win

And the shrunken electorate afforded him the kind of victory margins on the bylaw vote that he had not seen in more than five years—besides the rejection of his post-strike contract, Mr. Toussaint won reelection in December 2006 with just 45 percent of the vote, benefiting from a splitting of the opposition support among four challengers.

But at what price? A top official at another union, who spoke on condition that he not be identified, said Local 100 was not the only large union to experience relatively low returns from a mail ballot.

But asked whether the standards Mr. Toussaint had previously established for membership participation didn't make these results more glaring, he acknowledged, "I would be concerned if I was the TWU leadership to have such a low turnout. But part of it is a product of all the fighting within the union. It's a puzzlement to me why things are so contentious there."

The simplest answer may be that it's because Mr. Toussaint seems to thrive on combat, and resistance to his bruising management style has grown as a series of decisions he made over the past three years have wound up unhappily.

Building Sale Controversies

During his first contract negotiation in 2002, Mr. Toussaint found himself distracted by the machinations of then-International President Sonny Hall, a former Local 100 president who had stayed heavily involved in its operation until Mr. Toussaint took over, and his allies. Besides teaching him to watch his back, that experience should have been enough for Mr. Toussaint to want to avoid any diversions for internal battles before the 2005 talks, when Governor Pataki and the Metropolitan Transportation Authority leadership were being egged on by newspaper editorial boards to take a hard line with his union.

Shortly before the talks got serious, Mr. Toussaint decided to sell Local 100's West End Avenue headquarters for a reported $60 million. Mr. Samuelsen, who was still an ally of his and was a paid Local 100 staffer, questioned whether the transaction should be put on hold until after the contract was settled. Mr. Toussaint, in a reprise of his response countless times when a subordinate questioned his judgment, sent Mr. Samuelsen packing.

His handling of the matter came back to bite Mr. Toussaint twice. After the three-day strike produced a tentative contract deal, Mr. Samuelsen was among those most upset about the provision that required members to pay 1.5 percent of their total earnings—including overtime wages—toward their health coverage. With no reason to hold his tongue out of loyalty to Mr. Toussaint, he vociferously opposed the deal and is likely to have swayed a lot more than the seven votes that torpedoed it. Then, earlier this year, the union's headquarters, which it still occupies, was sold for $30 million more than Local 100 received for it a couple of years ago. It's not the only Manhattan property to be flipped quickly at a big profit, but the political ammunition this gave the anti-Toussaint faction of the union was fortified by the fact that the union still has no permanent home and lost a tax break it would have been entitled to had it purchased a new building within a year of the old one's sale.

Strike Rationale Dubious

Mr. Toussaint's decision to lead a strike continues to mystify, given that, unlike Mr. Quill at the time he led the 1966 transit walkout, he had the right to binding arbitration if he believed management was not bargaining in good faith. The rationale given by his supporters at the time—that asking for arbitration would have meant the MTA never again had to take a strike threat seriously—does not hold up under scrutiny. Local 100 in the past had gone to arbitration rather than risk a repeat of the disastrous 1980 transit strike, but that had not prevented Mr. Toussaint from credibly posing a strike threat in both 2002 and 2005.

Arbitration might have limited what he could have won for his members. But at the same time, it would have been an unlikely venue for the MTA to gain the right to impose less-generous pension or health-benefit plans for new employees, as it was seeking to do. Given that it already seemed likely at that point in late 2005 that Eliot Spitzer was going to be elected governor the following November and was expected to take a less-hostile position toward the union through his MTA chairman, the most-prudent course would have been to try the union's luck in arbitration and press for more-ambitious gains after the change of administrations.

Took the Bait, Then Pulled Back

Mr. Toussaint, however, feeling provoked—and not without justification in believing that—took the bait and led the walkout. Three days in, realizing that if he kept his members out and Scrooged the Christmas shopping season he would be facing ruin in the courts for violating the Taylor Law and have scant public support, he agreed to have his members return to work while a deal was reached with the help of mediators.

He emerged with a 37-month contract that provided 10.5 percent in raises and a number of small but important gains in other fringe-benefit areas. But he agreed to a major concession in requiring that members for the first time partly fund their own health coverage, and for much of the rank and file, this outweighed the gains in other areas. What particularly galled them was that the formula for deducting their premiums was tied to overall earnings rather than base salary.

In Mr. Toussaint's eyes, this was a necessary price to pay rather than forcing all future members to accept an inferior health plan compared to the one for those already on the job. Among his rank and file, however, the aim of going out on strike and incurring the salary losses required of them under the Taylor Law was to avoid givebacks, not spread them among the entire workforce.

So they narrowly voted down his deal, only to have its essential terms imposed in the arbitration that resulted. Arbitrator George Nicolau was constrained in crafting an award in ways that he wouldn't have been if the union had proceeded immediately to a third-party resolution without having already negotiated a deal.

Four months after the strike, Mr. Toussaint briefly went to jail for leading it. During an interview with NY1 anchor Dominic Carter while in custody, Mr. Toussaint was at his reflective best, talking about the impact that unions accepting lesser benefit plans for new members would have and asking, "Is that a future that we want for America— that we're harming our children?"

Back to Burning Bridges

But once he was back on the street, Mr. Toussaint turned his attention to burning more bridges with those who dared to question him. It became clear to me that the problem went beyond a union leader holding his subordinates to high standards and being unwilling to tolerate any failure to meet them 14 months ago, a few days before Local 100 was to lose its dues-checkoff rights.

An editorial appeared in this newspaper urging members to pay their dues, regardless of any hard feelings they might harbor toward Mr. Toussaint for the strike or other reasons. I got a call that afternoon from a representative of Local 100's outside public relations firm, Sunshine Sachs, not to comment on the editorial but to castigate me for running a letter to the editor from one of Mr. Toussaint's critics that the PR rep claimed was chock-full of distortions. When I suggested that we'd be happy to run a rebuttal letter, he responded by questioning the newspaper's ethics in running a letter without vetting it first for accuracy.

It occurred to me then, because I didn't think this young man was hectoring me on his own initiative, that Mr. Toussaint had gone off the deep end.

It wasn't even the absence of gratitude about the editorial, though that was notable. It was the notion that the letters page, the most-democratic part of any newspaper, should be cleansed of any opinions whose accuracy could not be certified.

Cursing the Darkness

Since then, the union's manner of officially communicating with this newspaper has settled into a peculiar routine. Our transit reporter, Ari Paul, calls with questions, which the Sunshine Boy refuses to answer; then, when stories appear noting the lack of response, he contacts Mr. Paul to squirt cider in his ear about the unbalanced nature of the articles and all the details he supposedly got wrong. It might seem simpler to try to affect that balance by answering the questions than to gripe about the stories after the fact, but Mr. Toussaint's vision may be too grand for logic to enter the discussion.

That appears to be at the root of the continued loss of dues-checkoff rights, nearly 14 months after the penalty was imposed—compared to the four-month loss the union suffered for the 11-day strike in 1980. Rather than petition a judge for relief on the grounds of economic harm, Mr. Toussaint is pursuing an appeal—on First Amendment grounds—of a judge's ruling last November denying checkoff restoration after he and the rest of his board refused to sign affidavits saying they would not strike again.

It's a noble fight to be sure, on principle. But the likelihood of another Local 100 strike when the current contract expires is less than great, for the simple reason that few union leaders call for job actions if they know that most of their members aren't going to follow them out to the picket line. And so it's hard to see what prerogative Mr. Toussaint is preserving, other than the right not to be humbled by saying you've done something wrong and learned your lesson.

'Shut Up' Still Echoes

He could argue the unfairness of the continued penalty, particularly since the MTA stated in court that the union should be given auto-matic dues-deduction rights again on a conditional basis. And so Mr. Toussaint might be justified in believing that the penalty has been prolonged solely to satisfy a grudge held against him by Mayor

Bloomberg, who surely realizes the chances of another transit strike six months from now are negligible.

Of course, Mr. Toussaint gave the mayor reason to be less than charitable toward him long before the transit strike disrupted life in the city: three years earlier, during a tense contract negotiation, the Local 100 leader responded to a reporter's question about statements Mr. Bloomberg had made by saying that the mayor should "shut up."

The remark was replayed numerous times on local television stations and embellished Mr. Toussaint's reputation as a tough guy who wouldn't bend the knee to anybody.

The image still holds nearly six years later. It has come with a large tab, however: a union that is hemorrhaging money while undoubtedly forced to dip into the proceeds from the sale of its headquarters, and a leadership that treats the spirited dissent that has long been a part of its tradition (with Mr. Toussaint in a previous life as an ordinary track worker once proudly partaking) as treason and grounds for removal from office.

It is a union where deep dissatisfaction among more than 10,000 members has left them, however wrongheadedly, withholding their dues and ineligible to vote, and where more than 20,000 who retain eligibility didn't bother to exercise that right regarding bylaws that radically altered the union's election process.

Not the Union He Promised

This wasn't what Mr. Toussaint had in mind early in his tenure, when he spoke of restoring Local 100's reputation as a great, fighting union. Nor does the current state of the union square with his remarks early in 2003 about members who had complained that, by addressing the most-pressing needs of some segments of Local 100, he had done more for them than the rest of the rank and file. "When you're voting," Mr. Toussaint said in an interview then, "you have to decide whether you're part of a union or a tribal association."

The bylaw vote suggests he can count on the support of 8 percent of his members. He may believe that's enough of a base to perpetuate his power. It's not enough to pass for a union, however.

What Killed Roger Rebel?
A Self-Inflicted Wound

(December 18, 2009)

In the 1974 movie *The Gambler*, the title character, Axel Freed, is asked by a bookmaker how he, a Harvard-educated college professor, could have gotten himself $44,000 in debt with his betting.

Axel, played by James Caan, replies, "I maneuvered."

That is essentially how Roger Toussaint squandered a career as a labor leader that once glowed with promise and became so radioactive among his own members that his handpicked successor was handily defeated by John Samuelsen December 7 in the Transport Workers Union Local 100 election.

It didn't matter that Mr. Toussaint and his cohorts did everything they could to stack the deck to protect their power, including a try at some chicanery on the morning of the actual vote count. They managed to get so many of the union's 37,000 members either declared ineligible to vote or too alienated to bother that only a shade over 10,000 took the trouble to mail in ballots. Nine years earlier, Mr. Toussaint by himself got 12,465 votes, justifying his claim that he had been given a mandate by his rank and file.

An Accelerating Descent
In the time since then, however, he went through all that goodwill like a gambler on a spree, losing it, as a Hemingway character once said, "gradually and then suddenly."

257

By the end of his first term, one of his closest allies was running against him as the most-visible example of a mounting list of union officials who earned Mr. Toussaint's wrath by expressing a point of view different from his own.

It might have been glossed over as an inevitable product of the friction that can develop when a union leader, knowing he's the one who shoulders the burden of making crucial decisions and takes the flak if they are wrong, bristles when one of his loyalists suggests he isn't sharing power enough.

But Mr. Toussaint's quarrels even at that relatively early point had spread beyond his erstwhile supporters, as he made clear that he wasn't sure his members were smart enough to be worthy of a leader like him. Two years into his tenure, negotiating his first contract with the Metropolitan Transportation Authority, he hinted at a strike but refrained from pulling the trigger when the contract deadline came, and later that morning got an offer reasonable enough to make a deal.

It wasn't a breakthrough by any means: to fix a major shortfall in the union's health fund that he had inherited from his predecessor, he was forced to forgo a first-year wage increase under the three-year agreement. It was solid enough to warrant ratification, not celebration, and it gained the approval of 60 percent of the union members who voted.

Rather than characterizing this as a good debut, Mr. Toussaint at some length lamented that too many of his members had allowed themselves to be hoodwinked by his political opposition and vowed to better educate them for the future.

At the end of 2003, he gained reelection by the same margin that the contract was approved but lost several key positions on the Local 100 executive board. Given his acrimonious relations with then-TWU International President Sonny Hall, some would have taken that result as a sign that he should mend a few fences if he wanted to consolidate his hold on the union, but not Mr. Toussaint. He continued to exact a price from those who disagreed with him.

A Fateful Building Sale
During the 2002 contract talks, he had been infuriated by a rebellion in the private bus-line ranks led by a union official who was close to Mr. Hall, blasting it as a hurtful distraction at a time when everyone's energy should be focused on improving wages and benefits.

Yet shortly before the 2005 negotiations grew urgent, Mr. Toussaint created a distraction of his own by agreeing to sell Local 100's West End Avenue headquarters for $60 million.

Speculation abounded as to his motives. Was he planning to lead a strike and figuring the money from the sale could tide the union over for an extended period when it lost dues-checkoff rights? Was he liquidating a key asset to ensure that it couldn't be seized to satisfy a strike-related judgment against the union?

Mr. Samuelsen, a track inspector whose skills at bringing grievance cases had endeared him to Mr. Toussaint, questioned whether this was the right time to be making a major decision on the building sale and asked at a union meeting that the issue be tabled until after a wage contract was reached.

This was too much for Mr. Toussaint; it constituted doubt, which to his mind bordered on disloyalty. Mr. Samuelsen was not only challenging his judgment but doing it in a room full of other union officials. That was outrageous and might prove contagious as well unless dealt with severely. Mr. Samuelsen was banished from his inner circle, an object lesson to all others that Mr. Toussaint would not tolerate being asked to explain or justify his decisions. (A couple of years later, the building was sold again for $30 million more than Mr. Toussaint got for it. The union continues to occupy space there but has no permanent home.)

And that same lack of debate figured into how the strike happened not long after. Mr. Toussaint had the guts to lead his members out but enough caution to realize it was not something to be done casually: about a month before the walkout he said in an interview that the trick was to convince management you were willing and able to go, giving the MTA incentive to offer you a viable alternative. But while there was discussion among the select few to whom he listened when it suited him about the MTA's proposal and its bargaining posture, one that seemed to be daring him to strike, he ultimately reached the conclusion that it was time to toss the grenade on his own and presented it to them as a fait accompli.

Wrong Time for a War
Prudence would have seemed to lie in taking the MTA up on its offer of binding arbitration. Governor Pataki was about to begin his final year in office, and it was already expected that Eliot Spitzer would be

elected to replace him, meaning a change in MTA management that figured to thaw out the relationship with Local 100. Arbitration presented a forum where the union didn't figure to get hurt in the interim.

But from the time he ran for office, Mr. Toussaint had talked about making Local 100 into the "great fighting union" it had been under Michael J. Quill, who became an immortal labor leader for the 1966 transit strike that welcomed in the mayoralty of John Lindsay and died shortly afterward. That spared Mr. Quill from any legacy reevaluations that might have occurred if his cantankerous nature at some later date had brought him into conflict with his subordinates.

Conditions were significantly different than what Mr. Quill had faced nearly 40 years earlier. For one thing, the Taylor Law was a much more effective tool of punishment for public employee strikes than the harsher Condon-Wadlin law had been. Perhaps as importantly, the TWU contract that spurred the 1966 strike ended on January 1; this time Local 100 would be striking at the heart of the holiday shopping season, meaning a much-greater inconvenience to the general public.

A Dare He Couldn't Refuse

However much Mr. Toussaint weighed these factors, they didn't balance his conviction that management was challenging his manhood, basically daring him to strike. And so he led the charge, taking his members out before dawn on December 20, right into the cannon fire of negative media coverage and mayoral condemnation.

He ended the strike 60 hours later, on the afternoon of the 22nd, later saying that the time had come to "get out of Dodge" before the strike blasted Christmas to smithereens and led Mayor Bloomberg and the business community to seek the same fate for the union. Working with mediators, he was able to craft a tentative contract settlement that provided some significant gains for his members beyond the wage increases.

But it also required that Local 100 members for the first time pay a portion of their health premiums, with the amount to be set based on their earnings, including overtime. Mr. Toussaint had called that a potential strike issue, along with the MTA's alternative demand that he accept an inferior pension plan for future members. He argued that it was fairer to extract a little bit of pain from the entire membership than to require the "unborn" to shoulder the entire load, but the rank and file didn't necessarily share that view. Most of them believed they were striking to avoid the health-benefit hit, and so his acceptance of the giveback, no matter what gains he'd made in other areas, stamped the strike as a failure, one that would also cost them six days' pay under the two-for-one employee strike penalty required under the Taylor Law.

An Exile Comes Home to Roost
Yet it also seemed clear that rejecting the contract would not lead to better terms. And so the deal might have been ratified due to a general sense of resignation, except that Mr. Toussaint's knee-jerk reaction to Mr. Samuelsen's questioning the building sale became the first excommunication that visibly came back to bite him on the posterior.

Already cast out of the flock, Mr. Samuelsen had little to lose in vigorously opposing ratification. The proposed pact was rejected by just seven votes out of more than 22,000 cast; there seems little question that he swung far more votes than the margin against the deal.

Mr. Toussaint was bloodied but unrepentant and insisted that the vote did not mean that only half his members still supported him. He stuck to that belief even after winning a third term in late 2006 with just 45 percent of the vote, saved by the fact that he had four challengers who split the anti-Roger ballots.

The bad choices continued to mount. After dues-checkoff rights were suspended in June 2007, even the discovery that many of his members were angry enough over the outcome of the strike that they wouldn't voluntarily make payments to the union didn't humble Mr. Toussaint. Rather than seek relief in Brooklyn Supreme Court based on financial hardship, which would have had to be accompanied by a pledge not to strike again, he based his case for checkoff restoration on the First Amendment. And so, where the 1980 strike lasted 11 days but dues rights were reinstated after a penalty of just over four months, the three-day walkout resulted in a checkoff loss that lasted 17 months. And in the end, he also made the no-strike pledge.

A Way to Disenfranchise
Somewhere along the way, Mr. Toussaint seemed to decide that this devastating financial blow to the union could be converted into a political opportunity. Since a majority of those who balked at keeping current on their dues were likely to vote against him, it was to his

advantage for them to fall so far behind that they couldn't catch up even if they wanted to in order to regain eligibility to vote in the next Local 100 election.

And when Mr. Samuelsen urged members to pay their dues no matter their feelings about Local 100's leadership but also noted that they had a right to expect that leadership to be accountable, Mr. Toussaint argued that he was really telling them not to pay dues and used it as an excuse to fire him as a shop steward. There would be other cases in which potential opposing candidates were ruled ineligible to run because of supposed dues arrears, even when they produced evidence that they were up to date.

And in the summer of 2008, Mr. Toussaint pushed through a bylaw change—approved by less than 10 percent of his rank and file—allowing the election to be conducted this June but with ballots not to be counted until December.

From Revolutionary to Wheedler

There were several theories as to why he sought what appeared to be a screwball process, and all of them pivoted on some political advantage for Mr. Toussaint. And so the man who had come to power as a kind of revolutionary trade-unionist vowing to mobilize his members to better take on management was now resorting to the sort of Byzantine election-law antics generally associated with the Brooklyn Democratic Party. It now was obvious that Mr. Toussaint was less intent on leading a movement than on creating a cult of personality.

By then, it was the only way he could have maintained power: his long-ago promise to develop and then empower a large shop-steward cadre had initially sputtered and, in the wake of the union financial cuts required when dues checkoff was lost, fizzled out. A man who spoke often about taking the long view and had tried to implement that belief in his contract bargaining had been thwarted by his short-sighted, short-fused decision to strike.

But the scheming and the wheedling on the staggered election process continued right up through the vote count last week. On the morning when the ballots were to be opened, Mr. Toussaint's United Invincible slate sought to have disqualified roughly 400 votes from those who had been union members when they cast ballots in June but subsequently left the bargaining unit, either because they were promoted out of it or departed the transit system altogether.

Couldn't Have It Both Ways

Given that the revised election rules barred those members who weren't current on dues when the June vote was held from becoming eligible to vote if they were paid up in full by the time that ballots were being given to new employees, this was an astonishing attempt to tilt the process once more. It was rejected, and it turned out Mr. Samuelsen had enough votes to win even if all the ballots at issue had been tossed and all came from his supporters.

One reason he won was that Mr. Toussaint's Maximum Leader governing style had ensured that he chose a potential successor who was no threat to his ultimate authority. Curtis Tate, who led the UI slate, never established himself as independent of Mr. Toussaint, in part because he rarely spoke to reporters, raising questions as to whether he could be the public face of the union in any context more complex than a speech at a rally where the primary requirement was to sound militant.

He had a reputation for affability, but anyone expecting that he might be a kinder, gentler president than his patron found scant evidence in the local's operations after he became acting president when Mr. Toussaint took a position with the TWU of America a year ago. When Darlyne Lawson, the recording secretary who came to power on Mr. Toussaint's slate nine years ago, had her car taken away earlier this month, she said she was told it was on Mr. Toussaint's order. When she reminded Mr. Tate that he was supposed to be running Local 100's day-to-day affairs, she said he responded that she wasn't going to put him in the middle of her dispute with Roger.

Still Settling Scores

Despite the local's claim that this was just a routine recycling of officer vehicles, it seemed clear that this was Mr. Toussaint, settling scores to the end, punishing a longtime loyalist who had incurred his wrath three years earlier when she balked at giving up her position to run for a vice presidency he thought could not be won by any other supporter.

That's an old, ordinary kind of political dispute, with the boss expecting his subordinate to defer to his judgment about what's good for the organization. She was rewarded for her defiance by being pushed as far from his orbit as one of the union's top officers could be, but toward the end Mr. Toussaint decided that wasn't penalty enough and had her notified the week of Thanksgiving that she was losing the union car that took her between the local's headquarters and her home in Rockland County.

It was an example of the basic character flaw that prevented Mr. Toussaint from becoming what a man of his intelligence and drive might have been for Local 100 and the labor movement at large.

He was so intent on fighting internal battles that he neglected to build a lasting organizational structure that empowered union shop stewards. Lacking that ability to transmit his message down the line to his rank and file, he left himself vulnerable to attacks from his critics, most notably in reaction to the post-strike contract, the rejection of which produced no tangible gains for Local 100 members and delayed by nearly a year their receiving the first-year raise under the deal.

Lack of Dialogue Hurt Him

And his attempts to stifle disagreements, which extended even to boycotting this newspaper because it printed letters from Local 100 dissidents, made it harder to consolidate his support in the union. Had he been more tolerant of those who spoke up against his policies, he might have convinced his members that they were wrong; he might even have won over some of those critics had he engaged in a meaningful dialogue in which they believed that at least they were given a fair shot to be heard.

Nine years ago, in the flush of their victory, Steve Downs, one of the prime movers behind the insurgent New Directions slate headed by Mr. Toussaint, spoke of reaching out to the incumbent union officers who had won reelection.

"We have to make clear that as long as they're doing a good job, they'll have the backing of the union," he said. "We have to, in many ways, build a new union in the shell of the old."

Last week, Mr. Downs was reelected as head of the Train Operators Division, running on a slate with Mr. Samuelsen, who in the first euphoria of his victory offered a variation on those remarks.

Asked what it said about Mr. Toussaint's tenure that the same statement could be applied when he left as when he took power, Mr. Downs said, "I certainly wouldn't say that Roger didn't have any accomplishments, because he did. But nine years after he took office, I would say that the union is in worse shape than it was when we got here."

'Didn't Honor Members' Will'

He continued, "One of the reasons is that he didn't make good on that promise to honor the will of the members and the people they selected as their representatives. The fruit of that is a weaker union. I think John and those who were elected with him—many of whom were victims [of Mr. Toussaint's high-handedness]—have learned a lesson from that and know the union paid a price for it. We'll make some mistakes, I'm sure [in the new administration]. I'm hoping that we avoid that one."

Mr. Samuelsen, still digesting that evening's victory, said, "It's surreal. It's been such a long fight."

In a larger context than he could provide on election night, it was the final half of Mr. Toussaint's tenure that was surreal. Mr. Samuelsen's victory offered the hope that there really was a light at the end of the tunnel.

Epilogue

The reelection of President Obama, with the union movement playing a vital role in get-out-the-vote efforts in battleground states such as Ohio, Michigan, Wisconsin, and Florida, was the major, if somewhat isolated, piece of good news for the city's public employees in 2012.

Mitt Romney's disdain for unions, whether they represented teachers or auto workers, was one of the few campaign positions on which there had been no apparent reversal from earlier stances he had taken while trying to appeal to a different audience than he played to during the Republican primaries. He had also made clear his belief that there was too much government regulation of private industry, and one little-noticed passage in his "47 percent" remarks at a fundraiser in May of that year concerned his plan to make sizable reductions in the staff of at least two Federal agencies if he was elected.

Mr. Obama had been something of a disappointment to public employee unions as well as their private-sector counterparts, who had seen him barely take office before he sent word that the time wasn't right to push for passage of the Employee Free Choice Act, which would make it easier to unionize unaffiliated workers. Teacher unions were less than thrilled that the president and his secretary of education, Arne Duncan, had pressed for more-demanding education standards, including stricter evaluations of instructors, without also calling for a lessened reliance on standardized testing in assessing their work. But these amounted to quibbles with a friend alongside the threat Mr. Romney—who exalted the power of the private sector while denigrating the capability of government to play a positive role in people's lives—had posed.

Instead of Mr. Romney continuing the Bush tax cuts if he had gained the White House, Mr. Obama won a second term while running on his pledge to discontinue them, meaning more money would be available for government operations without taking it out of employees' hides. This was of paramount importance not only to Federal workers who were in the midst of a three-year wage freeze but for those employed by state and local governments as well.

Beginning in April 2009, even as the private-sector economy began to rebound, over a period of more than three years there was a decline of 657,000 public-sector jobs, as cuts in Federal aid forced state governments and municipalities to balance their budgets in no small measure by reducing their workforces. That figure was what made Mr. Romney's remark after Wisconsin voters opted against a union-led recall of Governor Scott Walker—that the message being sent was, "It's time for us to cut back on government and help the American people"—emblematic of his insensitivity to public workers. It was as if he believed the cops and firefighters and teachers and government clerical workers were as divorced from "real Americans" as those including military personnel and retirees who paid no Federal income tax and were therefore unwilling to take responsibility for their own economic lives.

Public employee unions following the election would argue that the futile recall bid in Wisconsin had actually paid long-term dividends, because it had required mobilization of their forces in that state, just as had occurred in more-successful efforts to beat back attempts to curtail public union rights in Ohio and Michigan, that had been ideal tune-ups for the presidential election.

If that augured well for the long-term future, it was not enough to head off the surprise passage of right-to-work laws in Michigan just six weeks after the election, pushed through by a similar combination of forces—a Republican governor, a Republican-controlled legislature, and a lobbying campaign funded by the Koch brothers—that had sharply curtailed public employee rights in Wisconsin less than two years earlier, although those changes are tied up in a court battle.

Nor did the presidential outcome do much to change the present reality for public workers in New York City, where Mayor Michael Bloomberg continued to balk at granting any pay raises that weren't funded by union givebacks in other areas. A few days before Mr. Obama's reelection, the United Federation of Teachers marked the third anniversary of its members working under an expired contract; virtually every other important city union had been without a new pact since the summer of 2010. They all appeared resigned, as did their members, to not getting acceptable terms until after January 1, 2014, when a successor to Bloomberg would take office.

The absence of a contract was felt most acutely at District Council 37, since the majority of its members were among the city's lowest paid. The group that could least afford to go an extended period without a pay raise were the school employees represented by Local 372, which had experienced a change in leadership early in 2011 when President Veronica Montgomery-Costa retired, citing health issues. Her replacement, Santos Crespo, quickly made clear he would play a more-activist role in city labor, taking part not only in rallies against cuts to city services but turning out to support private phone-company workers during their extended bid for a new contract.

He also made good on a pledge to encourage more participation by members in union elections by expanding the number of work sites where ballots could be cast—but that didn't happen until after he gained a full term in office in June of that year when just 4 percent of his rank and file showed up at DC 37's headquarters, the only location for the walk-in vote.

At the other end of the economic spectrum within the union was its Local 375, representing engineers, architects, and other city professional employees. That local, however, was regularly mired in internal bickering, with two of its presidents removed in less than a decade for reasons that paled before the massive thievery that had wracked several other large DC 37 locals.

The second of them, Claude Fort, had incurred DC 37 Executive Director Lillian Roberts's wrath after she broke a promise to support him for a position with its international union when Ms. Montgomery-Costa expressed interest in the job and he then raised some unwelcome questions about the union's having spent more than $300,000 on a reception during the 2008 convention of the international, the American Federation of State, County and Municipal Employees.

Fort narrowly survived a reelection challenge in November 2009, but early the following year, he balked at giving check-signing authority to Behrouz Fathi, who had won a runoff election for first vice president of the union. It wasn't merely a case of giving a hard time to someone from the opposing slate; Fathi had been arrested the previous summer for allegedly shoplifting at a Suffolk County Home Depot store. This and the other minor power-sharing disputes Fort had with members of the opposing slate who had gained union office probably could have been worked out if Ms. Roberts was interesting in restoring peace, but instead Fort found himself facing charges before AFSCME, and in March 2010 he was removed from office.

This began to look like an overly hasty move when a further check into Fathi's background uncovered three previous convictions on misdemeanor larceny charges and, perhaps more significantly, that he had used six names besides his own during the period when he was being caught stealing. Each of them was relatively ancient—the most-recent one had occurred in 1982. Still, DC 37's constitution had a clause that barred from union office anyone who had previously been criminally convicted of a monetary crime.

Once again, the flexibility of the AFSCME judicial panel headed by Kangaroo John Seferian appeared to save the day, issuing a ruling that the convictions were too far in the past to disqualify Fathi from holding union office.

Mr. Fort's supporters at the Local 375 board weren't satisfied, and with the help of attorney Arthur Schwartz, they took the case to a more-neutral arbiter, a New York State Supreme Court justice in Manhattan. As had so often been the case over the previous decade, the court system took a jaundiced view of justice, AFSCME style. On May 31, 2012, Justice Lucy Billings ruled that the DC 37 constitution made no allowances for the amount of time passed since a crime had been committed and ordered Fathi's removal from office. He appealed, but the ruling was upheld, and later that summer Michael Rosenberg stepped up to become president of the local. Its fractiousness soon wore on him, however, and he decided not to seek a full term, setting up a rematch in December between Mr. Fort and the man he narrowly defeated three years earlier, Jon Forster. As had happened twice previously when the will of Local 375 members was undone by union higher-ups in questionable circumstances, the rank and file expressed its unhappiness via the ballot box: Fort won the second contest in a rout, with 63 percent of the vote.

DC 37 wasn't doing much better in the political arena, either, in cases where the choice wasn't as obvious as backing Obama's reelection. In June 2012, the Democratic Congressional primary for an open seat representing Brooklyn and a small slice of Queens offered a seemingly ideal candidate for the union to support in Hakeem Jeffries. He was a state assemblyman in his early 40s who in some political circles was being touted as a future mayoral candidate. Not incidentally, both his parents had been members of DC 37, with his mother having retired from her city job just a few years earlier.

Yet Roberts instead gave the union's endorsement to Charles Barron, a former Black Panther who still seemed more interested in radical rhetoric than in accomplishing much for his constituents. The reason given for backing him was that he had long supported issues that were important to the union, but it was questionable how much good it had done. He had long ago alienated City Council Speaker Christine Quinn, who to a large degree determined the fate of legislation at the local level, both by opposing her election to that post and appealing to other minority members to vote for one of their own, and by pursuing a bruising but unsuccessful bid to have a Brooklyn street named in memory of Sonny Carson, an activist with an incendiary bent that once led him to chide a reporter for describing him as "anti-Semitic" when what he actually was, he emphasized, was "anti-white."

Union officials and political analysts were shaking their heads at Roberts's decision long before the primary results were tallied, with Jeffries getting 72 percent of the vote.

She had more success internally, strongly backing Lee Saunders for president of AFSCME as her longtime ally Gerry McEntee faded into retirement. Saunders won by a surprisingly comfortable margin against Danny Donohue, the president of the Civil Service Employees Association, who just two years earlier had come within 4,000 votes of defeating him in a faceoff for secretary-treasurer of the international union. The one obvious explanation for the dramatic swing of close to 100,000 votes in Saunders's favor was the stinker of a contract Donohue had reached in the year between the two elections.

(Donohue at least retained his position as head of the largest state-employee union. Just a week after his drubbing in the AFSCME vote, his counterpart at the Public Employees Federation, the second-largest union of state workers, Ken Brynien, was swept from office along with the rest of his slate after challenger Susan Kent excoriated him for accepting the giveback-laden contract demanded by Governor Andrew Cuomo. The union, which retained its reputation for being more militant than the CSEA that dated back to its formation in the late 1970s by the leaders of what until then had been the professional, scientific, and technical wing of the CSEA, had voted down the terms accepted by the other union, and then accepted a slightly reworked deal only because many members were reluctant to risk the layoff of less-senior colleagues.)

Saunders, in an implicit criticism of his predecessor at AFSCME, said that he intended to be "more transparent" and "more aggressive in dealing with our members and listening to them." By the end of the year, some of McEntee's longtime advisers had moved on, and the following spring John Seferian retired as head of the judicial panel.

Roberts herself gave no indication that at age 87 she was thinking of moving on, and there was no reason for her to. In November 2012, when nominations were held for DC 37 offices, she had no opposition despite the union's continuing decline. Her mastery of the delegate process and her penchant for bruising campaign tactics had convinced potential opponents that it wasn't worth taking her on in what was certain to be a losing cause.

Roger Toussaint, the fiery former president of Transport Workers Union Local 100, found his combativeness less of an asset. On January 7, 2012, just eight days before his old local's contract was due to expire, from his perch as a highly paid staffer at its international union he fired off an e-mail accusing Local 100 President John Samuelsen of having no clue about getting a new deal except to "stumble from one blunder or fiasco to the next." He claimed Samuelsen planned to stall the bargaining until the union's next election was concluded in December of that year so that he would not be held accountable for a contract he predicted would be laden with givebacks.

It was an astonishing reentry in the local's political wars, given that when he was its president, Toussaint had bristled at what he considered efforts to undermine his own bargaining efforts as a contract deadline neared by then-TWU of America President Sonny Hall and his allies within Local 100.

Samuelsen, expressing determination not to be forced into a concessionary contract at a time when the Metropolitan Transportation Authority was insisting that any raises be offset by productivity gains, made clear his displeasure with Toussaint's attack. A short time later, Toussaint resigned from his position at the international, with some union officials saying that TWU of America President Jim Little had forced his hand.

When Toussaint in early February sought reinstatement to his old job as a track worker, speculation abounded that he was preparing to run for Local 100 president. It fizzled out when he ultimately decided not to return to transit service, but Toussaint again took a hand in the TWU election process in a way that once would have seemed unthinkable. The man who once had subordinates excoriate me for running what he called unsubstantiated accusations by his critics in the letters column of the *Chief* became a regular contributor to that column, delivering a series of attacks on Samuelsen, Hall, and the same Local 100 attorney, Arthur Schwartz, who for much of his own tenure had been among his primary confidantes.

Samuelsen contended that Toussaint was strongly behind the candidacy of his main reelection opponent, Joseph Campbell. Toussaint and Campbell both heatedly denied a campaign alliance, but although Toussaint discontinued his letter-writing activities by the end of the spring, he made several protests in September to the union's election monitor alleging improper activities by Samuelsen and his allies.

When the ballots were counted on December 7, Samuelsen won a second term by a 17-point margin over Campbell, notwithstanding the fact that more than 11 months had passed since the Local 100 contract expired and no resolution was in sight. Union leaders tend to live or die with their wage deals, yet Samuelsen had gained a second term handily without delivering a timely one.

There seemed to be two possible explanations for this result. One was that union members, burned by Toussaint's decision to force the issue just past the contract deadline in 2005 that led to losses from both the strike penalties and the imposition of a worker contribution toward health benefits, had decided that patience could be a virtue in a tough bargaining environment. The other possibility was perhaps that Toussaint's perceived support of Campbell—notwithstanding Campbell's denials late in the campaign of an alliance—had harmed him.

Index

29405078R00183

Made in the USA
Lexington, KY
24 January 2014